Classic
Mountain Bike
Rides

Classic
Mountain Bike
Rides

Thirty of the World's Most
Spectacular Trails

General Editor Nicky Crowther
Foreword by Mike Ferrentino

A BULFINCH PRESS BOOK
LITTLE, BROWN AND COMPANY
Boston   New York   London

FOREWORD

There's something magical and often overlooked about mountain bikes. While immense amounts of hyperbole are spewed out containing words like "edgy," "hip," and "extreme," the most understated magic about mountain bikes just keeps rolling along right in front of the eyes of an oblivious world—the magic is this: mountain bikes can go anywhere.

Per calorie burned, bicycles represent the most efficient form of transport known to man. Add to that efficiency a pair of fat tires, some racks, and a little imagination, and you have in your possession a vehicle that can be ridden around the world. This may seem like an adventurous proposal, and one that only increases in challenge, scope, and grandeur when the tarmac ends and the single-track begins, but *Classic Mountain Bike Rides* illustrates that it is also a very realistic proposal.

Featuring thirty different multi-day off-road epic rides, ranging from grueling sixteen-day treks in the Tibetan highlands to scenic three-day romps through England's Lake District, *Classic Mountain Bike Rides* contains a wealth of information for the destination hungry off-road cyclist. It represents an impressive breadth of research, the results of which are combined in one beautifully photographed, well written, coffee-table worthy piece of work. As a base resource for planning big out-of-the-way adventures, you would be hard-pressed to find an equal.

As mentioned above, mountain bikes can go anywhere. All they require is a rider up to the task of pedaling them. This book lays the foundation for adventure; it encourages you to revitalize your body, to use your bike to search out a far horizon, to wake up to a different language,and to taste the dust of another country. So, flip through the sumptuous pages, dream a little, and ask yourself: Where Do You Want To Go?

MIKE FERRENTINO
Editor-at-Large, *Bike* magazine

CONTENTS

First published in 2001 by Bulfinch Press

Copyright © 2001, Quarto Inc.

First North American Edition

ISBN 0-8212-2703-3

Library of Congress Control Number 00-111502

Conceived, designed, and produced for Bulfinch Press by Quarto Publishing plc

Bulfinch Press is an imprint and trademark of Little, Brown and Company (Inc.)

Printed In China

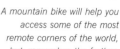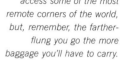

A mountain bike will help you access some of the most remote corners of the world, but, remember, the farther-flung you go the more baggage you'll have to carry.

INTRODUCTION "HOW FAR HAVE YOU COME, WHERE ARE YOU GOING, AND DO YOU WANT YOUR WATER BOTTLE FILLED?"

The great outdoors is the largest playground in the world, and is open to adults and children of all ages. Getting out into the countryside, and partaking of some energetic exercise will make you feel good about yourself, as well as being beneficial to your health.

The mountain bike is such an exultant instrument of adventure that it is amazing that it didn't predate tarmac and cars. The knobbly tires need no roads; the numerous gears give a top speed of 45 m.p.h. (70 k.p.h.) and a bottom speed of 2 m.p.h. (3 k.p.h.) (slower than walking pace); and it looks like a faithful workhorse but is designed to digest the miles rather than choke on them. Mountain-bike travel has become the number-one way to enjoy speed and distance without offending the earth. By comparison, the passive act of traveling by car cuts you off from the land and people. Hiking on foot is a fulfilling experience, but can leave you stranded in inhospitable weather while covering only a few miles per day. The honorable compromise has to be the bicycle built for trekking.

In a day, you can ride up to 100 miles (160km), cross entire regions, or dip into hostile territories and back without mishap. Only two inches (5cm) wide, tires can travel many of the trails used otherwise only by hikers. Culturally, cyclists are welcomed by local people the world over, as they are respected for traveling under their own steam, and for moving at a pace that allows a wave, a call, and a smile. Whatever the language, people want to know: "How far have you come, where are you going, and do you want your water bottle filled?"

We are still at the dawn of the mountain-bike age. In the two decades since they were first developed in northern California, knobbly tires have set out to explore the globe, bringing with them a form of sustainable tourism that is

INTRODUCTION

neither at odds with local resources nor polluting in any form. People use them to traverse continents, or to explore deeply the land in which they are traveling. They are also highly addictive when it comes to tackling exciting pieces of trail, either requiring skillful technique or simply offering a delicious long cruise downhill. For every climb, there is a descent, for every long hard day in the saddle, there is rest and recovery at the end, along with the great honest appetite and the powerful sense of achievement.

Cycling has much to do with personal empowerment. While the world encourages a greater consumption of energy-saving but alienating activities, the bike remains a simple tool with which to escape. The effort is all your own, the destination is up to you, and the excitement and satis-faction are guaranteed.

Such experiences jump off the pages of this book—a unique collection of extraordinary routes from all the continents. Here are tantalizing samples of what can be enjoyed or overcome in the saddle, with maps and travel

 ↑
*The one thing you can be
certain of when deciding
which of these wonderful trails
to experience, is that wide
open spaces will always be
your domain.*

→
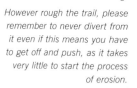
*However rough the trail, please
remember to never divert from
it even if this means you have
to get off and push, as it takes
very little to start the process
of erosion.*

Meeting the locals is one of the most satisfying elements of any trip into a foreign land, and mountain bikers tend to be warmly welcomed by all nations, even if the idea of the sport is alien to them.

perspective they bring to an established destination. Take the Tour du Mont Blanc, based on a well-known hiking trip around the mountain's great bulk and crossing the borders of France, Switzerland, and Italy; the biking route has been newly developed by a locally based expert, using roads and tracks where car tires cannot go, and completing in five days what would take ten on foot—an awesome experience without the blisters. In other areas, such as the Caribbean's Dominican Republic, the trek follows unmapped trails that link backcountry villages and are known only to the inhabitants. Thus it yields a vivid insider's impression of the land with the locals' blessing.

Every author is an experienced mountain biker—either a professional guide and/or an outdoor journalist—who personally completed the trek. Their inspiration is evident in their prose and photographs.

The mountain bike is a people-friendly beast rather than a stand-alone toy, designed to bring people together. On all trails, you are exhorted to give way to people and animals, to respect the land, and to look but not touch. Take care on descents, not only for your own safety, but for that of those who may be going about their daily business. Try to leave no tire marks, and stick to existing tracks wherever possible. Tread lightly and be gone, to ride another day in another wondrous part of our planet.

details to enable any inspired armchair adventurer to turn their dreams into reality. From outback trekking through crocodile country in Australia to a spectacular trip through Malawi's safarilands, from the thin air of occupied Tibet high up in the Himalayas to a full-length trek of America's Great Divide. Treks have been selected for the quality of the trail, for their sense of drama, and for the cycling

Nicky Crowther.

Beware of animals on your trips, as the native wildlife may not always be as docile as this yak, especially if you choose to visit the bear habitats of North America.

PRACTICAL ADVICE

It may be fun launching yourself spontaneously into a mountain-bike trip, turning left toward the country instead of right into town one morning. But you aren't likely to feel that way once lunchtime strikes and you forgot to pack enough food or when your pants begin to chafe. The thrill of adventure is partly throwing yourself in at the deep end, but sound preparation will help you swim rather than drown when you get there.

Good Travel Practice:

Whatever part of the world you intend to explore, equip yourself with the right travel guide. Check which immunizations are necessary, and get them done in plenty of time before your trip. A dental checkup before you depart is also a wise idea, and could save an emergency extraction in an out-of-the-way location. Keep separate photocopies of your passport, visas, and any travelers check numbers. If the language is not

your own, memorize a few phrases, such as asking the way, asking for food, and the simple courtesies—this will make your trip more enjoyable and perhaps win you friends. Note the season and study weather forecasts before you leave. Tell someone where you are going, with an estimate of dates when you'll be there. Don't mountain-bike alone.

The Bike: All the routes in this book require the willing services of a mountain bike, one with fat knobbly tires for grip and comfort and plenty of gears for extremes of gradient. To carry panniers the frame will need eyelets, and it can be useful to have braze-ons (screw-holes) for two water bottles if you expect to travel in arid areas. Suspension will add to your riding pleasure, especially if the off-road sections are single-track or rough, but this does take extra maintenance and you may not want to deal with that in a remote area. New bikes will need a period of wearing in before you set off; ride the bike for at least a

month to stretch the brake and gear cables, and then either service the bike yourself, or get a bike shop to do it for you. This will include readjusting the brakes and gears, ensuring that all bearings are done up (if they aren't permanently sealed anyway), checking the wheels for alignment and dents in the rims, and thoroughly lubricating moving parts. Set off with new or fairly new tires—they can last an extraordinary length of time, even on rough trips; equally, they can blow or tear within a week if you have a tumble, or if something rips the sidewall (carry at least one spare). Wheel rims should also be fairly new: they gradually get worn thin by the brake pads and eventually fail, causing the wheel to crumple. There is not really any need to buy a comfortable saddle

for a trip, because soreness is more a matter of your buttocks than the saddle. However, some women find they can ride only on wider women's saddles. Fit front and rear lights for the road riding after dark. The front one can double as a camping torch. Make sure you can get batteries locally, or carry a supply. Powerful bicycle headlamps allow you to enjoy the thrill of off-roading at night, but note that recharging requires a mains power supply. Needless to say, you must carry a puncture-repair kit, including a pump, plenty of patches, and fresh glue, plus spare inner tubes.

Mechanical repairs: All cyclists should be able to change a puncture and fit a tire themselves. But it will also help if you are familiar with the workings of the

↑
A good quality lightweight bike with 100 percent waterproof panniers could potentially transfrom your trip from a heavy, wet, exhausting ride to a veritable cruise.

main moving parts: chain, bottom bracket, cranks and pedals, brakes and gears, and wheels.

Get to know the bike and carry all the allen keys and spanners necessary for adjustment; also brake blocks. Take spare nuts and bolts, particularly good quality ones for the pannier rack, which bears the load and is subject to all sorts of shaking; lose a screw and you lose the rack's stability, a common hazard that can stop you in your tracks. Pack spare brake and gear cables, and a good lubricant. If all else fails, rags and zip-ties can keep things secure.

Daily Bike Checks: At the end of each biking day, clean the chain thoroughly with a rag and reapply lubricant—a ten-minute job that makes your bike feel like new every day. If you are using S.P.D. (Shimano Pedaling Dynamics) spring-clip pedals, keep them lubricated, otherwise you may tear the cleat out of your shoe when trying to disengage. Keep the gear changers smooth and replace the brake blocks when necessary. Keep an eye on the tires and test the pannier rack bolts.

←
The ability to mend a puncture and change a tire is essential for any biker, but the further you go into the wilderness the more reliant you will become on your own technical abilities.

↑
Always be prepared! Make sure your puncture repair kit and basic tool kit is complete and that everything is in full-working order.

Cycle Luggage: Good panniers make for good traveling; get fully waterproof ones if you can afford them. Load 35 percent of the weight at the front and 65 percent at the back. Buy the best pannier rack you can afford, since it will repay itself many times. On smooth trails use a trailer to carry more, although there is a weight penalty.

First aid: Carry a well-stocked first-aid pack, and know the rudiments of first aid, such as C.P.R. (cardiopulmonary resuscitation). Be prepared for cuts, grazes, and insect stings. The most common mountain-biking injury is a broken collarbone, caused by flying over the handlebars, and will require strapping and painkillers.

Navigation: Develop a good understanding of how to use a compass before you leave. Note that standing near a steel bike when you take a reading can affect the bearing, so step back. When not in a waterproof handlebar bag, maps should be packed in a sealed bag, as rain can destroy tens of square miles within seconds.

Clothing: The basic outfit is padded shorts, a cycling jersey and jacket, plus good cycling shoes (possibly S.P.D.-compatible to click into cleats in the pedals). Long and bib leggings are essential for cooler weather. For rainy times get good technical wear, preferably cycle-specific (long arms, long behind, and pants with a higher waist). Waterproofs rarely keep you completely dry, but their forte is in eliminating windchill. A helmet could save your brain in a crash, while most of the time just having a peak on it will keep out rays, rain, and bugs. Trendy shades may look out of place in

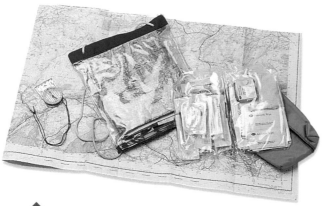

↑

Navigational skills, from basic map reading to advanced compass use will be extremely important on some of the rides; whereas a well-stocked first-aid kit is always indispensable.

remote areas, but U.V. rays damage eyes, as do flying insects and grit.

Your Fitness: The fitter you are when you begin your bike ride, the more you will enjoy it. You strengthen as you progress—riding for a few hours day after day is perfect training—and you will avoid first-day blues if your buttocks are tough and your legs are firm to begin with. Carrying baggage significantly increases the stress on legs, heart, and lungs, so expect it to take extra effort in the first few days. For beginners a three-month period of one long and three short rides per week is recommended, while regular cyclists will benefit from a half-dozen all-

day rides in the six weeks before departure—this will prepare the body for the endurance ahead.

Nutrition in the Saddle:
Hard pedaling uses around 500 calories an hour. Ride for four hours a day, say 40 miles off-road, and your total burn-up, including the 2,000 calories it takes to keep your organs going, comes to 4,000 calories a day. You need to gobble that amount to maintain your weight and energy—no wonder cyclists have enormous appetites. Most people lose weight and gain tone on a ride, even eating a lot. If you feel weak or dizzy, eat fruit or carbohydrates and feel your strength return within an hour or so. Fueling properly can be a serious issue when you're a long way from supplies. Plan your days' requirements—look ahead at your trip and calculate how much food

you need to carry to get you to the next depot. Camp food has improved a lot, and is designed to be light and easily packed.

Drinking in the Saddle:
Wherever you are cycling you must always carry enough water to avoid dehydration. Take water-purification tablets and exploit streams on the way. The method is to drink little and often while pedaling. The volume of fluid you use up is incredible, both in sweat and expelled on the breath—think how much water vapor you puff out with each breath on chilly mornings. The body can absorb about 1¾ pints (1 liter) of water an hour, but, if you leave drinking until you are thirsty and then down 2 pints at once, you'll expel some of it through urine, not because your

↑

Good quality gear, for everything from panniers and lights to shoes and helmet, will always be a worthwhile investment, and will make any trip you make infinitely more comfortable.

body doesn't need it, but because it can't process it that quickly.

Tread Lightly on the Earth:
Leave no trace of your presence. Carry your provisions in and your litter out. Bury human waste and toilet tissue. Mountain-bike tires, particularly in high or northerly areas where fauna has only a toe-hold, can leave a mark that takes years to disappear—so stick to existing tracks; and resist the temptation to skid.

→

Certain trails require self-sufficiency, on these there are certain foods that will serve you particularly well; such as bananas, which are very high in energy, and lightweight dried food to which you just add water from your water bottle for a quick and easy meal.

←

If you intend to travel long distances where water supplies are uncertain, be sure to carry copious amounts of water; it will make your bike heavy but dehydration is to be avoided at all cost.

HOW TO USE THIS BOOK

Through maps, photographs, illustrations, charts, and text, *Classic Mountain Bike Rides* brings alive rides from all over the world. From the comfort of your own armchair you can follow in the tire tracks of some of the world's most experienced mountain bikers, and be inspired to experience these trails for yourself. These two pages explain exactly how to follow each ride, what information you can expect to find within the main profiles of each ride, and where to locate that information.

Photographs:
These have been carefully selected not only to capture the true spirit of the trail and the region and to highlight the scenic splendor, but also to provide informative visual information on key points of the route.

Itinerary Text:
For each section the start and finish point is detailed along with the length of the section described. Where relevant, easier alternatives or shorter routes are suggested. In many instances, if the time you have available is limited, you can select only the portion you wish to complete.

Locator Map:
Where in the world? Get a general indication of what part of the world the ride takes place in by using this locator map.

Degree of Difficulty Logos:
All the rides have been graded into levels of easy, moderate, and difficult, taking into consideration the terrain, climbs & descents, overall distance, and climate. An orange border around the relevant icon provides a basic guide as to how tough or simple the ride is.

Introductory Text:
A colorful introduction leads to a descriptive analysis of the trail, which is broken down into manageable days or groups of days.

AFRICA & THE MIDDLE EAST

CANYONS and VOLCANOES

RÉUNION ISLAND

Chris Ford

RÉUNION ISLAND IS AN INCREDIBLE FEAT OF VOLCANIC GEOGRAPHY. FEW PLACES ON EARTH HAVE SUCH AN ARRAY OF LANDSCAPES AND ECOSYSTEMS IN SO SMALL AN AREA. WITH THIS COMES A VIBRANT MULTICULTURAL SOCIETY— ALTHOUGH THE ISLAND IS FRENCH, THE LOCAL CREOLE PEOPLE BRING THEIR OWN LANGUAGE, TRADITIONS, AND CUISINE INTO THE MELTING POT.

For mountain bikers this combination of landscapes and lifestyle is wonderful. After a ride across lava flows, or following the Galet riverbed (still half full of water!) into Cirque de Mafate, you can visit wonderful little Creole restaurants or relax at cafés on the beach.

This trip combines bike touring with serious off-road riding. You can load up the panniers to move around the island, then spend a few days at each location enjoying the great mountain biking without any baggage. For days off the bike there's an incredible variety of other adventure sports on offer too.

←
The rivers are a major form of access to the overgrown interior of Réunion for bikers.

142

DAYS 1–2 31 miles (50km)

St. Denis to St. Gilles-les-Bains

Spend Day 1 exploring St. Denis, the island's capital. The next morning, ride west along the coast, and, after crossing the Rivière St. Denis, turn off into the mountains. The views down to the Indian Ocean are beautiful, and the hairpin bends up the lower slopes of Cap Noir are a good warm-up! The road drops to follow the coast into St. Gilles-les-Bains.

DAY 3 47 miles (75km)

Cirque de Mafate

The Cirque de Mafate is the most inaccessible place on the island, with no roads reaching its sheer, hidden peaks and waterfalls. The only route into the cirque follows the bed of the Rivière du Galet during the dry season. This trail takes you through St. Gilles-les-Hauts, and down to Tours des Roches—a narrow, scenic road that winds through dense groves of coconuts, mangos, and bananas. You then rise up to the edge of the Galet river canyon at Sans Souci, before dropping onto a dirt trail. You're now on the riverbed, heading into the cirque. After 12 miles (20km) the valley opens up, and you ride through a tunnel to emerge at a clear pool, behind which is a canyon with swimming pools and dramatic "plongées" (12-foot-/4-meter-high jumps into a waterfall). The return along the river is no less exciting.

DAY 4 40 miles (65km)

Piton Maido

About 7,900 feet (2,400m) above St. Gilles-les-Bains is Piton Maido, a sheer ridge that rises up from the ocean and drops into Mafate on the other side. Your aim is to climb the road to the ridge, then descend to the ocean on a stunning mix of single-track, fire roads, and plantation trails.

The climb takes at least four hours, and setting off early is essential to avoid the heat on the lower slopes. At Petit France there is a great Creole café that serves takeouts. Grab your lunch and take it to the top of Piton Maido, where you can enjoy it with views across the sea of peaks within the cirque. This will also be your first view of Piton des Neiges—the central summit of the island.

The descent begins on tarmac, then you'll see a board describing the nearby biking. You should take the left turn onto a waymarked forestry trail, with challenging shortcuts through steep, narrow forest single-track. Pass through high mountain heathers, then dense cloud forests, before meeting farmers tending their patches of flowers, sugar cane, and palm groves. Eventually you'll come out onto the road at St. Gilles-les-Hauts, for the last blast down to the beach.

DAY 5 37 miles (60km)

St. Gilles-les-Bains to Cilaos

The first 22 miles (35km) of the day follow the coastal road past Réunion's most beautiful beaches. Heading inland, brace your legs for the hardest climb yet—nearly 6,000 feet (1,800m) with a fully loaded bike. As you twist and turn up the side of the St. Étienne river canyon, the road takes you through small villages, spaced by dense groves of bananas. The scenery gradually becomes more alpine—pine forests stretch from the road to the vertical cliff face that marks the east side of this rock amphitheater. At the village of Cilaos you will be surrounded by the giant rock walls of the cirque.

DAY 6 34 miles (45km)

Cirque de Cilaos

Cilaos's tourist information center has a giant [...] ing all the local mountain bike routes. A favor[...] option is to head out to the eastern edge of th[...] under the brow of Piton des Neiges, and retu[...] trails to the road you rode in on yesterday. For t[...] there are some great single-track routes that [...] region above the Hôtel des Thermes. The vie[...] here are fabulous. Some of these trails are bla[...] stick to the fire roads if you are unsure of yo[...] While in Cilaos, try canyoning—abseiling und[...] jumping into pools, and whizzing down rock s[...]

DAYS 7–8 80 miles (130km)

Cilaos to St. Philippe

Leaving the mountains, you can enjoy the swit[...] tunnels that you previously rode up, before[...] along the coast to St. Philippe. After the busy [...] Pierre, the traffic disappears as you head towa[...] Sauvage"—the Wild South. This area sits right [...]

Ride Profile:

To supplement the descriptive text, these charts assess the degree of difficulty of the route on a daily/group of days basis in terms of ascent and descent. They have been drawn in sufficient detail to allow quick visual reference. They are a very useful and easy guide to help determine just how tough each day's biking is going to be.

Map:

With the line of the route clearly marked, these have been drawn to provide an overall presentation of the complete trail. They show the key stages of the ride, start and finish points, major features, and alternative routes. A comprehensive key clearly explains any symbols and markings used. Please note that the coloration of the maps reflects the height of the ground above sea level, rather than being indicative of the terrain.

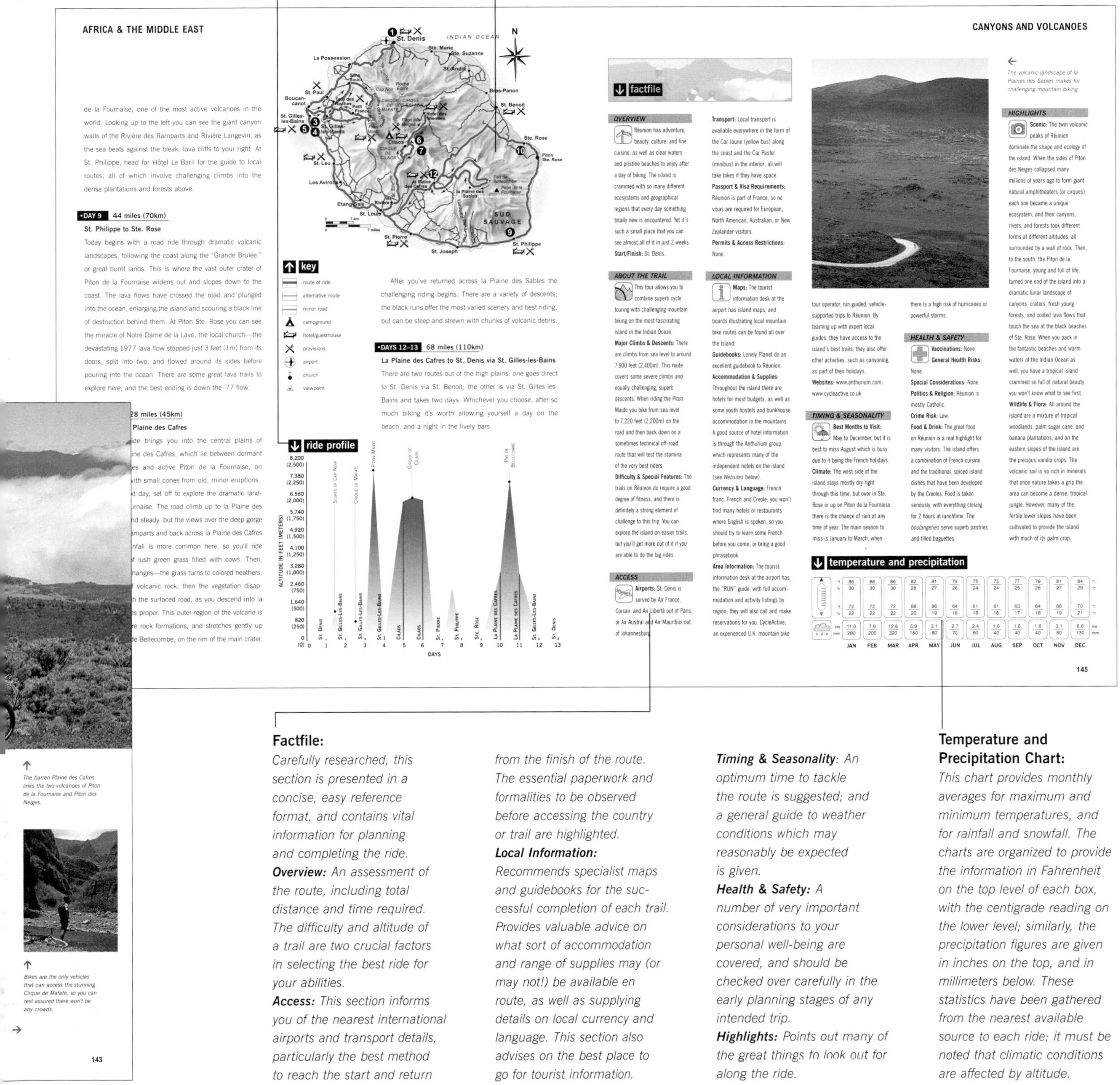

AFRICA & THE MIDDLE EAST

de la Fournaise, one of the most active volcanoes in the world. Looking up to the left you can see the giant canyon walls of the Rivière des Ramparts and Rivière Langevin, as the sea beats against the bleak, lava cliffs to your right. At St. Philippe, head for Hôtel Le Baril for the guide to local routes, all of which involve challenging climbs into the dense plantations and forests above.

•DAY 9   44 miles (70km)

St. Philippe to Ste. Rose

Today begins with a road ride through dramatic volcanic landscapes, following the coast along the "Grande Brulée," or great burnt lands. This is where the vast outer crater of Piton de la Fournaise widens out and slopes down to the coast. The lava flows have crossed the road and plunged into the ocean, enlarging the island and scouring a black line of destruction behind them. At Piton Ste. Rose you can see the miracle of Notre Dame de la Lave, the local church—the devastating 1977 lava flow stopped just 3 feet (1m) from its doors, split into two, and flowed around its sides before pouring into the ocean. There are some great lava trails to explore here, and the best ending is down the '77 flow.

•DAY ...   28 miles (45km)

... Plaine des Cafres

...de brings you into the central plains of ...ine des Cafres, which lie between dormant ...es and active Piton de la Fournaise, on ...with small cones from old, minor eruptions. ...t day, set off to explore the dramatic land- ...ournaise. The road climb up to la Plaine des ...nd steady, but the views over the deep gorge ...amparts and back across la Plaine des Cafres ...nfall is more common here, so you'll ride ...f lush green grass filled with cows. Then, ...hanges—the grass turns to colored heathers, ... volcanic rock; then the vegetation disap- ...h the surfaced road, as you descend into la ...s proper. This outer region of the volcano is ...re rock formations, and stretches gently up ...de Bellecombe, on the rim of the main crater.

↑ key

route of ride
alternative route
minor road
campground
hotel/guesthouse
provisions
airport
church
viewpoint

After you've returned across la Plaine des Sables the challenging riding begins. There are a variety of descents; the black runs offer the most varied scenery and best riding, but can be steep and strewn with chunks of volcanic debris.

•DAYS 12-13   68 miles (110km)

La Plaine des Cafres to St. Denis via St. Gilles-les-Bains

There are two routes out of the high plains: one goes direct to St. Denis via St. Benoit; the other is via St. Gilles-les-Bains and takes two days. Whichever you choose, after so much biking it's worth allowing yourself a day on the beach, and a night in the lively bars.

↓ ride profile

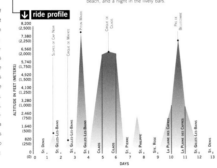

↓ factfile

OVERVIEW

Réunion has adventure, beauty, culture, and fine cuisine, as well as clear waters and pristine beaches to enjoy after a day of biking. The island is crammed with so many different ecosystems and geographical regions that every day something totally new is encountered. Yet it's such a small place that you can see almost all of it in just 2 weeks.
Start/Finish: St. Denis.

Transport: Local transport is available everywhere in the form of the Car Jaune (yellow bus) along the coast and the Car Pastel (minibus) in the interior; all will take bikes if they have space.
Passport & Visa Requirements: Réunion is part of France, no visas are required for European, North American, Australian, or New Zealander visitors.
Permits & Access Restrictions: None.

ABOUT THE TRAIL

This tour allows you to combine superb cycle touring with challenging mountain biking on the most fascinating island in the Indian Ocean.
Major Climbs & Descents: There are climbs from sea level to around 7,900 feet (2,400m). This route covers some severe climbs and equally challenging, superb descents. When riding the Piton Maido you bike from sea level to 7,220 feet (2,200m) on the road and back down on a sometimes technical off-road route that will test the stamina of the very best riders.
Difficulty & Special Features: The trails on Réunion do require a good degree of fitness, and there is definitely a strong element of challenge to this trip. You can explore the island on easier trails, but you'll get more out of it if you are able to do the big rides.

ACCESS

Airports: St. Denis is served by Air France, Corsair, and Air Liberté out of Paris, or Air Austral and Air Mauritius out of Johannesburg.

LOCAL INFORMATION

Maps: The tourist information desk at the airport has island maps, and boards illustrating local mountain bike routes can be found all over the island.
Guidebooks: Lonely Planet do an excellent guidebook to Réunion.
Accommodation & Supplies: Throughout the island there are hotels for most budgets, as well as some youth hostels and bunkhouse accommodation in the mountains. A good source of hotel information is through the Anthurium group, which represents many of the independent hotels on the island (see Websites below).
Currency & Language: French franc, French and Creole, you won't find many hotels or restaurants where English is spoken, so you should try to learn some French before you come; or bring a good phrasebook.
Area Information: The tourist information desk at the airport has the "RUN" guide, with full accommodation and activity listings by region; they will also call and make reservations for you. CycleActive, an experienced U.K. mountain bike

tour operator, run guided, vehicle-supported trips to Réunion. By teaming up with expert local guides, they have access to the island's best trails; they also offer other activities, such as canyoning, as part of their holidays.
Websites: www.anthurium.com
www.cycleactive.co.uk

TIMING & SEASONALITY

Best Months to Visit: May to December, but it is best to miss August which is busy due to it being the French holidays.
Climate: The west side of the island stays mostly dry right through this time, but over in Ste. Rose or up on Piton de la Fournaise there is the chance of rain at any time of year. The main season to miss is January to March, when

there is a high risk of hurricanes or powerful storms.

HEALTH & SAFETY

Vaccinations: None.
General Health Risks: None.
Special Considerations: None.
Politics & Religion: Réunion is mostly Catholic.
Crime Risk: Low.
Food & Drink: The great food on Réunion is a real highlight for many visitors. The island offers a combination of French cuisine and the traditional, spiced island dishes that have been developed by the Creoles. Food is taken seriously, with everything closing for 2 hours at lunchtime. The boulangeries serve superb pastries and filled baguettes.

CANYONS AND VOLCANOES

←

The volcanic landscape of la Plaines des Sables makes for challenging mountain biking.

HIGHLIGHTS

Scenic: The twin volcanic peaks of Réunion dominate the shape and ecology of the island. When the sides of Piton des Neiges collapsed many millions of years ago to form giant natural amphitheaters (or cirques), each one became a unique ecosystem, and their canyons, rivers, and forests took different forms at different altitudes, all surrounded by a wall of rock. Then, to the south, the Piton de la Fournaise, young and full of life, turned one end of the island into a dramatic lunar landscape of canyons, craters, fresh young forests, and cooled lava flows that touch the sea at the black beaches of Ste. Rose. When you pack in the fantastic beaches and warm waters of the Indian Ocean as well, you have a tropical island you won't know what to see first.
Wildlife & Flora: All around the island are a mixture of tropical woodlands, palm sugar cane, and banana plantations, and on the eastern slopes of the island are the precious vanilla crops. The volcanic soil is so rich in minerals that once nature takes a grip the area can become a dense, tropical jungle. However, many of the fertile lower slopes have been cultivated to provide the island with much of its palm crop.

↓ temperature and precipitation

	JAN	FEB	MAR	APR	MAY	JUN	JUL	AUG	SEP	OCT	NOV	DEC
°F	86	86	86	82	81	79	75	75	77	79	81	84
°C	30	30	30	28	26	24	24	24	25	26	27	29
°F	72	72	72	68	64	61	61	61	63	64	66	70
°C	22	22	22	20	18	16	16	16	17	18	19	21
in	11.0	7.9	12.6	5.9	3.1	2.7	2.4	1.8	1.6	1.8	2.6	6.6
mm	280	200	320	150	80	70	60	40	40	40	60	130

145

The barren Plaine des Cafres links the two volcanoes of Piton de la Fournaise and Piton des Neiges.

Bikes are the only vehicles that can access the stunning Cirque de Mafate, so you can rest assured there won't be any crowds.

143

Factfile:

Carefully researched, this section is presented in a concise, easy reference format, and contains vital information for planning and completing the ride.

Overview: *An assessment of the route, including total distance and time required. The difficulty and altitude of a trail are two crucial factors in selecting the best ride for your abilities.*

Access: *This section informs you of the nearest international airports and transport details, particularly the best method to reach the start and return from the finish of the route. The essential paperwork and formalities to be observed before accessing the country or trail are highlighted.*

Local Information:

Recommends specialist maps and guidebooks for the successful completion of each trail. Provides valuable advice on what sort of accommodation and range of supplies may (or may not!) be available en route, as well as supplying details on local currency and language. This section also advises on the best place to go for tourist information.

Timing & Seasonality: *An optimum time to tackle the route is suggested; and a general guide to weather conditions which may reasonably be expected is given.*

Health & Safety: *A number of very important considerations to your personal well-being are covered, and should be checked over carefully in the early planning stages of any intended trip.*

Highlights: *Points out many of the great things to look out for along the ride.*

Temperature and Precipitation Chart:

This chart provides monthly averages for maximum and minimum temperatures, and for rainfall and snowfall. The charts are organized to provide the information in Fahrenheit on the top level of each box, with the centigrade reading on the lower level; similarly, the precipitation figures are given in inches on the top, and in millimeters below. These statistics have been gathered from the nearest available source to each ride; it must be noted that climatic conditions are affected by altitude.

The Americas

Sitting on the Pacific Ring of Fire, the Americas are linked by a long chain of high mountains formed by the clash of continental plates. Extraordinary mountain bike trails in the Andes, around Lake Tahoe, along the Great Divide, and in British Columbia reveal dramatic segments of this awesome whole. By contrast, a Caribbean trip, a tour of the Appalachians, and a high desert trail showcase other shades of the continent's character.

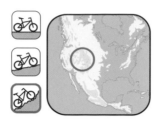

↓ itinerary

the GREAT DIVIDE

MONTANA, IDAHO, WYOMING, COLORADO, AND NEW MEXICO, U.S.A.

Michael McCoy

THE GREAT DIVIDE ROUTE FOLLOWS THE BACKBONE OF THE ROCKY MOUNTAINS, FROM THE NORTHERN REACHES OF MONTANA AT THE BORDER WITH CANADA, TO THE SOUTH OF NEW MEXICO. UTILIZING OLD LOGGING PATHS, MINING TRACKS, FOUR-WHEEL-DRIVE ROADS, AND SINGLE-TRACK TRAILS, THE ROUTE SURMOUNTS THE CONTINENTAL DIVIDE MORE THAN TWO DOZEN TIMES AS IT WENDS ITS TORTUOUS WAY THROUGH THE EMPTIEST YET MOST AWE-INSPIRING SCENERY ON EARTH.

The description given here breaks the Great Divide into 62 days, which is about the average time it takes a relatively fit cyclist to complete the ride. Because of the length and complexity of the route, the following description is not adequate for navigation. Moreover, the route runs through wilderness terrain and it is not signposted, so maps and a guidebook are essential (*see* Factfile).

←

The Great Divide is such a lengthy trail that you may choose to do it in sections, but be aware that snow will often catch you out if you decide to cover some ground during winter.

•DAYS 1–20   695 miles (1,118km)

Montana

Montana is aptly known as "Big Sky Country." Here, the Great Divide passes through five national forests: the Kootenai, Flathead, Lolo, Helena, and Deerlodge-Beaverhead. Precipitous mountains and vast forests of western larch, Douglas fir, and lodgepole pine typify the northern half of Montana. The southern reaches of the state are more commonly characterized by mining ruins and wide valleys filled with grazing horses and cattle. Views from lofty places up north are reminiscent of Alaska, whereas the big ranches of the south evoke images of the Wild West.

The route begins, rather humbly, in Roosville, amid the quiet farms of the Tobacco Valley, situated south of the Canadian border. But on entering the wild lands of Kootenai National Forest, you'll climb past clear-cuts and through stands of old-growth timber, earning chances to spot moose, gray wolves, bald eagles, and pileated woodpeckers.

From the Whitefish Divide, the route descends through the valleys of Yakinikak and Trail creeks, places so isolated that grizzly bears too rambunctious to live close to human habitation are sometimes relocated here by fish and game officials. You'll then spin along the western boundary of Glacier National Park, through the valley of the Flathead River's North Fork. From Whitefish—home to the Big Mountain, Montana's pre-eminent ski resort—the route twists its way over paved and gravel roads through the pastoral, mountain-surrounded upper Flathead Valley. A puzzling system of old logging roads then leads through the Seeley-Swan Valley to the shores of Seeley Lake and its eponymous town.

Helena, Montana's capital city, is a beautiful and historic community—one of relatively few mineral boom towns of the nineteenth century that made it big and stayed that way into the twenty-first. From Helena, ride on to the unique and colorful city of Butte, whose residents refer to their hometown simply as Butte, America. Butte and Helena are

the two most populous cities located along the entire 2,470-mile (3,976-km) Great Divide.

From Butte you'll head up, then down, then up and down again, and over Fleecer Ridge, the most remarkable downhill found along the length of the Great Divide. From tiny Wise River you pedal onto the paved Pioneer Mountains National Scenic Byway—this road provides one of the finest road rides in the West as it meanders amid the spectacular Pioneer Mountains. A descent past Elkhorn Hot Springs delivers you to the valley of Grasshopper Creek, which you follow to Bannack. Montana's original territorial capital is now a well-preserved ghost town protected by its status as a state park. From there, it's southward through the ranching country surrounding the Lewis and Clark

National Historic Trail. The ensuing ride on the Big Sheep Creek Backcountry Byway provides mile after mile of empty country, probably looking not much different than it did in the 1860s when horse-drawn coaches stormed through.

From Dell (home to Calf-A, one of southwest Montana's best and most unusual eateries), you'll parallel Interstate 15 on a gravel road to Lima, then travel through a wild, desiccated terrain to Red Rock Lakes National Wildlife Refuge. Here, in one of Montana's best-kept secrets, you may have the opportunity to see and hear trumpeter swans, a large, pure-white bird that faced near extinction in the early part of the twentieth century. Finally, the easy spin over the Continental Divide at Red Rock Pass takes you into Idaho.

Wyoming's lofty Tetons are considered by many to be among the world's most spectacular mountain ranges. The Great Divide passes through so many other ranges that you will have plenty of opportunities to find out if you agree with this claim.

→

•DAYS 21–32 553 miles (890km)

Idaho and Wyoming

Island Park, Idaho, is a popular destination for fly-fishers, who arrive from all over the world to try their skill and luck with the wily fish of the legendary Henrys Fork of the Snake River. From near Big Springs, where the Henrys Fork springs forth, the Great Divide follows for 31 miles (50km) a former Union Pacific Railroad spur line that delivered early-day tourists to the doorstep of Yellowstone National Park. The rail trail terminates at the pleasing Warm River Campground. Beyond there, you'll pedal onto the Ashton–Flagg Road, which squeezes its way eastward between Yellowstone and Grand Teton national parks. More than 60 miles (100km) of paved road follow in Jackson Hole and the upper Wind River Valley as mountain bikes are off-limits on the trails in America's national parks and wilderness areas. The incredible Tetons and other mountain ranges will vie for your attention as you try to keep your eyes on the road.

From outside Dubois, the route crawls up historic Union Pass, an important passageway for the fur-trapping mountain men of the 1820s and 1830s, and for the Native Americans who preceded them. After leaving behind acres of wild-flower-filled, high-elevation meadows, you'll enter the valley of the upper Green River, with its jaw-dropping views of the high Wind River Range to the south and east. South of the busy ranching and outfitting town of Pinedale, the terrain turns from mountainous to high desert as it falls away from the flanks of the Wind Rivers. In certain high, lonely places you'll pedal directly atop the Continental Divide, before the Great Divide brings you to South Pass City, where a state park encompasses the evocative remains of a town key to the settlement of Wyoming.

From South Pass City, the route pushes into the Great Divide Basin, a 2.3-million-acre, high-elevation depression where waters drain neither east toward the Atlantic Ocean nor west toward the Pacific. It is one of the longest

The Wise River, which runs through Montana's Pioneer Mountains, is one of many outstanding trout-fishing streams encountered along the route.

↓

Gravel byways are characteristic of a majority of the roads followed by this trail.

key

▬▬▬	route of ride
▬▬▬	major road
▭▭▭	minor road
▦▦▦	continental divide
- - - -	country border
▭ ▭ ▭	State border
▲	peak
⊔	pass
Ⱥ	campground
🛏	hotel/guesthouse
✕	provisions
☍	bike shop/repairs

↑
Montana's remote Centennial Valley is home to Red Rock Lakes National Wildlife Refuge—the area was set aside in 1935 to protect the then-endangered trumpeter swan.

segments of the route holding no services, and you'll need to prepare for it by stocking up on water and food at Boulder. Herds of wild horses and pronghorns are plentiful; the shade of a tree, however, is virtually non-existent. America's most important pioneer trails including the Oregon Trail and Pony Express Trail cut through this big empty space.

From the full-service desert town of Rawlins, the Great Divide climbs into the high Sierra Madre, and back to the forests, before continuing south into Colorado.

•DAYS 33–46   548 miles (882km)

Colorado

The first town encountered in Colorado is the popular ski resort of Steamboat Springs. From there, you'll follow segments of the Yampa River Trail prior to commencing the climb over Lynx Pass. Enjoy the high-country chill while you can, for it's not long before an unforgettable downhill delivers you back to desert at a Colorado River crossing at Radium. After a visit to the town of Kremmling and yet another stretch of broad, treeless basin, you'll cross Ute Pass and enter Summit County, a name that is virtually synonymous with winter and summer recreation in Colorado.

A brief stretch on all-too-busy State Highway 9 links with the absolutely car-free Blue River Bikeway, a hard-surfaced recreational pathway leading to the historic mining

and skiing village of Breckenridge. From there, you'll bump up and over Boreas Pass, the Great Divide's fifteenth Continental Divide crossing (11,482 feet/3,500m). After pedaling through the high, dry basin known as South Park, you will climb over a mountain ridge to free fall into the attractive town of Salida, which lies beneath several of Colorado's famous Fourteeners—peaks that top out at over 14,000 feet (4,270m).

At Marshall Pass, southwest of Salida, a trio of mountain ranges converge: the Cochetopa Hills, Sawatch Range, and Sangre de Cristo (Blood of Christ) Range. Here you'll note signs marking the way for hikers following the Continental Divide National Scenic Trail and the popular Colorado Trail. As you will have come to expect in Colorado, high valleys alternate with even higher mountains, as you continue through places such as Doyleville, La Garita, and Del Norte. From the last of these, a fair-sized settlement, you'll approach one of the Great Divide's most demanding climbs, ascending more than 4,000 feet (1,220m) in 24 miles (38km), to the Great Divide's apex, Indiana Pass, at 11,910 feet (3,631m).

Summitville, a shockingly poisoned and eroded mining site (and one of the U.S. Environmental Protection Agency's notorious Superfund sites), is followed, in great contrast, by →

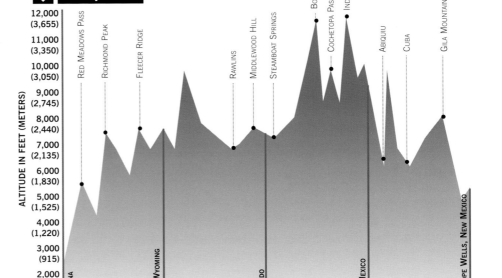

ride profile

Altitude in feet (meters) / Days

12,000 (3,655)	
11,000 (3,350)	
10,000 (3,050)	
9,000 (2,745)	
8,000 (2,440)	
7,000 (2,135)	
6,000 (1,830)	
5,000 (1,525)	
4,000 (1,220)	
3,000 (915)	
2,000 (610)	
0 (0)	

Labeled peaks/points: Red Meadows Pass, Richmond Peak, Fleecer Ridge, Rawlins, Middlewood Hill, Steamboat Springs, Boreas Pass, Cochetopa Pass, Indiana Pass, Abiquiu, Cuba, Gila Mountains

Regions along bottom: Montana / Idaho/Wyoming / Colorado / New Mexico / Antelope Wells, New Mexico

Days axis: 0   1–21   21–32   33–46   47–62

DAYS

some of the most gorgeous alpine meadows you'll find anywhere in the Rockies. A trip over Stunner Pass and downstream along the Conejos River quickly leads to your entry into the final state traversed by the Great Divide.

•DAYS 47–62 **674 miles (1,085km)**

New Mexico

Guaranteed to surprise and delight you, New Mexico is the most diverse state on the Great Divide—almost like a composite of Montana, Idaho, Wyoming, and Colorado, with a little bit of Mexico thrown in for good measure.

From the Tusas Mountains, the route twists southerly through federal lands, past private ranches, and amid Native American tribal lands. The Spanish Colonial villages of Vallecitos, El Rito, and Abiquiu are as alluring to the eye as their names are appealing to the ear. Artists and spiritual seekers/healers have been drawn to this area throughout the centuries, and you'll understand why after visiting.

From Abiquiu, the route ascends the volcanic ramp known as Polvadera Mesa, which, according to veteran Great Divide through-bikers, is even tougher than the climb up Indiana Pass in Colorado. From Cuba, weather permitting (don't try it if it looks like rain), you will zip up, down, and around one of the most isolated and remarkably eroded regions of the western United States. Subsequently, in Grants, you'll cross ways with the historic Route 66, America's legendary Mother Road, before passing through the solidified-lava landscapes of El Malpais (Bad Country) National Monument. From curiously-named Pie Town, the route crosses the arid, forbidding Plains of San Agustin before climbing back into the mountains of Gila National Forest. Here, for many miles, you'll flirt with the Continental Divide, crossing it no fewer than seven times.

At Silver City, a town straight out of the Wild West, you'll bid farewell to the mountains at last, as the final 125 miles (200km) of the route traverse Chihuahuan desert lands. The last crossing of the Continental Divide, along one of the loneliest paved roads in America, is perhaps most memorable for being a barely noticeable rise in the landscape. The Great Divide ends on the threshold of Mexico, at the tiny international border crossing of Antelope Wells.

A biker tackling the Great Divide is dwarfed by the immense terrain near Stunner Pass in the San Juan Mountains, Colorado.

OVERVIEW

The Great Divide is the longest designated, mapped mountain-bike route in the U.S. It has been called "the mountain biker's answer to the Appalachian Trail," referring to the historic footpath of lore that is located in the eastern United States. The total distance is 2,470 miles (3,976km).
Start: Roosville, Montana.
Finish: Antelope Wells, New Mexico.

ABOUT THE TRAIL

The route is made up of approximately 80 percent dirt and gravel roads and double-track, 10 percent single-track, and 10 percent paved roads.
Major Climbs & Descents: Climbs and subsequent descents ranging between 1,500 and 4,000 feet (450m and 1,220m) are the norm. The daily average elevation gain is around 3,200 feet (1,000m). The route's low point of 2,500 feet (760m) is near the beginning, in Eureka, Montana. The high point of 11,910 feet (3,631m) is at Indiana Pass, Colorado.
Difficulty & Special Features: The route was designed specifically so that cyclists carrying—or hauling in trailers—a full complement of camping and cooking gear can tackle it. Still, to complete the

route is a physical and mental challenge with few peers. Almost the entire Great Divide is ridable by a fit cyclist, although weather conditions may occasionally make parts of the route impassable. The one segment that has proven unridable is the mile-long (1.5km) descent from Fleecer Ridge, southwest of Butte, Montana. It must be walked, and even that is not easy.

ACCESS

Airports: Cities on or in close proximity to the trail with major airports include Kalispell, Montana; Helena, Montana; Jackson, Wyoming; and Steamboat Springs, Colorado.

Transport: No public transport is available to the start or the terminus of the route. Private shuttles can possibly be arranged at the trip's beginning through bike shops in Kalispell and Whitefish, Montana; and at the trip's end through shops in Silver City and Deming, New Mexico.

Passport & Visa Requirements: Passports and visas or visa waiver forms are required for all visitors.

Permits & Access Restrictions: None—the entire route is either on public lands or public-access roads that cross private property.

LOCAL INFORMATION

Maps: Detailed navigational maps are available through the Adventure Cycling Association, P.O. Box 8308, Missoula, MT 59807-8308. These maps also include information on services, such as grocery stops and campgrounds.

Guidebooks: *Cycling the Great Divide: From Canada to Mexico on America's Premier Long-Distance Mountain Bike Route*, by Michael McCoy (Mountaineers Books) includes a wealth of information on history and natural history; also

→

The trails on this route are often deserted, and you may well have only the lakes and the mountains for company.

details an itinerary that breaks the route into 62 riding days.

Accommodation & Supplies: This is primarily a camping trip, so riders must carry gear and be prepared to haul up to 4 days' worth of supplies at a stretch. Occasional indoor overnights are feasible, but generally you will be camping, which is permitted anywhere on U.S. Forest Service and Bureau of Land Management lands not posted to the contrary. The route also crosses private lands, which are generally off-limits to camping.

Currency & Language: U.S. dollars; English.

Photography: Please use common courtesy before photographing Native Americans and other residents of the region by asking their permission first.

Area Information: The Adventure Cycling Association maps include addresses and phone numbers for the many national forests and Bureau of Land Management districts crossed during the course of the route; Adventure Cycling, P.O. Box 8308, Missoula MT 59807-8308 (tel.: 406-721-1776).

Website: www.adventurecycling.org

TIMING & SEASONALITY

Best Months to Visit: July, August, and September, except for southern New Mexico, which is most pleasant in May, June, October, and November. Best-case scenario: leave from the north in mid-July, ending in southern New Mexico in early October. Many through-bikers are breaking the route into segments, covering the entire

Great Divide by riding quarters or thirds of it during successive summers.

Climate: Nearly any type of weather imaginable is possible along this route, including cold rain and snow at the highest elevations, and extreme heat (in excess of 100°F/37.5°C) in the desert areas of Wyoming and New Mexico. Wind is also common in the vast open areas of Wyoming, Colorado, and New Mexico. Warm and waterproof clothing is a must. Some portions of the route, because of clay soils, will be impassable when wet; for these stretches the Adventure Cycling Association maps outline paved options. The climate chart provided below is for Jackson, Wyoming, a community that is fairly representative of the mountain towns along the way. Typically, you will find the desert areas to be much hotter and drier.

HEALTH & SAFETY

Vaccinations: None required.

General Health Risks: Be aware of the possibilities of hypothermia in cold, wet weather, and heatstroke in extremely hot conditions. Rattlesnakes and other poisonous wildlife, such as scorpions, may be seen in the low-lying deserts of New Mexico. Potentially disease-carrying ticks may also be encountered in areas of brush throughout the route.

Special Considerations: Many mountainous regions along the northern part of the route, from the Canadian border to approximately Pinedale, Wyoming, are inhabited by grizzly bears. Take special care to keep a clean camp and hang food from a high tree limb, away from your tent. The U.S. Forest Service can provide details on how to remain bear aware.

Politics & Religion: No concerns.

Crime Risk: Low.

Food & Drink: Surface water from lakes and streams must be filtered to protect against giardia, which is increasingly common, and can cause severe intestinal sickness.

HIGHLIGHTS

Scenic: There are many wild, remote stretches along the trail. It will take you through forests, over mountains, past rivers, and even through dusty plains, ensuring that there is something for everyone.

Wildlife & Flora: The Rocky Mountains are known throughout the world for their remarkable scenery and abundant wildlife, and this route will not disappoint those expecting these things. Bear, moose, elk, deer, gray wolves, mountain lions, and javelina (a wild pig residing in the southern desert areas) are some of the larger mammals you may encounter.

↓ temperature and precipitation

		JAN	FEB	MAR	APR	MAY	JUN	JUL	AUG	SEP	OCT	NOV	DEC	
▲	°f	27	32	41	52	67	72	81	80	71	58	39	28	°f
	°c	−3	0	5	11	19	22	27	27	22	14	4	−2	°c
▼	°f	5	8	16	24	31	37	40	38	31	23	16	6	°f
	°c	−15	−13	−9	−4	−1	3	4	3	−1	−5	−9	−14	°c
🌧	ins	1.5	1.0	1.1	1.1	1.9	1.7	1.1	1.2	1.3	1.1	1.5	1.6	ins
	mm	38	27	29	28	48	43	27	29	33	29	38	42	mm

→

At Buck Canyon, where the Island in the Sky mesa dominates the horizon, the trail runs perilously close to the rim.

↓ itinerary

the WHITE RIM

UTAH, U.S.A.

Steve Callen

DESERTS ARE HOSTILE ENVIRONMENTS OFFERING LANDSCAPES OF SURREAL BEAUTY THAT HAVE BEEN FORMED BY THE EXTREMES OF NATURE. THE HIGH DESERT OF SOUTHEASTERN UTAH IS NO EXCEPTION TO THIS CRITERION, AND THE WHITE RIM TRAIL RIDES FOR 80 SPECTACULAR MILES (130KM) THROUGH THE APTLY NAMED "ISLAND IN THE SKY" DISTRICT OF CANYONLANDS NATIONAL PARK.

The trail mainly follows a geological fault that comprises the middle of three distinct shelves. This allows you to cycle with relative ease, avoiding heart-stopping canyons and rims, while gazing upward at the burned orange mesa of the "Island," the many soaring towers and buttes that penetrate the skyline, and catching glimpses of the mighty Colorado and Green Rivers as they slice their way slowly through this arid landscape.

The trail came into being through the early cattle ranchers, who used the area for winter grazing. Later came the Atomic Energy Commission, who completed the road to its present form to aid the exploration of uranium mining. The finished result is a mecca for mountain bikers, giving them the opportunity of sampling the harsh delights of desert travel on a hard-packed, easy trail.

Fast riding takes you past the spectacular Monument Basin.

•DAY 1 | 18½ miles (30km)

Shafer Trail to Airport Tower

The start of the Shafer Trail keeps you guessing as to where and how it is going to descend the 1,400 feet (430m) from the Island in the Sky mesa. You cycle next to vertical cliffs and suddenly catch sight of the trail as it stretches into the distance far below. To get there will certainly give you an adrenaline rush as the trail switchbacks steeply down the cliff face. Admire the view and the fast ride, but not at the same time. At approximately 6 miles (10km) a trail comes in from the left. Take a rest here and stare back in amazement to where you've just descended from. Two miles (3km) further on, leave your bikes just off the trail and walk to the Goose Neck Overlook. You will be rewarded with a view of the Colorado River as it turns on itself, and very likely catch a glimpse of a raft trip floating with the current.

You're back in the saddle for a short while until at 10 miles (17km) you park up and walk a short distance to Musselman Arch. This is a vertigo-inducing natural arch; walk across if you dare but bikes are strictly forbidden.

There is now a short climb to stretch the limbs before a rapid descent leads you past the entrance to Lathrop Canyon. A mile (1.5km) further on are the four independent campgrounds of Airport Tower, with its namesake monolith rising 1,400 feet (425m) above. Set up camp and then cycle back to Lathrop Canyon and prepare for the 4-mile (6.5-km) descent to the Colorado River. This will test your skills on everything from steep loose rock through to lung-bursting soft sand. The bottom is an idyllic picnic spot with welcome shade and a chance to cool off in the river. The wise will take a support vehicle to avoid the steep return leg.

Back at the camp, enjoy your first sunset in the desert as the rocks turn blood red, bats flutter through the dusk, and a myriad of stars appear. The landscape is timeless, and the silence helps you reflect on life's great experiences.

→

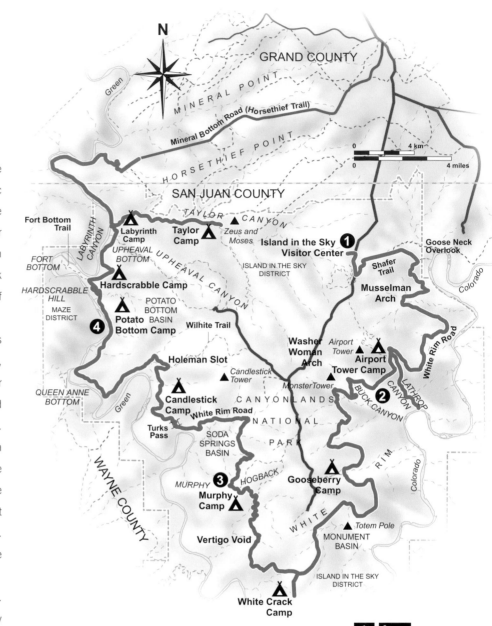

•DAY 2 26 miles (42km)

Airport Tower to Murphy Hogback

Make an effort to break camp early to avoid riding in the afternoon heat. Early risers will also witness the fantastic spectacle of the sun's rays bringing color and warmth to the desert. As Airport Tower disappears from view, so Monster Tower and Washer Woman Arch take its place. This is an easy start to the day with plenty of opportunity to sit back and enjoy the scenery. The trail skirts the overhung lip of Buck Canyon, so make sure you keep a steady line.

Ten miles (17km) from Airport Tower you pass Gooseberry Camp. Keep going for a further 3 miles (5km), where the outlook into Monument Basin will catch your breath—crumbling pillars topped with capstones stand erect out of the basin, like an imaginary lunar landscape. Further round from this viewpoint, the pencil-like Totem Pole is spotted rising 305 feet (93m) from the floor of the basin. Another 3 miles (5km) and the road forks to White Crack Camp. There are many archaeological artifacts of pot shards and projectile points spread throughout this site. Please leave them undisturbed. The site has expansive views and is worth reserving for an overnight stop.

Back on the trail, a fast downhill leads to Vertigo Void. Look across and under the lip of this canyon and you may

key

	route of ride
	major road
	minor road
	vehicle track
	path
	USA area boundary
	park border
	seasonal river
▲	peak
⊔	pass
🛖	campground

←

The primeval beauty of Monument Basin, with its multitude of crumbling pillars, is one of the route's most impressive scenic highlights.

well see the swifts and swallows that play in the updrafts of the rim. The easy going now gives way to the first big climb—Murphy Hogback. This is a steep, remorseless climb of 400 feet (122m) that will get your pulse racing. Crawl, breathless, over the top knowing you are camping here for the night. There is plenty of shelter from the sun plus panoramic views of the surreal Land of the Standing Stones to Soda Springs Basin and Candlestick Tower.

•DAY 3 21 miles (34km)

Murphy Hogback to Potato Bottom

Prepare yourself mentally for the descent off Murphy Hogback. Check for any vehicles coming up before launching yourself down the steep track and accompanying switchbacks. So long as your eyes aren't firmly rooted on the trail then glimpses of the Green River will flash past. As the track straightens out, don't be surprised to find yourself occasionally airborne as you rattle over the slickrock bumps. The Soda Springs Basin is still fast and generally downhill until your enjoyment is abruptly halted—ahead lies Turks Pass, which is overcome by a short steep struggle. Take a rest at the top and follow the trail with your eyes back across the flat shelf toward the steep rise of Murphy Hogback. If you are quiet, chipmunks may begin to play →

The Shafer Trail descends 1,400 feet (430m) by a series of fast, loose switchbacks that have been carved out of the cliff face.

The ascent of Hardscrabble Hill is one of three testing climbs best done in the cool of an early morning.

↓ ride profile

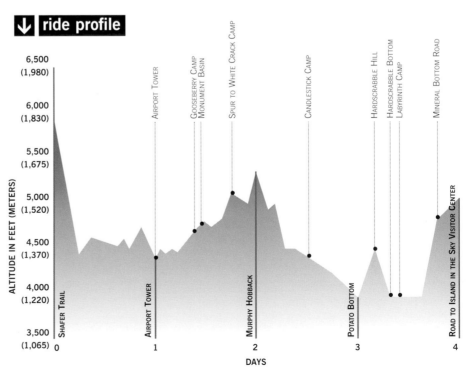

Ride profile chart — ALTITUDE IN FEET (METERS) vs DAYS

Altitude axis: 6,500 (1,980), 6,000 (1,830), 5,500 (1,675), 5,000 (1,520), 4,500 (1,370), 4,000 (1,220), 3,500 (1,065)

Labels: SHAFER TRAIL, AIRPORT TOWER, GOOSEBERRY CAMP, MONUMENT BASIN, SPUR TO WHITE CRACK CAMP, CANDLESTICK CAMP, MURPHY HOGBACK, HARDSCRABBLE HILL, HARDSCRABBLE BOTTOM, LABYRINTH CAMP, POTATO BOTTOM, MINERAL BOTTOM ROAD, ROAD TO ISLAND IN THE SKY VISITOR CENTER

DAYS: 0, 1, 2, 3, 4

among the rocks. More quick downhill follows from Turks Pass as you head past Candlestick Tower and Camp. Two miles (3km) past this site is the Wilhite Trail. Dismount here and take time to explore the fascinating Holeman Slot, where you will see at close quarters the textures and effects of erosion.

The trail is now quite rocky and technical in sections, though still steadily descending. The Green River is getting closer all the time. If you need to replenish water supplies, then look out for a water wash approximately 4 miles (6.5km) from the Wilhite Trail that leads down to Queen Anne Bottom. There are many signs of settlers along these shores, plus old anchors used by ferries that once transported cattle across the river. A further 4 miles (6.5km) brings you to the Potato Bottom campgrounds. These riverside sites offer plenty of cool shade but do attract large numbers of insects. If you are looking for a cool dip then the wash north of Campground C has the easiest access.

•DAY 4   14 miles (22.5km)

Potato Bottom to Mineral Bottom Road

Camping at Potato Bottom gives the advantage of tackling Hardscrabble Hill—an unrelenting climb with two very steep sections—early in the morning. A couple of miles (3km) after the top you come to the hiking trail of Fort Bottom. Leave your bike and hike the mile (1.5km) to some ruins at the bottom. The cabin near the river was built as a hospice for tuberculosis patients on their way to a refuge that was never built at the confluence of the Green and Colorado Rivers. There is a ruined tower that dates back to 1260 and is thought to have been defensive or ceremonial in purpose.

Back at the top, a fast sandy descent leads you past the Hardscrabble campgrounds. You are now in Upheaval Bottom, which can be very heavy going in the soft sand. These sands are the product of flash floods, so take care in inclement weather. At Labyrinth Camp the track splits. The right fork will take you up Taylor Canyon for 5 miles (8km), to a viewpoint of the impressive Zeus and Moses Towers. You will ride through some sandy sections that preserve wildlife footprints extremely well; bobcats and lizards are

common ones. The return trip to Labyrinth Camp is quick and exhilarating.

The trail is now right next to the Green River with its forest of tamarisk. Old uranium mines can be spotted close to the track. These are still unstable and emit dangerous radiation so do not enter. The end is now in sight as you come to Mineral Bottom Road, formerly known as Horsethief Trail. This route was supposedly used by the Robbers Roost gang that included Butch Cassidy. The ascent is the longest of the whole trail, 1,000 feet (305m) in approximately 1 mile (1.5km). It is ridable all the way, though one or two rest stops may be needed. Those with any sense will meet a support vehicle at the top of the switchbacks to avoid the 21-mile (34-km) uphill stretch to the visitor center.

On completion of such a journey there is cause for much celebration, and long after you have returned home you will dream of those few special days spent in a different world.

The first half of the route follows a road built for mining exploration; glimpses of the Colorado River can be caught as the road meanders through the canyons.

factfile

OVERVIEW

The route follows a four-wheel-drive trail that was built for mining exploration. The distance covered is 80 miles (130km), which can be cycled in 1 day but is more usually done in 3 or 4 days under favorable conditions.

Start: Top of the Shafer Trail, just north of the Island in the Sky Visitor Center.

Finish: Top of the steep climb on Mineral Bottom Road.

ABOUT THE TRAIL

The trail is relatively easy, being all on double-track.

Major Climbs & Descents: There are three major climbs: Murphy Hogback, Hardscrabble Hill, and Mineral Bottom Road. The last is the hardest with a climb of 1,000 feet (305m) in 1 mile (1.5km). The descent of the Shafer Trail is steep and loose in places, and particular care must be taken.

Difficulty & Special Features: Four-wheel-drive vehicle support is strongly recommended to carry water and supplies. Adventure companies in Moab offer this support if needed. Cycle and walk on the trail only—do not diverge from the track as the desert ecosystem is protected by a surface crust called cryptobiotic soil. This soil is normally dark and crunchy but can also be reddish or brown. Once this surface crust is broken, it can take up to 200 years to regenerate.

ACCESS

 Airports: The closest international airports are Denver, Colorado (355

miles/570km), and Salt Lake City, Utah (236 miles/380km).

Transport: Moab is the town to base yourself in. Most people tend to rent their own vehicle from the airport but a shuttle is available from Salt Lake City. There is no public transport to the start or finish of the route. Use a support vehicle or cycle the 33 miles (53km) from Moab.

Passport & Visa Requirements: Passports with visa or visa waiver form (available on incoming flights) for all visitors to North America.

Permits & Acess Restrictions: Permits are required for overnight camping. You must camp at one of the designated campgrounds, where a reservation is essential. Only one group (up to 15 people) is allowed on a particular site, so a feeling of seclusion is assured. Reserve early, allowing 6 months to guarantee your chosen sites.

LOCAL INFORMATION

 Maps: Moab West: Mountain Biking and Recreation by Latitude 40° Inc.

Guidebooks: *Mountain Biking Moab* by David Crowell (Falcon Publishing); *Above and Beyond Slickrock* by Todd Campbell (University of Utah Press).

Accommodation & Supplies: You must camp at the designated campgrounds and carry all your own supplies. Moab offers all the amenities and stores to supply the trip, and it has a wealth of bike shops.

Currency & Language: US dollars; English.

Area Information: Moab Tourist Information Center, Center & Main Street, Moab, Utah 84532.

Canyonlands National Park Reservation Office, 2282 West Resource Blvd., Moab, Utah 84532 (tel.: 435-259-4351; fax: 435-259-4285).

Website: www.nps.gov/cany

TIMING & SEASONALITY

 Best Months to Visit: Spring and fall. Avoid the summer months of June to August because of the extreme heat— temperatures can rise to as high as 130°F (54°C).

Climate: Storms are a common hazard and can close the access trails (Shafer and Mineral Bottom Road). If caught by a storm be extremely cautious of flash floods.

HEALTH & SAFETY

 Vaccinations: None.

General Health Risks: Protect yourself from the desert sun and be aware of the dangers of

heatstroke.

Politics & Religion: No special concerns.

Crime Risk: None.

Food & Drink: You will need a minimum of 2 gallons (7.5 liters) of water per person per day. If you're self-supported you can obtain water from the Colorado River in Lathrop Canyon, but not again until you reach the Green River before Potato Bottom. The water in these rivers is heavily silted, so an efficient filter system is essential.

HIGHLIGHTS

The White Rim Trail travels through a high desert. The vast openness and complete silence will indelibly imprint themselves on your memory.

Scenic: The desert architecture is one of primeval beauty. Arid land-

↑

The trail descends quickly to the open expanses of Soda Springs Basin. In the background, the monolithic butte that is Candlestick Tower can be seen rising out of the canyon.

scapes sweep out to the horizons with no sense of depth or scale. This changes dramatically as you turn a bend and catch sight of a great meandering river ribboned with fertile green foliage.

Wildlife & Flora: Lizards and snakes are common, and the latter will avoid you unless disturbed. Bighorn sheep graze on the slopes above and below the White Rim, while golden eagles and peregrine falcons soar the thermals. At ground level, shadscale and four-wing saltbush are dominant shrubs along with a variety of sparse grasses and cacti.

↓ **temperature and precipitation**

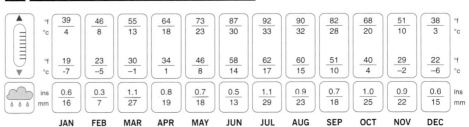

	JAN	FEB	MAR	APR	MAY	JUN	JUL	AUG	SEP	OCT	NOV	DEC	
°f	39	46	55	64	73	87	92	90	82	68	51	38	°f
°c	4	8	13	18	23	30	33	32	28	20	10	3	°c
°f	19	23	30	34	46	58	62	60	51	40	29	22	°f
°c	-7	-5	-1	1	8	14	17	15	10	4	-2	-6	°c
ins	0.6	0.3	1.1	0.8	0.7	0.5	1.1	0.9	0.7	1.0	0.9	0.6	ins
mm	16	7	27	19	18	13	29	23	18	25	22	15	mm

the SHENANDOAH MOUNTAIN TOUR

VIRGINIA, U.S.A.

Chris Scott

THIS FIVE-DAY RIDE HEADS SOUTH ALONG SHENANDOAH MOUNTAIN ON THE VERY RIDGES THAT CONFEDERATE SCOUTS MONITORED UNION TROOPS FROM DURING THE AMERICAN CIVIL WAR. "SHENANDOAH" WAS THE NAME OF A NATIVE AMERICAN PRINCESS AND MEANS "DAUGHTER OF THE STARS."

The first two days are relaxing and scenic with most of the travel on dirt roads. The ride gradually covers more and more single-track until the final day, when you traverse over 20 miles (32km) of ridge-top single-track—sheer bliss! Shenandoah Mountain is a highly prized section of the ancient Appalachian Mountains. It spans the length of the Dry River and Deerfield Ranger Districts in the George Washington National Forest and serves as the boundary of Virginia and West Virginia for many miles. The George Washington National Forest was previously known as the Shenandoah National Forest, but changed its name in order not be mistaken with the close-by Shenandoah National Park.

•DAY 1   20 miles (32km)

Blue Hole to Hall Spring Road

The start of the ride is at Blue Hole, a picnic area and beautiful swimming hole on the North Fork of the Shenandoah River. The first half of the day is pleasant riding on country roads along stocked trout rivers and lush green fields until the road turns to dirt and starts climbing the massive mountain for just over 20 miles (32km).

Start pedaling up the headwaters of the Shenandoah River. Pick up Rt. 865 in Bergton and follow it to Rt. 824, leaving the flat river valleys behind. Climb along Bennett Run up onto Shenandoah Mountain. At 2,802 feet (850m) you will reach the ridge; head south toward Cow Knob at 4,036 feet (1,230m) and then descend 3 miles (5km) toward Long Run Road. Continue onto Hall Spring Road, where there are some clearings that are good for camping.

•DAY 2   18.5 miles (30km)

Hall Spring Road to Wild Camp

Follow Hall Spring Road south across the ridge for 6 miles (9.5km) to the single-track of Road Run Trail (see VARIATION below). Continue for 3 more miles (5km) before taking a left onto the top of the ridge; the views to the east of Switzer Dam are fabulous from here. Continue east to a double-track trail on your right, which drops in and descends 1,100 feet (335m) over 2 miles (3km) down to Dunkle Hollow Road.

The climb up Dunkle Hollow along the lake to Flag Pole Knob is spectacular, even though Dunkle Hollow seems to keep you in its dark hardwood shadow for most of it. From the summit, where the view of the Shenandoah Valley is breathtaking, take a right and continue climbing to Flag Pole Knob.

Continuing south you will see an old stone wall appear on the right with a pipe gushing delicious spring water out of the mountain—fill up for the night here. Proceed for another mile (1.5km) until you see a turnout on the left, which goes over a big mound and up onto a peak. This is a great camp spot; it is not as popular as Flag Pole Knob and has more protection from bad weather.

The views across the wonderful woods and forests of Virginia and West Virginia never fail to impress. This trail is particularly beautiful in fall when the area becomes awash with golden and fiery hues.

A host of amazing downhills are available to you if you want an adrenaline burst of major proportions, but these high-speed trails are not obligatory and easier dirt roads can be taken if you are carrying a heavy load, or if common sense prevails!

VARIATION: Road Run Trail is a steep downhill off the west side of the mountain into West Virginia, descending 1,800 feet (550m) in 2 miles (3km). To take full advantage of the rocky drops and twisting steepness, leave any gear at the top. To reclaim your gear, from the bottom take a left heading over to U.S. 33, then left again climbing back up to Hall Spring Road, and then yet another left for 3 miles (5km).

•DAY 3   19.5 miles (31km)

Wild Camp to North River Campground

Continue south, past a turnout on the left to Hone Quarry Ridge Trail (see VARIATION below), until you reach Briery Branch Gap. From here, a tarmac road leads up to great views from Reddish Knob (4,397 feet/1,340m).

From Reddish Knob, backtrack to the intersection with the F.R. 85 and take a left onto the dirt road, which you follow south to Bald Mountain Road. Bald Mountain Road provides the sweetest dirt-road downhilling on the ride—the best mountain view is ahead of you, and wide-open fields

come and go in a blur. At 3,530 feet (1,075m), take the road that climbs to the summit of Little Bald Knob.

From Little Bald Knob, take the Chestnut Ridge Trail that shoots off to the left and goes mostly downhill for 7 miles (11km)—a difficult yet fun downhill that blasts along a ridgeline for 3 miles (5km) before you have to take a right at the Grooms Ridge Trail intersection. The descent remains tricky over the next 2½ miles (4km), until you pass a pond and connect with the Little Skidmore Trail. The final 1½ miles (2.5km) of the descent is a high-speed, grassy road trail down to F.R. 95. Stokesville Market is 3 miles (5km) to your left and the camping destination for the night is 2 miles (3km) to your right at the North River Campground.

VARIATION: Hone Quarry Ridge Trail is a 9-mile (14.5-km) ridge ride; it has a few short, steep pitches uphill, but for the most part it goes downhill over 2,000 feet (610m) to Rt. 257. It is a 10-mile (16-km) road climb back up to Briery Branch Gap. This option is only recommended if you are traveling with no extra gear.

•DAY 4 ▮ 18.7 miles (31km)

North River Campground to Signal Corps Knob

The campground is at the base of Hankey Mountain; climb to the mountain's summit by heading south, crossing the North River, and taking a left onto Hankey Mountain Road.

From the summit, downhill along double-track to where it becomes single-track, then climb to the junction of Dowell's Draft Trail and the Wild Oak Trail. Take a left onto Dowell's Draft and begin 4 miles (6.5km) of fantastic, off-camber single-track that hugs the contour of the mountain. At the bottom, take a right until you reach a left turn onto Rt. 715, which you follow to U.S. 250. Head west on Rt. 250 to grab final provisions at Carpenters Convince, and then continue west to Mountain House. In the early 1900s there was a roadhouse here for travelers passing over Shenandoah Mountain. During the American Civil War, Stonewall Jackson's first victory—the famous 1862 Valley Campaign—started at this location: Jackson's troops encountered Union soldiers at Ramsey's Draft and chased them up and over Shenandoah Mountain to McDowell, where most of the battle took place.

Double back 100 yards (90m) to the east side of the ridge and take a right toward the Shenandoah Mountain Trail to a great camping spot on Signal Corps Knob.

↑ key

▭	route of ride
▭	major road
▭	minor road
┈	bike trail
╌	U.S.A. state boundary
▲	peak
⛺	campground
🛏	hotel/guesthouse
✕	provisions
🚲	bike shop/repairs

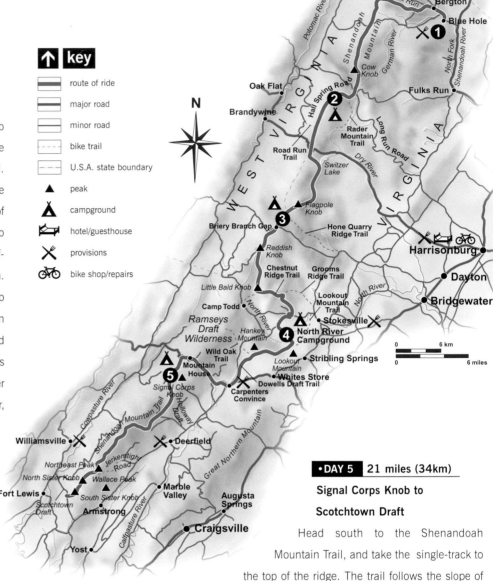

•DAY 5 ▮ 21 miles (34km)

Signal Corps Knob to Scotchtown Draft

Head south to the Shenandoah Mountain Trail, and take the single-track to the top of the ridge. The trail follows the slope of the mountain in a magical way, eliminating the steep climbing yet providing long, plush downhills over the next 5 miles (8km) to the Holloway Draft saddle.

The trail continues south and, at 3,634 feet (1,100m), begins to climb toward the summit. This 11-mile (18-km) section of single-track has long straights that are tight, twisty, and smooth, scattered with technical rocky sections.

Be careful at the Jerkemtight junction to take the Shenandoah Mountain Trail, as there are two different single-track trails heading off the west side of the ridge; the one you want is that which heads more southerly, and drops only slightly to meet up with the ridge again. The trail skirts around North Sister Knob at an elevation of 3,292 feet (1,000m) and then coils you up onto South Sister Knob at 3,088 feet (940m) for a screaming-fast, 1,100-foot (330-m) descent to Scotchtown Draft, the end of the route.

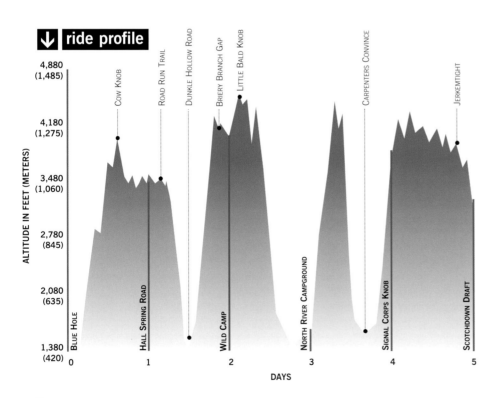

↓ ride profile

(Altitude in feet (meters) vs. Days)

Peaks labeled: Cow Knob, Road Run Trail, Dunkle Hollow Road, Briery Branch Gap, Little Bald Knob, Carpenters Convince, Jerkemtight

Valleys labeled: Blue Hole, Hall Spring Road, Wild Camp, North River Campground, Signal Corps Knob, Scotchdown Draft

Altitude scale: 4,880 (1,485); 4,180 (1,275); 3,480 (1,060); 2,780 (845); 2,080 (635); 1,380 (420)

factfile

This trail is ridable in all seasons, and although it may be bitterly cold in winter the numerous climbs should still cause you to work up a sweat.

OVERVIEW

This route covers the best riding in Virginia. Experience the Shenandoah Mountain Trail at its finest, by taking 5 days to cover 88 miles (140km)—that might not sound like hard going, but the propensity of single-track and technical riding will leave you exhausted and exhilarated at the end of each day.

Start: Blue Hole.

Finish: Scotchdown Draft.

ABOUT THE TRAIL

The majority of the ride is on dirt tracks, with 31 miles (50km) of glorious single-track, 15 miles (24km) of scenic tarmac, and 12 miles (19km) of grassy double-track.

Major Climbs & Descents: Day 1 climbs over and past Cow Knob; Day 2 descends to Switzer Dam and climbs back out to Flagpole Knob; Day 3 descends off Little Bald Knob down to North River Campground; Day 4 climbs up Hankey Mountain, descends Dowell's Draft, and climbs again to Signal Corps Knob; Day 5 is a medley of climbing and descending the Shenandoah Mountain Trail's fantastic single-track.

Difficulty & Special Features: If you are having problems with the downhills or are carrying a heavy load on Day 3 do not divert from the dirt tracks all the way to North River Campground. Bikes should be set up with wide ratio gears for all the long climbs.

ACCESS

Airports: Washington Dulles and Regan National are 2 hours from the trail head.

Baltimore/Washington International is 3 hours from the trail head.

Transport: Shenandoah Mountain Touring in Harrisonburg offers shuttles to and from the ride's beginning and end (see below for contact details).

Passport & Visa Requirements: Passports and visas or visa waiver forms (available on international flights) are required for all visitors.

Permits & Access Restrictions: No special-use permits are needed for the route. Stay on the roads when it is posted "No Trespassing," as the roads are public rights of way. Wilderness areas in the U.S. forests are off limits to bikes.

LOCAL INFORMATION

Maps: Shenandoah Mountain Touring offers detailed maps of the ride. Dry River and Greenfield Ranger District maps of the George Washington National Forest provide a great overview. Without a guide you should purchase topographical maps of the region from United States Geological Survey.

Guidebooks: This trail isn't detailed in any guidebooks, but general mountain biking books for the area include *Mountain Bike America Virginia* by Scott Adams, (Beachway Press) and *Mountain Biking in West Virginia* Frank Hutchins (Quarrier Press).

Accommodation & Supplies: Camping spots can be found along the route, and the best ones are recommended in the itinerary. You will pass near several towns on the route—apart from on the final day—to which you can detour to supplement your provisions. A fully supported trip is run by

Shenandoah Mountain Touring, Shenandoah Bicycle Co., Harrisonburg, Virginia (tel.: 540-434-2087; e-mail: mountaintouring@aol.com).

Currency & Language: U.S. dollars; English.

Area Information: Harrisonburg–Rockingham Convention & Visitors' Bureau (tel. 540-434-2139).

Website: www.virginia.org; www.mountaintouring.com.

TIMING & SEASONALITY

Best Months to Visit: The riding is great from late March to late October.

Climate: June can become warm and you can expect afternoon

thunderstorms in July and August. By the end of September the leaves are changing, and colors peak in hue and tone in early October. Be aware of the weather and how fast and drastically it can change, particularly at higher elevations (4,000 feet/1,200m).

HEALTH & SAFETY

Vaccinations: None required.

General Health Risks: Eastern rattlesnakes are seen, but not too frequently, sunning themselves on rocks along the ridge. Be alert to symptoms of hypothermia. It can occur at temperatures well above freezing. Outdoor skills are important, and using a compass is

a must, because the trails are generally unmarked.

Special Considerations: Avoid riding during the deer hunting season, late November to early December. At other times always wear bright colors and frequently whistle or talk to make hunters aware of your presence.

Politics & Religion: America is a stable, democratic, multicultural country.

Crime Risks: Low.

Food & Drink: Be sure to treat the water to prevent various parasitic diseases such as giardiasis. To protect against black bear attacks, hang your food from a tree high above the ground and well away from your tent.

HIGHLIGHTS

Scenic: Shenandoah Mountain provides great views to the east of the Shenandoah Valley, the Shenandoah National Park, and to the west of West Virginia's high country and countless ridges. Reddish Knob provides a 360 degree view that can be breath-taking on a clear day.

Wildlife & Flora: Wildlife you may see includes deer, bear, bobcat, turkey, grouse, squirrel, rabbit, racoon, and fox. The dogwoods bloom in April and mountain laurel blooms in late May.

temperature and precipitation

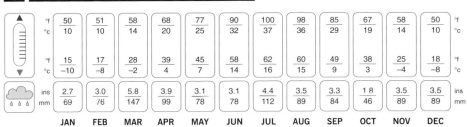

	JAN	FEB	MAR	APR	MAY	JUN	JUL	AUG	SEP	OCT	NOV	DEC	
°f	50	51	58	68	77	90	100	98	85	67	58	50	°f
°c	10	10	14	20	25	32	37	36	29	19	14	10	°c
°f	15	17	28	39	45	58	62	60	49	38	25	18	°f
°c	−10	−8	−2	4	7	14	16	15	9	3	−4	−8	°c
ins	2.7	3.0	5.8	3.9	3.1	3.1	4.4	3.5	3.3	1.8	3.5	3.5	ins
mm	69	76	147	99	78	78	112	89	84	46	89	89	mm

The immense depth of Lake Tahoe means that this lake never freezes over, even in the coldest of winters.

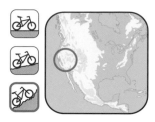

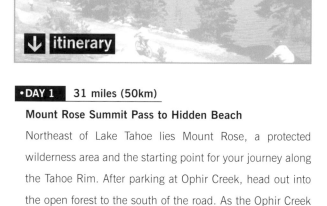

↓ itinerary

the TAHOE RIM TRAIL

NEVADA & CALIFORNIA, U.S.A.

Chris Ford

LAKE TAHOE IS THE JEWEL OF THE HIGH SIERRAS—A PURE, SPARKLING ALPINE LAKE, HIDDEN IN THE JAWS OF THE HIGHEST MOUNTAIN RANGE IN THE U.S.A., THE SIERRA NEVADA. THE SURROUNDING WILDERNESS HAS BEEN CAREFULLY PROTECTED, GIVING BIKERS ACCESS TO REMOTE BACKCOUNTRY TRAILS WITHOUT SPOILING THE SERENE BEAUTY OF THE REGION.

From the forests of giant ponderosa pines to the pristine sandy beaches that line the shores of Lake Tahoe, it's a summer wonderland. And for the mountain biker there is no better way to experience it than on the classic Tahoe Rim Trail. It's an awesome roller-coaster ride, over 90 percent of it on breathtaking single-track, and by the end of three days you'll just want to head back and start again!

→
The startlingly bright blue of Lake Tahoe forms a fantastic backdrop to much of this trail.

•DAY 1   31 miles (50km)

Mount Rose Summit Pass to Hidden Beach

Northeast of Lake Tahoe lies Mount Rose, a protected wilderness area and the starting point for your journey along the Tahoe Rim. After parking at Ophir Creek, head out into the open forest to the south of the road. As the Ophir Creek Trail branches off left, keep right on the first climb of the day. The trail soon narrows to a sliver of single-track, and won't get any wider for many hours.

The riding here is a great challenge for all levels of riders, as the trail snakes up and down the mountain side. Some sections will have novices walking, while the faster sections test the courage and skill of any rider. There are rocky descents, technical climbs, big boulders, and a few steps thrown in, too.

Climbing high into the Toiyabe National Forest, you break free from the trees for the first breathtaking views down to Lake Tahoe. As the trail twists and turns you speed down toward the distant water, then climb around behind the next row of peaks for a view into Carson's Valley. This ridge marks the borderline between mountain forests and the dry lands of high desert, which can be seen on the slopes down into the edges of Nevada.

The final descent of the morning comes out at the Tunnel Creek Trail, your first sight of double-track and a good place for lunch. Don't eat too much, though, as a quick left onto this track then a right onto the rim trail brings you to a stinging climb. There are 1,200 vertical feet (366m) to ascend, all on twisting, but thankfully quite smooth, single-track. Below is the Carson Valley, while above is one of the best viewpoints on the trail—a bald top of scented heathers and wild herbs, with views across Marlette Lake, perching above the massive blue of Lake Tahoe.

A full hour after the summit, following a downhill of awesome proportions, you'll find yourself spinning along beside Marlette Lake. As you catch your breath at the dam, it's now time to ride the world-famous Flume Trail. This old →

, trail was cut into the mountainside by the early loggers, to get their precious timbers down from Marlette to the mills below. When the flume disappeared the trail became derelict, until some smart outdoorsman realized what great potential it had as a trail.

For bikers this is a uniquely thrilling ride—twisting along a pencil-line of dirt, with sheer cliffs above and steep precipices below. It may not be technical to ride, but if you have vertigo this is a no-go. At the end you rejoin Tunnel Creek Trail, below the spot where you had lunch. It's now an incredibly fast 3-mile (5-km) blast down to Hidden Beach for an after-ride swim.

• DAY 2   28 miles (45km)

Hidden Beach to Castle Rock

Today starts with a bit of backtracking. The reason for this is that to enjoy the full three-day ride there are limited cut-out points where you can get back to paved road and your waiting vehicle (or ride the road back). So today you get to ride back up Tunnel Creek Trail and blast along the flume to Marlette Lake.

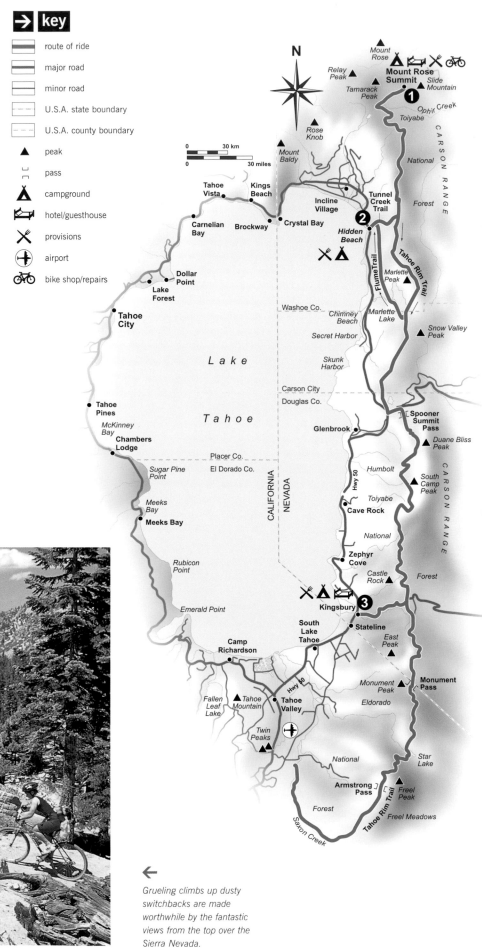

key

- ▬▬▬ route of ride
- ▭▭▭ major road
- ▭▭▭ minor road
- ┄┄┄ U.S.A. state boundary
- ┄┄┄ U.S.A. county boundary
- ▲ peak
- ⊔ pass
- ⛺ campground
- 🛏 hotel/guesthouse
- ✕ provisions
- ✈ airport
- 🚲 bike shop/repairs

←
Grueling climbs up dusty switchbacks are made worthwhile by the fantastic views from the top over the Sierra Nevada.

The Tahoe Rim Trail has a solitude and beauty that will take the breath away of even the most well-traveled visitor.

with some fairly challenging climbs in between. After this the going gets a little easier, as you follow the contours through the wild forests all the way to the Castle Rock parking area.

Castle Rock marks the edge of the Heavenly Ski Area, and the end of today's ride. If you left your car at Hidden Beach (or Sandy Harbor, which has plenty of parking) you'll find it's an easy road ride back down to the shore from here, then along the shoreline highway back to where you started.

•DAY 3 31 miles (50km)

Castle Rock to Saxon Creek

This is the toughest and most rewarding day on the Rim Trail. Continuing southward from Castle Rock, you soon hit the single-track once again, and just like before it varies from smooth and fast to twisting, rocky, and technical. The difference today is the altitude. Up to now you haven't gone over 8,500 feet (2,590m), but today you top 10,000 feet (3,000m)—a climb that will make your lungs feel like bursting; just keep thinking about the downhill that's coming.

The route winds through the open forests below higher and higher peaks, and at Monument Pass it crosses into California. For a long while you follow the gentle contours of

A short climb from Marlette brings you to the high point above Spooner Lake, ready for a high-speed double-track descent to Spooner parking lot—at least it would be, if this weren't a popular trail with 15-m.p.h. (24-k.p.h.) limits posted all along it. So, instead of speeding, enjoy the rich fragrance of the forests, the occasional bobbing tail of a deer, and the colorful wildflowers that spread like a carpet between stands of silvery aspen.

At the Spooner parking lot, you hit the pavement for about 2 miles (3km)—first turn left, then, at the Highway 50 intersection, turn left again. This leads to the Spooner Summit pass, where the trail turns off south once again. This time, though, it's a lot less populated by other bikers and hikers, and climbs high almost immediately. Now the route sticks to the Tahoe side of the ridge, passing Duane Bliss Peak and South Camp Peak,

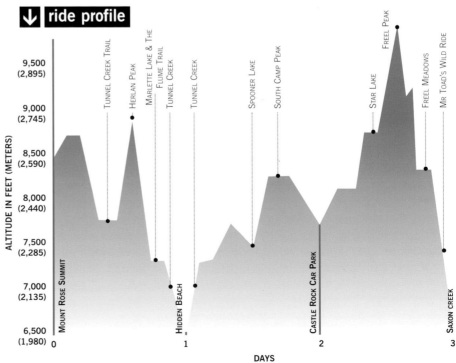

⬇ ride profile

Glimpses of the clear, enticing waters of Lake Tahoe through the branches of ancient firs is one of the most memorable features of the Tahoe Rim Trail.

the mountains to the beautiful, hidden gem of Star Lake. It's a short, steep climb to get here, so cool off by diving into the icy fresh water, if you can stand the cold—it'll prepare you for what is to come. After two full days on the trail your technical climbing skills should be well honed, if they weren't already. Hopefully you'll be feeling fitter, too, because now it's time to scale the side of Freel Peak. It's a superb challenge and something that every biker will love—pitting yourself against this 10,200-foot-high (3,110-m) trail, surrounded by pristine wilderness, and the blue skies and sunshine of California.

Once the triumph of the climb is over you need to prepare for a challenging descent, with plenty of roots, rocks, and ruts to keep you focused. Being less ridden, this part of the trail has fewer clear signs of the best lines through the more difficult parts. This all adds to the enjoyment of riding such remote single-track. At Armstrong Pass you start to climb again, before coming to a long, fairly level stretch across Freel Meadows. Lake Tahoe is out of sight now, and will be until the end of the ride, so it's just you,

the forest, and the snaking trail in front of you.

At Tucker Flat turn off the Rim at last, for possibly the best 3 miles (5km) of downhill you'll ever do. The Saxon Creek Trail is known by the locals as "Mr. Toad's Wild Ride"—and for a very good reason: you really do have to be wild to ride it! So sharpen your wits for an incredible, twisting and diving, thrilling, and, hopefully, not spilling descent. The first part is the toughest, with drops and steps and sections so tight between the rocks you'll want to hold your breath. Any rider with a bit of skill and a dose of courage can do most of it, but to ride it all or ride it fast you have to be quite an expert. The second part is everyone's favorite, where the banked hairpins and rolling descents kick in, sometimes on a trail just a few tire widths broad.

After three days of tough riding this last section is a great reward. When it's over you turn out onto Pioneer Trail Road, to spin your way back to South Lake Tahoe. It's time to ride to the beach, splash into the cooling waters, and laze on the golden sand savoring your achievement.

factfile

OVERVIEW

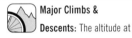

The 3-day route described here covers the very best of the Tahoe Rim Trail. To complete the coverage of Tahoe's best rides it also includes the Flume Trail and Mr. Toad's Wild Ride, both classic routes in themselves. When you put it all together you have a truly unique journey, through the most stunning region of the Sierra Nevada Mountains.

Start: Mount Rose Summit.
Finish: Saxon Creek.

ABOUT THE TRAIL

Major Climbs & Descents: The altitude at Lake Tahoe can affect riders who have come up from the coast. With the Tahoe shore being at 6,600 feet (2,000m), much of the trail over 8,000 feet (2,440m), and going above 10,000 feet (3,000m) on Day 3, be prepared for shortness of breath and slower pedaling.

Difficulty & Special Features: Spending almost all of your time on single-track means that this trail is not for the novice, but you don't need to be an expert, either. Just as long as you're fit, enthusiastic, and ready for some challenges, then you'll love this route. If you can do it with a friend and use two cars, then it's even better, as you can park at the finish of each day's ride to save a return road ride.

ACCESS

Airports: The Reno/Tahoe International Airport has good domestic but limited international connections. The best access point for international flights is San Francisco.

Transport: You will need your own

transport to get to and around Lake Tahoe. Rental cars are available from either the Tahoe or San Francisco airports.

Passport & Visa Requirements: Most visitors to the United States can enter under the Visa Waiver scheme.

Permits & Access Restrictions: The section of trail from Mount Rose to Tunnel Creek can be ridden only on the even days of the month as part of a trail-sharing program in this part of the region. The section from Tunnel Creek to just above Marlette Lake can be ridden only southbound. All other areas have unlimited access.

LOCAL INFORMATION

Maps: A detailed trail map is available from the Lake Tahoe Visitor Center, just outside of South Lake Tahoe on Highway 89.

Guidebooks: Both Lonely Planet and The Rough Guides produce guidebooks for California and Nevada.

Accommodation & Supplies: The cheapest and most easily available accommodation in the area is at South Tahoe. Here motel rooms cost between $50 and $100 per night, depending on season and motel. Along the trail there are no places to get food or drink, so be sure to take all you need into the mountains each day. By the lake shore, though, these are plentiful.

Currency & Language: U.S. dollars. English.

Area Information: Lake Tahoe Visitors Authority, 1156 Ski Run Blvd., South Lake Tahoe, CA 96150 (tel.: 530-544-5050). Lake Tahoe is on the itinerary of a 2-week trip

to California run by U.K.-based tour operator, CycleActive (tel.: 01768 881111; fax: 01768 881100; e-mail: sales@cycleactive.co.uk). **Website:** www.tahoe.com; www.cycleactive.co.uk.

TIMING & SEASONALITY

Best Months to Visit: June to October.

Climate: Summers in Tahoe are warm and clear, but with the chance of brief rain or storms. June can be hit by late snowfall that will block the trail for several days. By September the weather in the high peaks can be cooler, so come prepared for this.

HEALTH & SAFETY

Vaccinations: None.
General Health Risks: None.

Special Considerations: The remote location combined with

challenging terrain means riders must travel prepared for all eventualities. Come with a good tool kit and bike spares, as well as clothes for weather changes and a comprehensive first-aid kit.

Politics & Religion: America is a stable, multiracial, democratic country.

Crime Risk: Low.

Food & Drink: Always fill your bottles or water packs before riding as the water you will come across may harbor giardiasis.

HIGHLIGHTS

Scenic: The greatest highlight of the region is, of course, Lake Tahoe itself. This is the largest alpine lake in North America, filled with water that's 99.9 percent pure from the surrounding peaks of the Sierra Nevada Mountains. Despite the high altitude and hard winters, the

↑
The typical narrow single-track of this trail is easy when riding the flat, but can be daunting on the downhills.

lake never freezes over—its great depth means the cold water keeps circulating and never gets frozen.

Wildlife & Flora: Huge areas of land on both the California and Nevada sides are protected wilderness or forest reserves. These provide a safe environment for every bird, mammal, plant, or insect you could imagine living in the mountains. On your ride you may see bears and white-tailed deer; you'll pass under the arms of giant Jeffrey and ponderosa pines, and smell the wild herbs, thickly spread across the bald-topped peaks. A detailed guide to the flora and fauna of the region is available from the visitor center, a great source of advice and information.

↓ temperature and precipitation

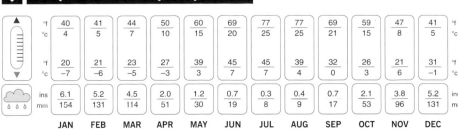

		JAN	FEB	MAR	APR	MAY	JUN	JUL	AUG	SEP	OCT	NOV	DEC	
	°f	40	41	44	50	60	69	77	77	69	59	47	41	°f
	°c	4	5	7	10	15	20	25	25	21	15	8	5	°c
	°f	20	21	23	27	39	45	45	39	32	26	21	31	°f
	°c	−7	−6	−5	−3	3	7	7	4	0	3	6	−1	°c
	ins	6.1	5.2	4.5	2.0	1.2	0.7	0.3	0.4	0.7	2.1	3.8	5.2	ins
	mm	154	131	114	51	30	19	8	9	17	53	96	131	mm

→

The clear, late summer sky creates striking glacial blues and forest greens in the Warner Creek Valley.

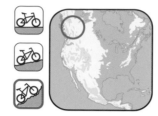

↓ itinerary

the WARNER PASS

BRITISH COLUMBIA, CANADA

Brent Henry

PARALLELING THE DRY SIDE OF THE RUGGEDLY BEAUTIFUL COAST MOUNTAINS, THE WARNER PASS ROUTE RUNS THROUGH THE SPECTACULAR HIGH VISTAS AND DRY, CLEAR SKIES OF THE CHILCOTIN REGION OF BRITISH COLUMBIA. PACKHORSE TRAILS, FOUR-WHEEL-DRIVE TRACKS, AND EMPTY BACK ROADS LEAD THE INTREPID FROM THE TINY RAILROAD STATION OF SOUTH SHALALTH ACROSS A REMOTE AND WILDLY CHALLENGING SECTION OF THE PROVINCE TO TATLA LAKE ON THE BELLA COOLA HIGHWAY.

After a day of gravel back roads, the route makes a hardy single-track climb up to the 7,800-foot (2,380-m) Warner Pass, accessing the long, exhilarating descents of the Taseko River watershed. The route described is of an advanced level in difficulty, taking eight to nine days and covering 208 miles (335km). Bikers must be self-sufficient through challenging territory. The single-track section is remote, with no inhabitants until after Red Pass. This is a trail for the hardy, but with great rewards, in both the ride and scenery. Keeping travel gear to the necessary minimum will pay off in a more enjoyable single-track ride. Although most of the trails are evident, they are not always signposted. Therefore, use of maps and a compass are essential.

←

The occasional stretch of rocky single-track will require you to push your heavily-laden bike.

•DAY 1   20 miles (32km)

South Shalalth to Bighorn Creek

Having utilized the breathtaking BC Rail train for drop-off, the route will not start until noon in South Shalalth. You're now on the drier side of the Coast Range, and the route uses two half-days of back-road riding to warm up. The first challenge is a thirst-making climb over Mission Pass to reach the Carpenter Lake Valley. Although road, the grade, with a loaded mountain bike, makes walking seem faster at times. To make up for it is the thrilling hairpin descent, with its exposed rock chutes—a classic interior back road!

The trail leaves the coastal Douglas fir forest for white-bark and ponderosa pines. At the Terzaghi Dam, the route heads west along the north shore of Carpenter Lake toward Goldbridge. Keep an eye on the surrounding cliffs for California bighorn sheep or mountain goats. A great BC Hydro campground at Bighorn Creek ends the day.

•DAY 2   27 miles (43km)

Bighorn Creek to Eldorado Creek

After continuing along Carpenter Lake, the route follows, successively, the Tyax and North Gun Creek roads, to finally access single-track. The steep trail head is uncharacteristic of the well-established track through the coastal interior forest. Pines predominate, with aspen starting to appear.

The route follows the picturesque creek valley, with the occasional challenging creek bed or downed tree trunk. The Jewel Creek forestry bridge marks the last vehicle access point. Northern flickers, yellow-bellied sapsuckers, and pileated woodpeckers inhabit the area, but so do bears, so start making noise periodically with your bike bell. Eldorado Creek, a horse packers' camp, makes a pretty destination.

•DAY 3   11 miles (17.5km)

Eldorado Creek to Trigger Lake

On this section of the route, the trail leaves the forest and you get your first look at broad ridges and valleys, →

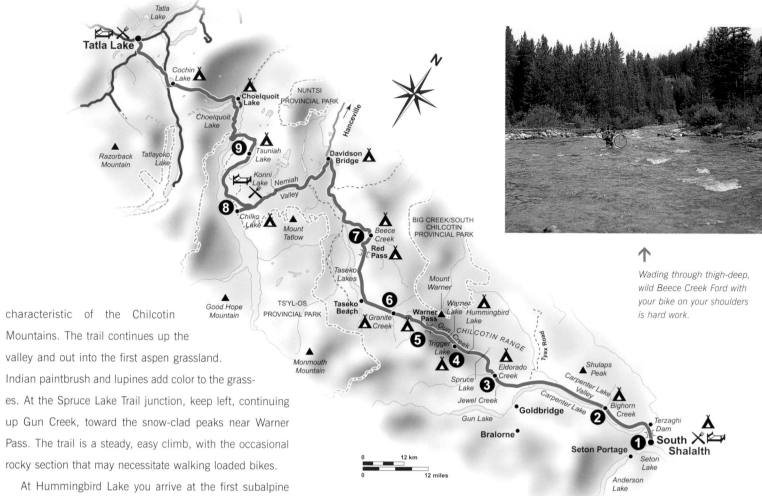

↑

Wading through thigh-deep, wild Beece Creek Ford with your bike on your shoulders is hard work.

characteristic of the Chilcotin Mountains. The trail continues up the valley and out into the first aspen grassland. Indian paintbrush and lupines add color to the grasses. At the Spruce Lake Trail junction, keep left, continuing up Gun Creek, toward the snow-clad peaks near Warner Pass. The trail is a steady, easy climb, with the occasional rocky section that may necessitate walking loaded bikes.

At Hummingbird Lake you arrive at the first subalpine lake. The forestry campground is tempting, but pushing on will bring you to another pristine site at Trigger Lake. Scat lining the trail is evidence of a healthy bear population in this area. Silent high-speed riding is not recommended—let bears know that you are present.

•DAY 4 **7½ miles (12 km)**

Trigger Lake to Warner Camp

Leaving Trigger Lake, you begin the most challenging and breathtaking section of the trail. The forest thins out toward Warner Lake, and riding is more frequently interspersed with walking. Loop trails leave the main route west of Trigger Lake, but you continue up Warner Creek. You'll often hear the unique whistle of the pika coming from the scree slopes. The superb view looking back shows the milky blue waters of glacially fed lakes and the striking profile of Mount Sheba.

The assault on Warner Pass is rocky and arduous, but the route is evident, and your 7,800-foot (2,380-m) goal is close at hand. This desolate

key

▬▬	route of ride
▭	alternative route
▭	major road
- - -	vehicle track
- - -	park border
▲	peak
⊔	pass
⛺	campground
🛏	hotel/guesthouse
🍴	provisions

←

After four days of hard work, Warner Pass is the gateway to the descent of the Taseko Valley, and a whole lot of fun!

The descent from Warner Pass is a subtle transition from stark open alpine to lush subalpine meadow and forest.

windswept spot, with its magnificent viewscape, marks the entrance to the Chilcotin, and the start of your deserved long open descents. Even in August, portions of snowfields remain and bike-skiing can be given a shot! Camp on the shores of an alpine pond just down from the pass.

• DAY 5   10 miles (16km)

Warner Camp to Taseko River–Granite Creek Confluence

This segment of the route exemplifies the longer valleys and gentler grades of the Chilcotin Mountains, and their exhilarating descents. Prepare for fun! The landscape starts completely open, and bear viewing will be at its safest. The surrounding ridges are perfect for animal sightings. However, the trail rapidly enters open pine forest and pasture land where the use of bike horns is advised. Where the trail has widened and is harder to follow in the grassland, slow down and fan out until the most apparent track is found. Look out for mountain daisy and the colorful Indian paintbrush here. In the thicker copses of trees, beware of fallen leaves snagging your derailleur.

Denain and Feo Creeks must be crossed on foot and make great spots for breaks. After crossing Battlement Creek, an old four-wheel-drive mining road is followed down to the campground at the Taseko River–Granite Creek confluence. The view of the open river bar with its surrounding ridges is spectacular. And it's bath time!

• DAY 6   24 miles (38.5km)

Taseko River–Granite Creek Confluence to Beece Creek

Although accessed by a rough road, the vast glacial-milk waters and unpopulated shoreline of Taseko Lake will convince you of the remoteness of this area. A variety of animal prints are seen on the beach, and you could be in for a thrilling sighting of wolves. The four-wheel-drive track continues to guide you up the 2,000-foot (600-m) assault on Red Pass. Views back over Taseko Lake toward the →

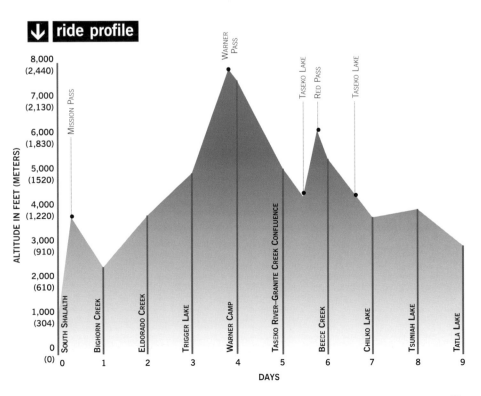

↓ ride profile

Pacific Range are humbling. Travel through a subalpine environment before making the descent to Beece Creek.

•DAY 7   46 miles (74km)

Beece Creek to Chilko Lake

The challenging ford of mountain-fed Beece Creek is followed by a brisk 1,000-foot (300-m), 7-mile (11-km) descent return to Taseko River, near the Taseko Lodge. Being so isolated, the lodge often welcomes visitors. The route continues over a smooth four-wheel-drive track through river valley grassland and open forest. At the Davidson Bridge, on the Taseka River, the route turns and heads west. (At this junction, heading out to Hanceville on Highway 20 can shorten the trip. With no public transportation on this highway, this is the shortest ride out to Williams Lake.) The route continues toward the broad farming valley of the Nemiah people. The road was not pushed through to here until the 1970s, and there's still no phone line. The day's reward, besides any packet you may have mailed to the Nemiah Post Office, is apparent at the end of the main road. Tsyl-os Provincial Park, with its majestic peaks of the Pacific Range, provides a roadside campground without equal!

•DAYS 8–9   62 miles (100km)

Chilko Lake to Tatla Lake

The route twists over rough country road along the perimeter of Tsuniah Lake, known for its trout fishing. This is a quiet, pleasant back road with few vehicles. Having a swim and making a peaceful camp here makes this a short travel day. From this point on to Tatla Lake, there are several campgrounds that could break up the two-day ride. The remainder of the route uses gravel road through scenic forest and meadow to the highway. Surrounding peaks and lakes dot the land, and rustic split-wood cariboo fencing borders the fields. With time permitting, a ride to Tatlayoko Lake and its steep fjord-like valley is a recommended side trip. At the Tatla junction, take the paved road down the highway to the community of Tatla Lake, where a well-deserved restaurant meal and accommodation await!

With loaded bikes it is wise to break the 2,000-foot (610-m) climb up to Red Pass up into segments.

↓ factfile

OVERVIEW

The Warner Pass Trail offers a unique touring experience in the southwest corner of British Columbia. It accesses remote scenic wilderness, with exhilarating descents. For years only utilized by horse packers, this route is perfect for mountain bikers heading in a south-to-north direction. The long gentle slopes of the Chilcotin valleys provide great rewards for challenging approach rides. You rise out of forest to view the alpine snowfields and glacial lakes of the rugged Chilcotin and Pacific ranges of the Coast Mountains. The route spans 208 miles (334km) in 9 days

Start: BC Rail train station at South Shalalth.
Finish: Tatla Lake.

ABOUT THE TRAIL

Because of the remote nature of this route, the trail described is suitable for loaded mountain bikes (with packs for rougher sections) or bikes with single-track trailers. The route consists of 62 percent gravel back road, 20 percent four-wheel-drive track and 18 percent single-track. The final few miles to Warner Pass require some pushing.

Major Climbs & Descents: There are three major climbs on the route. The first is the Mission Pass road climb out of South Shalath (2,850 feet/869m in less than 5 miles/8km). It is followed by an exciting 1,500-foot (460-m) descent. The second climb is the more gradual ascent to Warner Pass, rising 4,100 feet (1,250m) in 19 miles (30km). Then, single-track drops 2,100 feet (640m) to the Taseko River in 10 miles (16km). The final push is up Red Pass, a 2,000-foot (600-m) climb in 9 miles (14km), with a final drop of 2,000 feet (600m) in 11 miles (18km).

Difficulty & Special Features: The final ascent to Warner Pass crosses some coarse scree slopes. Take care if you're attempting to ride, as the large loose rocks could easily cause a fall. During the summer, the tributaries after Warner Pass are all fordable, with only two difficult crossings. Cross the homemade bridge at Powell Creek carefully. Beece Creek has the deepest and fastest waters to be crossed. Use a safety rope in thigh deep water.

ACCESS

Airports: Major airports in Vancouver and Williams Lake. Smaller carriers make scheduled stops at Williams Lake, Anihim Lake, and Bella Coola. Check current bicycle baggage regulations in advance.

Transport: Take the scenic BC Rail train route from North Vancouver to South Shalalth. Bikes are allowed on if space is available, although they will always be allowed on if they are packed in a box or bag. No public transportation is available at the route's end. You must ride from Tatla Lake to one of the airports, the train in Williams Lake, or to Bella Coola, to catch the *Discovery Coast* ferry to Vancouver. Check with local establishments in Tatla Lake to see if you can catch a lift

Classic cariboo fencing and summer grasses appear more frequently as one nears the Bella Coola Highway.

out in a truck. At the Davidson Bridge junction, you can opt to ride the 96 miles (154km) out to Williams Lake.

Passport & Visa Requirements: Citizens of Australia, New Zealand, the U.K., and the U.S. require passports and one other piece of photo identification.

Permits & Access Restrictions: None.

LOCAL INFORMATION

Maps: The Forestry Recreation Maps for Spruce Lake Trails and Cariboo Forest Region West are available through Canadian Cartographics Ltd., 57B Clipper Street, Coquitlam BC, V3K 6X2 (tel.: 1-877-5243337 toll-free). The Canadian topographic maps, 92J/15, 920/3, 920/4, and 920/5 are available from Crown Publications, 521 Fort Street, Victoria, BC, V8W 1E7 (tel.: 250-386-4636).

Guidebooks: There are no guidebooks for this region, but of interest may be *Nemiah: The Unconquered Country* by Terry Galvin (New Star Books).

Accommodation & Supplies: You must be self-sufficient regarding camping, food, and bike repairs. You'll have to carry food until you reach Konni Lake, where there is a small store. It's a good idea to send a food parcel to the Nemiah Post Office, Konni Lake, BC, V0L 1X0. There is a bed-and-breakfast in the Nemiah Valley (tel.: 250-394-4286). The Snow Mountain Outfitters run a guesthouse (tel.: 250-392-4761; fax: 250-392-4756). The Konni Lake Resort also has a few cabins. A provincial

campground is located at Tsyl-os Provincial Park on Chilko Lake. If you end your trip at Tatla Lake, the Tatla Lake Motel (tel.: 250-476-1184) or Graham Inn (tel.: 250-476-6112) can provide lodging and perhaps help find rides out. Williams Lake has full services.

Currency & Language: Canadian dollars. English.

Photography: No restrictions; carry all film with you.

Area Information: The Cariboo Chilcotin Coastal Tourism Association can provide current information about accommodation (tel.: 1-800-663-5885 toll-free). Information on the *Discovery Coast* ferry from Bella Coola can be obtained from BC Ferries (tel.: 1-888-223-3779 toll-free).

TIMING & SEASONALITY

Best Months to Visit: July, August, and early September.

Climate: Although this is the drier side of the Coast Mountains, cold rain can happen at any time with a slight chance of snow higher up. Good-quality, layered clothing and rain gear are a must. It is extremely exposed above the timberline. Some creeks may be more difficult to cross early in the season.

HEALTH & SAFETY

Vaccinations: None required.

General Health Risks: You should be aware of the risks of hypothermia in a wet, temperate climate. Having a set of thin, polypropylene underwear is advisable. Carry sunscreen and insect repellent.

Special Considerations: This is grizzly and black bear country. Be aware of their habitat and regularly use a sound-signaling device. It is common practice in remote areas to carry bear spray, which is

available from hardware or outdoors stores. Keep your camp meticulous, don't have food in your tent, and bring a light rope to hang your food from a tree. This is a remote area, so have at least one group member proficient in survival first aid.

Politics & Religion: No concerns.
Crime Risk: Low.
Food & Drink: Water from lakes and streams should be filtered or treated, especially for giardia.

HIGHLIGHTS

The Coast Mountains are a rugged young range heaved up by the Pacific Plate. The route lies between the Pacific and Chilcotin ranges, and takes you through breathtaking territory that is traveled by few. The descents are exhilarating.

Scenic: The alpine surroundings offer clear views of rugged peaks and pristine glacier-fed lakes. It's well worth the ride to the Nemiah Valley and Tsyl-os Provincial Park. The Nemiah people didn't gain road access to their territory until the 1970s, and neighboring Tsyl-os Provincial Park, with milky Chilko Lake, offers views of some of the wildest glaciers and peaks in the province.

Wildlife & Flora: Wildlife includes grizzly bear, black bear, muledeer, bighorn sheep, mountain goat, cougar, gray wolf, pika, woodpeckers, bald eagle, and songbirds. Horses can be found grazing on ranges. Open grassland and alpine areas provide excellent wildflower viewing.

⬇ temperature and precipitation

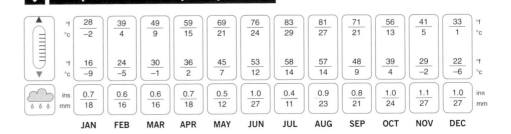

	JAN	FEB	MAR	APR	MAY	JUN	JUL	AUG	SEP	OCT	NOV	DEC	
°f	28	39	49	59	69	76	83	81	71	56	41	33	°f
°c	−2	4	9	15	21	24	29	27	21	13	5	1	°c
°f	16	24	30	36	45	53	58	57	48	39	29	22	°f
°c	−9	−5	−1	2	7	12	14	14	9	4	−2	−6	°c
ins	0.7	0.6	0.6	0.7	0.5	1.0	0.4	0.9	0.8	1.0	1.1	1.0	ins
mm	18	16	16	18	12	27	11	23	21	24	27	27	mm

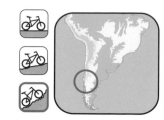

ACROSS the ANDES

CHILE & ARGENTINA

Chris Ford

THE LAKE DISTRICT OF CHILE AND ARGENTINA IS ONE OF THE MOST PICTURESQUE STRETCHES OF THE VAST ANDEAN CHAIN. GIANT SNOWCAPPED VOLCANOES RISE UP FROM THE MOUNTAINS IN PERFECT CONES TO BE REFLECTED IN LAKES OF GLACIAL MELTWATER. THERE ARE DENSE, WILD FORESTS, GUSHING RIVERS THAT CARVE GREAT CANYONS OUT OF THE MOUNTAINS, AND A MIX OF NEW AND ANCIENT LAVA FORMATIONS.

This tour cuts right through the heart of the South American Lake District on a challenging route across the spine of the Andes and back. It's a real wilderness adventure, requiring full camping gear and space for several days' food; it is definitely for fit riders only. If you are up to the task the rewards are great, as few explorers have access to this remote and beautiful region in quite the same way as a mountain biker.

↓ **itinerary**

•DAYS 1–2 420 miles (675km)

Santiago to Temuco

After flying into Santiago you must get the train south to Temuco. It's worthwhile going for a first-class sleeper car—the little extra gets you a proper bed with sheets and pillow and access to a fresh, clean toilet!

Once in Temuco, ride a little out of town to a wild campground. Although you are still close to civilization, it already feels like the wilderness, and mountain lions from the national park you are approaching have been sighted here.

•DAYS 3–4 75 miles (120km)

Temuco to Cunco

Your first biking destination is Conguillo Los Paraguas National Park. This 114,000-acre reserve is home to forests of beech and giant araucaria (monkey puzzle) trees—one of the few places in Chile where these can still be found. Its most dramatic feature, though, is snowcapped Llaima Volcano, which dominates the whole landscape.

The good road out to the gates soon becomes a rough track, passing through fields of thick grass grazed by large herds of cattle. After a night at the basic campground by the gates, this all suddenly changes. The horizon rises up to a series of steep ridges, each capped by a line of giant araucarias. The road is coated in fine lava ash, which provides a smooth, hard surface when dry.

The route twists and turns through thick forests, then abruptly clears cover at the towering volcano. The timberline ends at a vast lava flow, and you can see its path of destruction right to the summit. In nearly 40 years very little has grown here, but, if you look closely, you can see that ferns and lichens are starting the process. The track continues through the lava, and on to Cunco, a little village on the far side of the park. Head down to the river to camp.

•DAY 5 43 miles (70km)

Cunco to Villarrica

The rough road to Villarrica is hard work—mostly on the level, on rough gravel, with no respite—and an early start is needed if you're to make it all the way before dark.

The bright, white slopes of Lanín Volcano lie behind you on the descent into Argentina.

The South American Lake District is a land of awe-inspiring scenery, where thundering waterfalls compete with volcanoes for your attention.

Villarrica will be your first exposure to tourist Chile, camping at a site full of other travelers. This is a great place to visit, with its superb volcano, quiet lake, and bustling small center where you can stock up on provisions.

•DAYS 6–7 **80 miles (130km)**

Villarrica to the Argentine Border

The next stage of the ride may be tough but it will also be incredibly rewarding. Your destination is Puerto Tromén—the pass at the top of the Andes ridge and the border with Argentina.

From Villarrica head due east, climbing steadily. The road soon ends to put you back on gravel, often muddied by the rains. The first night is at a wild site on the edge of Currarehue, the last village in Chile. After this, the road quickly becomes steep and narrow; it is also completely devoid of traffic. As you pedal up through a valley the forests around seem to be closing in, thicker and thicker, and you're

unlikely to see any signs of habitation. After several hours you reach the Chilean customs post in Puesco, then head out into no-man's-land. The Argentine border is now about 10 miles (16km) away, but the road is very steep and, with full panniers, you may have to walk some sections.

The trail now enters a real mountain wilderness. All around, appearing out of a swirling mist, you'll see bleak crags and snow patches on the other side of the gorge. After 6 miles (9.5km) the track levels for a short section at a vast silvery lake—not shown on some maps. There are 4 more miles (6.5km) of steep and slippery climbing before you reach the "Bienvenido à Argentina!" sign. If the sky is clear you'll also get a stunning view of Lanín Volcano, which towers directly above the border post. After completing your customs paperwork just head on down the road to find a roadside spot at which to camp. You've now completed the toughest section of the route, and camping under the gaze of Lanín is a just reward.

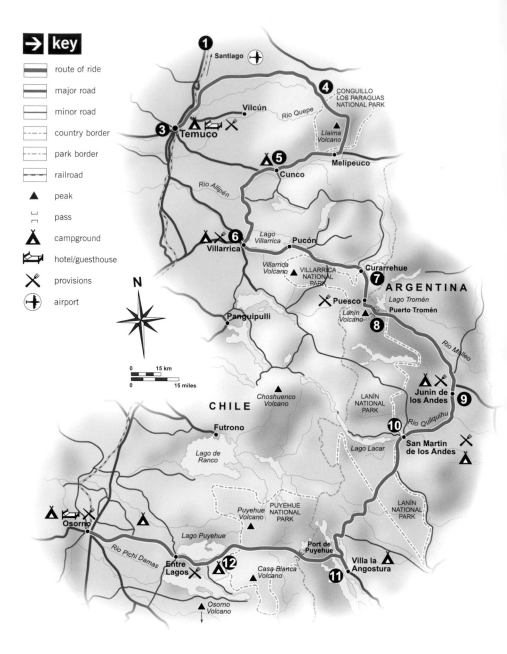

key

	route of ride
	major road
	minor road
	country border
	park border
	railroad
▲	peak
⊐⊏	pass
⚠	campground
🛏	hotel/guesthouse
✕	provisions
✈	airport

•DAYS 8–10   130 (210km)

The Argentine Border to Villa la Angostura

The descent from the border is a dramatic piece of biking. The rough and sandy track can be challenging as you wind your way out of the high section of the Andes, and the views are stunning, especially if you stop and look back up to the pass you've just crossed. At the end of Day 8 you reach Junin de los Andes, a small town where you can buy all the food you'll need and enjoy a good meal out.

The next day is spent entirely on a good road, as you continue south to San Martin de Los Andes, perched on the shores of Lake Lacar. From here you return to rough dirt roads that cut a winding trail through mountains, lakes, and wild forests to Villa la Angostura. This is one of the most scenic stretches in Argentina, with waterfalls splashing out of the mountains and the peaks of the Andes ever present.

Villa la Angostura is the last staging post before the climb back into Chile over the Port de Puyehue pass, and has a large campground. Unlike the Puerto Tromén, the Port de Puyehue is a smoother climb from both directions, and links some of the major southern towns on the two sides of the border. Even though this is the route chosen by local drivers wanting to cross the Andes, it still sees very little traffic.

•DAYS 11–12   100 miles (160km)

Villa la Angostura to Osorno

Leaving early, you begin your last major climb. The long dirt road is smooth and gentle. A short way out of town you'll be surrounded by wilderness, and a mist often obscures the view up into the peaks. The steady gradient allows you to settle into a good rhythm and enjoy the climb.

As you cross the final ridge and reach the Chilean border, you'll be able to make out several major summits. The Osorno, Puyehue, Casa Blanca, and Chushuenco volcanoes are all within sight.

From the border, the dirt gives way to a proper road once again and it's a fast descent to the shores of Lago Puyehue. In the morning, the road takes you out of the mountains and through rich farmlands. The destination is Osorno, a busy little town located on the main rail and road links. From here you can catch the train back to Santiago.

⬇ ride profile

ALTITUDE IN FEET (METERS)

4,100 (1,250)
3,280 (1,000)
2,460 (750)
1,640 (500)
820 (250)
0 (0)

SANTIAGO · SLEEPER TRAIN · TEMUCO · CONGUILLO LOS PARAGUAS NATIONAL PARK · CUNCO · VILLARRICA · CURRAREHUE · ARGENTINE BORDER · PUERTO TROMEN · JUNIN DE LOS ANDES · LAGO LACAR · VILLA LA ANGOSTURA · PORT DE PUYEHUE · LAGO PUYEHUE · OSORNO

DAYS

0   1–2   3–4   5   6–7   8–10   11–12

factfile

OVERVIEW

 This Andean adventure takes you through a rare landscape of giant, snowcapped volcanoes, high mountain passes, and beautiful glacial lakes. You'll be far from the crowds and will need to be self-sufficient for several days at a time. You'll also be at the mercy of the elements—experiencing everything from blazing heat to erratic hailstorms. These factors all combine to make for a unique, challenging, and highly rewarding journey through one of Chile and Argentina's most beautiful regions. Fit and determined bikers could complete the 848-mile (1,357-km) route (including the train journey) in 12 days, but there are many options for side tracks, rest days, or days to explore on foot. Allowing at least 15 days will give time to explore the region as you travel, and to enjoy each destination to the full.
Start/Finish: Santiago, Chile.

ABOUT THE TRAIL

 Major Climbs & Descents: Altitude is not a problem on this tour, with the highest pass being just under 9,800 feet (3,000m). However, the climb to get there is steep, slippery, and long, so a good level of fitness and determination are essential.
Difficulty & Special Features: This is a challenging trip for fit and experienced travelers. You need to be equipped for all weather conditions, carrying full camping and cooking gear with space for 4 days' worth of food. You need to be on a tough mountain bike, as the rough lava trails through the parks and across the border take their

toll on any machine. You must be sure that you can fix any bike problems, since a serious breakdown in some areas could result in several days on foot before you can find help—so be sure to pack all the necessary tools and spares.

ACCESS

 Airports: Santiago International Airport.
Transport: The railroad service in Chile is excellent. An overnight sleeper is good value and provides a good bed for a night. Bikes travel free in a separate part of the train, but be sure the rail officials know where the bike is going as carriages do get dropped off along the way. Off the railroad, the only option for bikers is to hitch. Although there is little traffic, most vehicles will stop to help a cyclist when off the beaten track.
Passport & Visa Requirements: A full passport only is required for both Chile and Argentina.
Permits & Access Restrictions: None.

LOCAL INFORMATION

 Maps: The best map available locally is produced by Touristel, the telephone company. This is fairly accurate and marks all roads, passes, campgrounds, and major peaks. It crosses over to the Lake District region of Argentina, but in slightly less detail.
Guidebooks: Lonely Planet do an excellent *Chile* guidebook.
Accommodation & Supplies: In the main towns and cities there are accommodation choices ranging from backpacker hostels through to luxury hotels. In national parks and

small villages there are plenty of basic campgrounds. The supermarkets in most towns and villages are well stocked with fresh and packet foods.
Currency & Language: Chilean peso and Argentine peso (different values). The language is Spanish.
Area Information: National Parks information can be obtained from CONAF, Department 303, Avenida Bulnes 285, Santiago, Chile (tel.: 696 6749).

TIMING & SEASONALITY

Best Months to Visit: October to March.
Climate: The Chilean Lake District has a climate similar to the United Kingdom, but being south of the equator their summer season runs from October to March. Summer doesn't mean constant sunshine, so you must come prepared for foul weather, especially on the high passes.

HEALTH & SAFETY

Vaccinations: None required.
General Health Risks: None.
Special Considerations: The often remote nature of the journey means that you must carry food and appropriate clothing.
Politics & Religion: Both Chile and Argentina are stable democracies and predominantly Catholic.

Crime Risk: Low.
Food & Drink: Water at most campgrounds is safe to drink, often coming directly from high mountain streams where there is no giardia; if in doubt, it should be filtered.

HIGHLIGHTS

This is a wild place, and you'll get a great sense of exploration and challenge as you journey where few bikers or tourists have gone before. Being alone in this vast and dramatic landscape is at once daunting and exhilarating, making it the perfect destination for a real biking adventure.
Scenic: The South American Lake District is characterized by its volcanoes and the landscapes that surround them. The sharp contrast between snowy peaks, thick forests, clear lakes, and barren lava flows is quite remarkable.
Wildlife & Flora: The rich volcanic soils of Conguillo produce the giant araucaria, mixed with cypress and southern beech at lower elevations. In Villarrica, the lava flows have not reached below 5,000 feet (1,500m), and dense forests of beech and pehuen cover the flanks of the volcanoes. Above this canopy you can occasionally spot the majestic Andean Condor.

← *A fantastic view of lake and volcanoes greets you as you arrive at the wilderness campground in Conguillo Los Paraguas National Park.*

↓ temperature and precipitation

		JAN	FEB	MAR	APR	MAY	JUN	JUL	AUG	SEP	OCT	NOV	DEC	
	°f	88	88	91	95	93	93	93	97	95	93	91	90	°f
	°c	31	31	33	35	34	34	34	36	35	34	33	32	°c
	°f	57	61	61	63	66	68	68	70	70	68	64	61	°f
	°c	14	16	16	17	19	20	20	21	21	20	18	16	°c
	ins	2.0	1.6	2.1	3.1	5.9	2.3	2.0	2.3	3.9	3.9	4.3	2.3	ins
	mm	50	40	55	80	150	60	50	60	100	100	110	60	mm

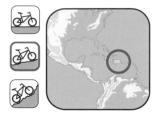

the DOMINICAN REPUBLIC

THE CARIBBEAN

Tom Hutton

FROM A DISTANCE, THE DOMINICAN REPUBLIC LOOKS LIKE ANY OTHER CARIBBEAN ISLAND: CLEAR BLUE WATERS LAP WHITE, SANDY BEACHES, SHADED FROM THE TROPICAL SUN BY SWAYING PALM TREES. BUT TOUR THE COUNTRY BY MOUNTAIN BIKE AND YOU WILL DISCOVER TINY VILLAGES, RICH IN A COLORFUL BLEND OF CARIBBEAN AND LATIN AMERICAN CULTURES, LINKED BY DUSTY TRACKS THAT WIND THEIR WAY THROUGH LUSH FORESTS AND CLIMB OVER SOME OF THE WEST INDIES' HIGHEST MOUNTAINS.

This five-day tour around the northern flanks of the Dominican Alps, and onto the surf-swept beaches of the north shore, combines the thrills of hard-core mountain biking with the sights, sounds, and smells of a fascinating developing country. However, a word of warning: maps of the Republic leave a lot to the imagination. Where main roads exist, many of the dirt roads are no longer shown, and the island is a maze of tracks. A good command of Spanish will help to extract plenty of route information from the helpful locals. Otherwise, take a guided tour, and just concentrate on enjoying the riding!

↓ **itinerary**

•DAY 1 **16 miles (26km)**

Cabarete to Constanza

Starting from the small coastal resort of Cabarete, the first leg of the tour crosses the Cordillera Septentrional, a narrow chain of mountains that stretches right across the north coast from the Haiti border to the Samana Peninsula. With no obvious off-road crossing, the climb is best tackled in a support vehicle, using the road from Sabaneta del Yásica to Moca. The views from the top, across the huge expanse of the Cibao Valley, are really quite spectacular. This is one of

Away from the ocean, the interior of the Dominican Republic is a hilly patchwork of every conceivable shade of green.

Cool breezes, blue skies, and miles of dirt track, what more could you wish for on the descent toward Santiago?

the Republic's more prosperous areas, and the fertile soil is ideal for growing both coffee and tobacco.

From the top, the next objective is the small town of Moca. There are a few good off-road options for the descent. Starting around Puerto Grande, a good track traverses around the hillside and links with a few perilously steep and incredibly rocky single-track paths—described locally as being "OK for horses but far too rough for bikes!"

Take a little time to look around Moca, in particular the rather grand church—Iglesia Corazón de Jesús—and then press on south, by road, through La Vega and on to Constanza for the first night. At over 3,280 feet (1,000m) above sea level, you'll notice a considerable difference in the temperature between here and the coast.

•DAY 2   29 miles (47km)

Constanza to Jarabacoa

With an abundance of good dirt roads in this area, it's possible to complete the whole journey from Constanza to the small mountain town of Jarabacoa with only a few yards of tarmac. Climb steeply out of Constanza and follow some excellent undulating dirt roads to the small town of El Rio. From El Rio, climb steeply north on a switchback track that leads through countless small villages. Although the climbing is steep, the surfaces are pretty good and the miles seem to fly by. Extra encouragement is plentiful, as groups of locals rush out onto the streets to wave you by.

The drop into Jarabacoa passes the stunning waterfall known as Salto de Jimenoa. The most spectacular but least visited of Jarabacoa's waterfalls, Jimenoa, is set back from the main track, about 15 minutes' walk, but well worth a visit. The cold clear water falls into a deep pool that's ideal for cooling you down after a hard day on the trail.

From the falls, it's downhill all the way into Jarabacoa. The track is steep in places with plenty of sharp turns to keep concentration levels high. If that's not enough, you'll probably also have to navigate a way past the odd logging truck and a few locals on motor scooters, weaving all over the road.

Jarabacoa is a charming mountain town with a really lively atmosphere. It's fast becoming the adventure capital of the Republic, from where you can sample the excellent rafting, canyoning, and hiking available in the area.

•DAY 3 | 28 miles (45km)

Jarabacoa to Santiago

This is probably the toughest day of the whole trip with some pretty monumental climbs that are rewarded by huge views and a long, bone-shaking descent at the end of the day.

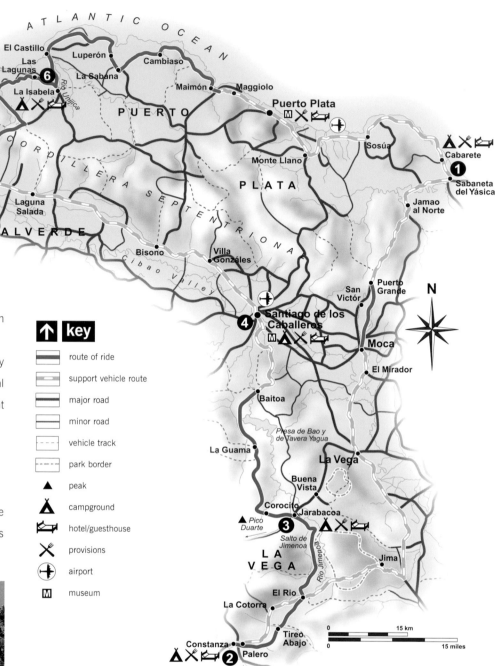

key

	route of ride
	support vehicle route
	major road
	minor road
	vehicle track
	park border
▲	peak
⛺	campground
🛏	hotel/guesthouse
✕	provisions
✈	airport
Ⓜ	museum

← On Day 4, a long, rocky, and very technical descent leads back toward the heat of the coast and the crystal waters of the Atlantic Ocean.

→ River crossings are commonplace wherever you ride in the Republic. Some are ridable, others involve carrying the bike. Either way, the cool, clear waters are always inviting.

Early starts are essential to avoid big climbs at the hottest part of the day. Constanza will feel remarkably chilly after a few days on the coast.

After a steep road climb, the track heads west toward Corocito. Again, you'll pass numerous small settlements along the way and the scenery is absolutely fantastic with lush green forests stretching almost as far as the eye can see. To the west, the skyline is dominated by the highest mountain in the Caribbean, Pico Duarte (10,400 feet/3,175m). Another steep pull gains a roller-coaster track that heads due north before a long descent, on a mixture of surfaces, drops you to La Guama. Continue off-road to the huge lake of Presa de Bao y de Tavera Yagua and pick up the support vehicle near the dam. Continue, by road, to the country's second city, Santiago.

Santiago will seem like a huge sprawling city after the smaller towns of the Cibao Valley but its population only just tops the half-million mark and it's still got a fairly relaxed feel to it. Sadly, the city has been struck by more than its fair share of earthquakes and consequently there's not that much history left standing for a visitor to see.

•DAY 4   28 miles (45km)

Santiago to La Isabela

After three days in the mountains, Day 4 of the tour returns to the Atlantic coast. It's not quite as simple as it sounds, since there's still one large obstacle in the way: the Cordillera Septentrional, the western end of the ridge that →

↑ *This river crossing near Cabarete might cool you down, but it won't do your bike any good, so carrying is a must.*

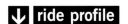

↓ ride profile

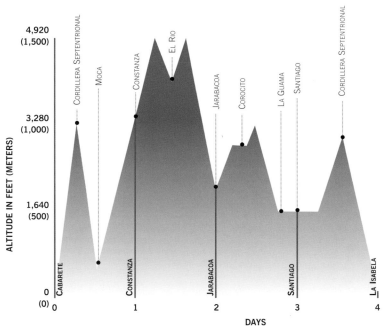

you climbed on Day 1. Take the support vehicle west toward Monte Christi and take to the saddle again at Hatillo Palma. From here, it's a long steady pull up over the ridge. The landscape here is almost desert-like with scrubby bushes replacing the pines and palms. It'll also feel a lot hotter.

From the top of the ridge, it's a superb descent all the way to the coast. There's a choice of tracks ranging from well-surfaced dirt roads, which take most of the traffic, to rocky and often muddy trails that see only horses and pedestrians.

The final leg into La Isabela comes as a welcome change on flat tracks that allow you to really spin. It's worth cracking on at this stage: the sunset over the ocean, from the coast at La Isabela, is one of the highlights of the tour.

•DAY 5 24 miles (38km)

La Isabela to Cabarete

With the mountainous sections over, this should be one of the easier days. However, back at sea level, the heat and humidity start to take their toll and it feels every bit as tough as the rest of the tour. From La Isabela, a well-hidden track runs parallel to the coast, passing some spectacular limestone caves and one or two deserted beaches. It's worth leaving early in order to enjoy both. The route then tracks back inland a little before hitting the surf again at the small resort town of Luperón.

On Day 5 you will be back on the coast, but there are still plenty of big climbs to contend with.

Descending into a small village near the north coast, where a welcome drink should be available.

The next stage takes the road around a large inlet to La Sabana. Here it returns to the coast, following a variety of dirt roads and donkey tracks and occasionally crossing beautiful beaches. There are still plenty of stiff climbs to navigate as the tracks head back inland over numerous steep hills. It's possible, however, to keep fairly close to the ocean and enjoy the cooling effect of the trade winds.

The last few miles rise and dip many times on a fairly major dirt road that terminates on the outskirts of Puerto Plata, one of the country's larger tourist destinations. The tour ends where the track meets a major road, near Maggiolo, and from here, unless you relish the idea of a fairly major road ride, it's best to take a lift back to Cabarete—hopefully in time for Happy Hour.

 factfile

OVERVIEW

 This 5-day tour—with a total riding distance of 125 miles (203km)—starts and finishes in Cabarete, a surfer's paradise on the north coast, and travels around the central northern area of the country. By using a guide and a support vehicle, it's possible to travel light and enjoy each day as an all-out mountain bike ride. To undertake a similar tour unaided would require a good knowledge of Spanish in order to dig out information from the locals on the best trails.

Start/Finish: Cabarete.

ABOUT THE TRAIL

The majority of the riding is on broad, loose-surfaced tracks that are used by jeeps, motorcycles, and donkeys. There are a few steep and technical trails in some areas but these are the exception rather than the rule, and all of the climbs are ridable for a fit person.

Major Climbs & Descents: The big climbs come on Days 2, 3, and 4. Each is approximately 1,000–1,600 feet (300–500m) but the surfaces are generally good and the gradient never too steep. The descents, in general, mirror the climbs, but there are some narrower, more gnarly trails on Days 1 and 4.

Difficulty & Special Features: Van support makes this a thoroughly enjoyable and fairly compact tour, cherry-picking the best trails and using the support vehicle to avoid long road sections. The real challenge comes from the heat, as you'd expect in this kind of climate.

ACCESS

Airports: The best airport for the tour is Puerto Plata, which is served by regular flights from all over Europe and North America.

Transport: Cabarete is approximately 30 minutes from the airport by taxi.

Passport & Visa Requirements: Visitors from Europe, Australasia, and North America will need a full passport and a tourist card, purchasable at the airport.

Permits & Access Restrictions: There are no permits required for any of the route.

LOCAL INFORMATION

Maps: Maps of the Republic show few of the trails and can give little more than a general overview.

Guidebooks: For a general guide to the country, it'd be hard to beat the Lonely Planet's guide to the *Dominican Republic and Haiti*.

Accommodation & Supplies: By following the itinerary set out here, each night is spent in a fairly large town with a wide choice of accommodation and food outlets. Away from the main tourist areas, there's plenty of opportunity to sample authentic local dishes.

Currency & Language: The Dominican peso is the local currency, although U.S. dollars are accepted quite readily also. Spanish is the local language; and English is only spoken in the large tourist centers.

Area Information: There are tourist offices in the U.S.A., Canada, and many European countries. This tour, like numerous others, is the brainchild of

Cabarete Adventure specialists, Iguana Mama. They use helpful and knowledgeable guides who speak good English and also offer rental of up-to-date, top quality, mountain bikes (tel.: 571 0734).

Websites: www.iguanamama.com; www.hispaniola.com is particularly useful for information about Cabarete.

TIMING & SEASONALITY

 Best Months to Visit: January to August.

Climate: The notorious Caribbean hurricane season is from September to December, otherwise the climate is pretty consistent all year round.

HEALTH & SAFETY

Vaccinations: There are no specific immunizations required but those against tetanust,

polio, and typhoid should be seen as essential. Hepatitis is also worth considering.

General Health Risks: The biggest health hazard on the bike tour will be the heat and the sun. Ensure that you carry plenty of water at all times and use a high-protection sunscreen. Malaria is present in some areas.

Special Considerations: None.

Politics & Religion: No concerns.

Crime Risk: Crime risk is small outside of the main tourist resorts but it always pays to be vigilant.

Food & Drink: Tap water is not drinkable anywhere.

HIGHLIGHTS

 Scenic: The coastline is beautiful with sandy beaches, clear blue water, and many coral reefs offshore. The central area of the interior is

↑
Riding through the small villages will provide an insight into the culture and lifestyle of the Dominican people beyond the tourist centers.

spectacular; here, huge mountains, covered in pine trees, rise up from miles and miles of rolling green fields. The rivers, too, provide spectacle; in particular the waterfalls around Jarabacoa.

Wildlife & Flora: You may catch the odd glimpse of a hummingbird or an occasional sighting of a turkey vulture; crocodiles can be seen at Lago Enriquillo; and the magnificent humpback whale returns year after year to calve in the waters off the Samana Peninsula. The mountainous regions are covered with indigenous pine trees while elsewhere king and coconut palms dominate the landscape.

⬇ temperature and precipitation

		JAN	FEB	MAR	APR	MAY	JUN	JUL	AUG	SEP	OCT	NOV	DEC	
▲ ▼	°f	88	88	91	95	93	93	93	97	95	93	91	90	°f
	°c	31	31	33	35	34	34	34	36	35	34	33	32	°c
	°f	57	61	61	63	66	68	68	70	70	68	64	61	°f
	°c	14	16	16	17	19	20	20	21	21	20	18	16	°c
☁	ins	2.0	1.6	2.1	3.1	5.9	2.3	2.0	2.3	3.9	3.9	4.3	2.3	ins
	mm	50	40	55	80	150	60	50	60	100	100	110	60	mm

Europe & Asia Minor

The soaring glories of the Alps and the Pyrenees are well known to mountain lovers. Expeditions around the Mont Blanc Massif and along the Hautes Pyrénées are popular challenges. Then, there are the less expected routes—across the Caucasus Mountains, a railroad trail in Norway, upland riding among the lakes of northwest England, and a fling in the Scottish highlands.

the ENGLISH LAKE DISTRICT TOUR

ENGLAND, U.K.

Dave Willis

THE ENGLISH LAKE DISTRICT, IN NORTHWEST ENGLAND, HAS WITHOUT DOUBT THE MOST BEAUTIFUL PANORAMAS IN THE COUNTRY. ONE OF BRITAIN'S FIRST NATIONAL PARKS, IT CONTAINS ENGLAND'S HIGHEST PEAK, SCAFELL PIKE, AND LARGEST LAKE, WINDERMERE.

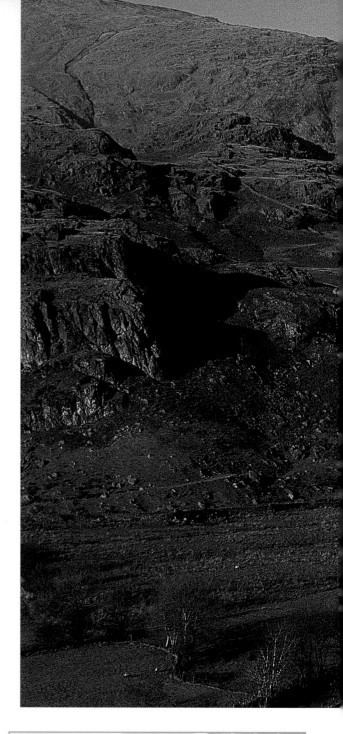

For such a compact area, only 900 square miles (2,330km^2), the Lake District National Park has an amazingly varied landscape. Peaceful lakes, jewel-like tarns, imposing fells, crags, and passes, picture-postcard hamlets, and white-painted farms nestling in the valley bottoms all make the Lakes almost too pretty for its own good. Set out like the spokes of a wheel with the central fells and Scafell as its hub, the Lake District lends itself perfectly to a circular mountain-bike tour.

At only 104 miles (165km) over three days, it should be a relaxing tour. But taking in nearly every valley, lake, pass, and forest takes effort and willpower with plenty of energy-sapping off-road climbs requiring riders to shoulder their bikes more than once. The rewards, when they come, are well worth the effort: some of the best descents found anywhere, set amid stunning mountain scenery, fabulous lakes, tarns, and swimming holes; challenging single-track and sweeping forest roads; and, of course, many excellent pubs.

↓ itinerary

•DAY 1   38 miles (60km)

Windermere Ferry to Skiddaw House

The obvious place to start and finish this tour is the Windermere ferry. It's the only place where you have to cross a lake and is convenient for trains, buses, and cars entering the Park. The bustling tourist town of Bowness-on-Windermere has all the conveniences to stock up with and the lake makes a pretty backdrop for the first day. Starting up the Crook Road (B5284) on tarmac gets the legs warmed up before you turn off onto the old gated road

Kentmere Valley is enclosed by dramatic mountains and provides a scenic route into the high fells of the Lake District.

Row boats caress the waters of Windermere, the spectacular lake at Bowness, on a glorious summer's day.

across to Ings, and continue up the Troutbeck Road to Dubs Road and the first off-road section. Dubs Road is a bridle path leading to Garburn Pass, a stunning vantage point that gives views over the Troutbeck Valley and down into Kentmere. Suddenly, you've left the traffic and the tourists behind and the fells are before you. The descent into Kentmere is wild and rocky. A climb up Hallow Bank on a farm road leads to the Sadgill bridle path and a descent into Longsleddale. Again, it's steep and technical. The bridle paths are well marked with blue arrows by the National Park Authority, so look out for them. This is sheep-farming country, mostly the indigenous Herdwicks, some Rough Fell, and others; wild ponies are seen up here too.

The long bridle path climbs up Brownhowe Bottom to

Mosedale Cottage via an unusual cobbled section, but then gives way to boggy conditions to Swindale via a long grassy descent. Enjoy the descent, as a climb to Haweswater is next. Steep at first, it eases into a traverse to bring you down to Naddle Farm, near to the Haweswater Reservoir. In a dry spell, the village of Mardale, which was drowned when Haweswater filled up, can still be seen at the head of the reservoir. There's a short road section to Bampton Bridge and Helton before heading off-road again on the ancient Roman road over Askham Fell, crossing the more famous Roman "High Street," a fell-top military road that spans the Lake District, north to south. Ullswater doglegs from Pooley Bridge to Patterdale and it's Pooley Bridge that you will descend to before taking the scenic road down →

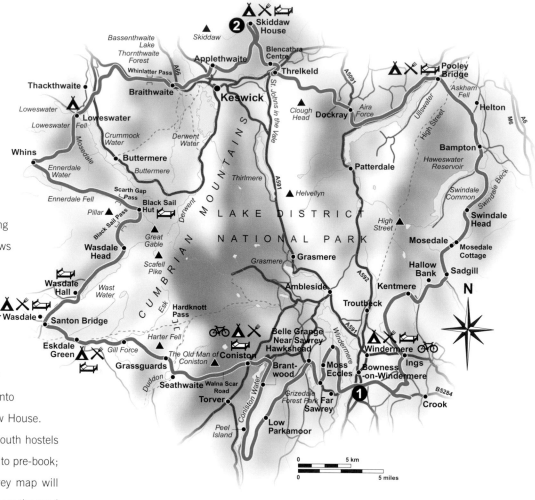

Ullswater to Aira Force—a popular waterfall that is worth a stop before you continue to Dockray and off-road again.

The Old Coach Road that once ran from Dockray to St. Johns in the Vale now serves as an excellent bridle path on a good stony surface for most of its length. Traversing the fells below Clough Head, you get great views of Blencathra. There's a steep descent to St. Johns and a short road section to Threlkeld village. The end of Day 1 brings you through Threlkeld, past the Blencathra Centre, the Lake District National Park Authority's field study center, and onto the fine bridle path that runs into the Back O' Skiddaw all the way up to Skiddaw House.

Skiddaw House is one of the most remote youth hostels in the country. It's very small and you will need to pre-book; otherwise, a quick scan of the Ordnance Survey map will show many other campgrounds; Keswick is just up the road if you fancy a guesthouse and a beer.

•DAY 2 | 32 miles (50km)

Skiddaw House to Nether Wasdale

Backtrack to the guidestone skirting the lower flanks of Skiddaw and follow the Cumbria Way path around to Applethwaite. This drops you onto the A591, then down to the A66 near Keswick, which is followed west for almost 2 miles (3km) to the B5292 at Braithwaite. Whinlatter Pass is where you are heading, climbing steeply on tarmac, all the way up through the pine trees of Thornthwaite Forest to the visitor center, where you can stop for tea, a view, and a great introduction to the flora and fauna of this area. The view over Bassenthwaite Lake is tremendous on a clear summer morning, and Basenthwaite is the only "Lake" in the Lake District; all the others are "Meres" or "Waters"!

Downhilling Whinlatter Pass on tarmac is fun and fast. Look out for the turn-off at Blaze Bridge and make for Loweswater Church at Church Bridge. Pick up the boggy bridle path over to Ennerdale via Mosedale and Loweswater Fell. The ground is pretty flat but, if it's been raining, you're

↑ key

▬▬	route of ride
▭	major road
▭	minor road
┅	vehicle track
▲	peak
⊔	pass
⛺	campground
🛏	hotel/guesthouse
✕	provisions
🚲	bike shop/repairs

←

Garburn Pass—the rocky descent over the fells from Troutbeck to Kentmere—is the first major hurdle to be encountered.

The Troutbeck Valley is the first chance to escape the bustle of Windermere and take in Lakeland's real charms.

going to get wet. A great descent down to Ennerdale will put you on the forestry track, which takes you 6 miles (10km) up the side of Ennerdale Water to the even more remote Black Sail Youth Hostel, where you should take a break—you're going to need it for the next section. Take a look around. Great Gable is looming right over you; up on the right is the famous climbing ground of Pillar Rock. If you go up Scarth Gap there are fantastic views right over Buttermere and Crummock Water, but not today; rather you have to shoulder the bike and climb Black Sail Pass—budget for an hour's climb. When you get up, you'll struggle to ride down until you get to Mosedale, then it's a reasonable bridle path to Wasdale and a well-earned rest at the Wasdale Head Inn.

Wasdale Head has a pub, a hotel, a shop that sells food and climbing/camping gear, a campground, one farm, and heaps of rock-climbing history. This is the birthplace of rock climbing: the pioneer Victorians all stayed here and, surprisingly, little has changed since. Scafell Pike is up on the left and the bulk of Great Gable with the famous Napes Needle rock climb is behind you. Wast Water is the deepest lake in the park, at over 300 feet (90m) deep, and probably the coldest. Wasdale Hall Youth Hostel is 4 miles (7km) down the lake at Nether Wasdale and is a wonderful old half-timbered lodge right by the lakeshore.

The long grassy rake down to Swindale from Mosedale Cottage makes a fantastic and challenging descent.

↓ **ride profile**

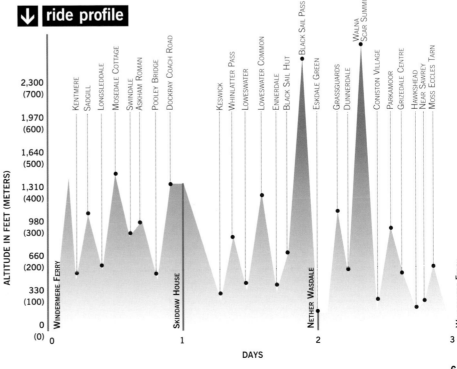

The old Roman road over Askham Fell and High Street is well used today, as it was when it was built as a military road to Ullswater.

•DAY 3   34 miles (55km)

Nether Wasdale to Windermere Ferry

Taking the quiet lanes through Nether Wasdale and Santon Bridge, then left over the hill to Eskdale Green, makes a relaxed start to the day. Eskdale Green is peaceful and unspoiled, very different from the tourist draws of Winder-mere or Ambleside. The only thing that gets busy here is the "Laal Ratty," a narrow gauge railroad that runs tourist trips from Boot village to Ravenglass on the coast. It started out as a quarry railroad but is now owned and run by a trust.

Pick up the bridle path just past the King George pub at Forge Bridge. This pretty bridle path, beside the clear waters of the River Esk, goes past the thundering Gill Force water-fall, and up the valley to the foot of Hardknott Pass—the steepest hairpin road in the country. Luckily the route doesn't go up here; instead it winds up Grassguards, under the shadow of Harter Fell, but you still have to shoulder the bike. It soon eases off and leads gently, if a bit damply, down to Dunnerdale. Stepping stones take you across the River Duddon, then the road winds south to Seathwaite Bridge, where the Walna Scar Road takes you over to Coniston. This is another ancient route, once used for mining and quarrying. Coniston is famous for the water speed record attempts of Donald and Malcolm Campbell, and for the Coniston copper mines, which can still be seen

and explored, at your own risk. The Walna Scar Road skirts The Old Man of Coniston to Coniston village. Head north out of the village to the east shore of Coniston Water. The ride beside the lakeshore is relaxed and scenic: past the great literary figure John Ruskin's house at Brantwood; past Peel Island, made famous as Wild Cat Island in Arthur Ransome's *Swallows and Amazons*; and Coniston Water Park, where the beautiful steamboat *Gondola* that cruises Coniston Water was rescued from rot and abandonment.

Parkamoor overlooks Coniston Water and leads you into the fantastic myriad forestry roads of Grizedale Forest. Look out for the sculpture trail, where dozens of unique, natural material sculptures have been erected. The visitor center is easily found, or keep going to the picture-postcard village of Hawkshead. Next, head down the road following signs for Near Sawrey and the Windermere ferry. If you're a *Peter Rabbit* fan, you may want to visit Hill Top, Beatrix Potter's house; otherwise, take the bridle path left, just before the Far Sawrey Arms pub, to Moss Eccles Tarn. After an undemanding climb past the three tarns, a fantastic descent through woodland and forestry plantations brings you out onto the shore of Windermere at Bell Grange, where a gentle ride takes you back to the ferry landing. Catch the ferry across Windermere to complete the circle and the most amazing mountain bike circuit in the country.

 factfile

OVERVIEW

 Circular tour of the Lake District National Park in Cumbria that encompasses most of the principal valleys and lakes. The total distance covered will vary from rider to rider, as there are innumerable opportunities to digress from the basic route, exploring alternative descents or detouring into towns and villages, but 104 miles (165km) over 3 days is a rough guide.

Start/Finish: Windermere Ferry.

ABOUT THE TRAIL

The tour takes the rider around the park on a challenging yet well-marked and graded route, using a combination of legal bridle paths, ancient tracks, and surfaced roads. About 60 percent is off-road and 40 percent on tarmac, plus one ferry crossing at the end.

Major Climbs & Descents: The route follows the perimeter of the Lake District but inevitably climbs into and out of each valley in turn, so expect big climbs and big descents. There are four major climbs where you should expect to shoulder the bike: Garburn Pass into Kentmere, Black Sail Pass in Ennerdale, Grassguards in Eskdale, and Walna Scar in the Duddon Valley.

Difficulty & Special Features: This is quite a tough tour, owing to the switchback nature of the landscape. Route finding can be very tricky with many options available, so you should study the maps carefully and understand contours, path markings, and distances given.

ACCESS

Airports: The nearest international airport is Manchester (75 miles/120km south).

Transport: The starting point at Windermere is arbitrary, in that you can start a circular route at any point. But it does have the advantage of good access, with railroad and bus links, and is the first town on the way into the Lakes from the M6 motorway for anyone traveling from the south. Also there are all the usual town facilities, a good tourist information office, and access to good bike shops at Staveley (between Kendal and Windermere) and Ambleside (4 miles/6.5km north).

Passport & Visa Requirements: Passport with tourist visa for all non-Europeans.

Permits & Access Restrictions: Mountain bikers in the national park must ride on bridle paths only, except where permissive paths have been granted; e.g., the Old Coach Road at Dockray. Bridle paths are marked on maps with a long, green, dashed line—check the map legend if you are unsure.

LOCAL INFORMATION

 Maps: You should take all four of the Ordnance Survey 1:25,000 Outdoor Leisure maps, numbers 4, 5, 6, and 7. These are the best maps available and detail every inch of the route described.

Guidebooks: *The Lake District: The Rough Guide* by Jules Brown (Rough Guides); *Mountain Bike Route Guide: Lake District* by Tim Woodcock (Dalesman Publishing Company Ltd.).

Accommodation & Supplies: Youth Hostel Association at Windermere (tel.: 01539 443543); Tourist Information accommodation service (tel.: 01768 775757); for camping barns contact the Lake District National Park at Bowness (see below). Food can be bought at most villages along the route.

Currency & Language: Pounds sterling; English (with a broad Cumbrian accent).

Area Information: Contact the Tourist Information office at Windermere (tel.: 01539 446499); the Lake District National Park Information office at Bowness (tel.: 01539 442895); and Biketreks at Ambleside for ride information and service (tel.: 01539 431245).

TIMING & SEASONALITY

 Best Months to Visit: May to September gives the best weather. The summer vacation season begins in mid-July and runs through to September, which makes it busier. Also, you get British Summer Time, so longer daylight hours. May is the very best month.

Climate: England has a temperate climate, mild and wet, but the weather can be incredibly varied and each day can be quite different from the next in any season.

HEALTH & SAFETY

 Vaccinations: None required.

General Health Risks: Midges, tiny flying bugs, the same as you get in Scotland. They bite and itch like crazy. They love water and trees and come out after rain and in the evening. If you react badly to them, carry a midge hat and repellent and keep away from campgrounds under trees by the side of lakes. They can't fly in wind

← *Coniston Water, scene of Donald Campbell's fatal water speed record attempt in the 1960s, shelters under the watchful eye of The Old Man of Coniston, the highest peak in this valley.*

so a breezy evening can be a real break. The adder, England's only poisonous snake, inhabits this area, but its bite is not fatal.

Special Considerations: Wear a helmet as the descents on this tour can be fast and rocky.

Politics & Religion: No special considerations.

Crime Risk: Low.

Food & Drink: If you drink water out of the streams (becks) and are not used to it you will fall ill. The locals are used to it and drink straight out of streams all the time, but don't be tempted unless you know you'll be fine. Watch out for dead sheep upstream!

HIGHLIGHTS

Scenic: Windermere is the largest lake in England at over 11 miles (18km) long, but it is the wild beauty of the higher fells and hidden lakes and tarns that are the real attraction of the Lake District. White painted cottages, huge waterfalls, and pretty market towns with an unspoiled feel.

Wildlife & Flora: Windermere is home to several rare species of fish, including char, and waterfowl such as tufted ducks. Deer patrol at night; golden eagles ride the thermals; and brown trout, mink, and otters swim the rivers.

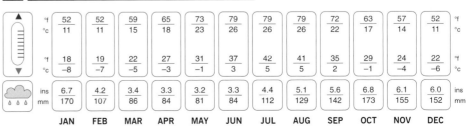 **temperature and precipitation**

		JAN	FEB	MAR	APR	MAY	JUN	JUL	AUG	SEP	OCT	NOV	DEC	
	°f	52	52	59	65	73	79	79	79	72	63	57	52	°f
	°c	11	11	15	18	23	26	26	26	22	17	14	11	°c
	°f	18	19	22	27	31	37	42	41	35	29	24	22	°f
	°c	−8	−7	−5	−3	−1	3	5	5	2	−1	−4	−6	°c
	ins	6.7	4.2	3.4	3.3	3.2	3.3	4.4	5.1	5.6	6.8	6.1	6.0	ins
	mm	170	107	86	84	81	84	112	129	142	173	155	152	mm

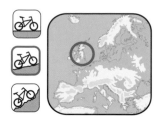

COAST-to-COAST

ENGLAND, U.K.

Dave Willis

THE COAST-TO-COAST (C2C) JOURNEY HAS BEEN A POPULAR CHALLENGE FOR WALKERS EVER SINCE ALFRED WAINWRIGHT PUBLISHED HIS COAST TO COAST GUIDEBOOK IN 1972. THE C2C WAS ENVISAGED TO PROVIDE THE SAME SORT OF CHALLENGE ON TWO WHEELS. THE FRAMEWORK FOR THE ROUTE WAS LARGELY IN PLACE ALREADY, OWING TO AN EXTENSIVE NETWORK OF DISUSED RAILROAD TRACKS ONCE USED BY THE THRIVING MINING AND QUARRYING INDUSTRY IN THE NORTH OF ENGLAND.

The C2C cycle path has become one of the most popular long-distance routes in the U.K., due largely to the "Sustainable Transport" group, known as "Sustrans." Sustrans, in partnership with local authorities, adopted this route, promoted it, equipped it with signposts and waymarks, ensured access, and published guides and maps.

Traversing the northern counties of Cumbria, Northumberland, and Durham, from Whitehaven or Workington to Sunderland or Tynemouth, the route takes in the stunning mountains of the Lake District National Park, crosses the wild and lonely Pennines (the backbone of England), and heads down into the urban landscape of Newcastle—all the way from the Irish Sea to the North Sea.

This is a stunningly varied roller-coaster journey through a landscape that twists and turns from awesome mountain and lake scenery, moody moorlands, and gentle pastoral villages to a historic industrial landscape represented in mining, shipbuilding, the proud heritage of the Rivers Tyne and Wear, and the rich Geordie cultures of Newcastle and Sunderland.

↓ itinerary

•DAY 1   31 miles (50km)

Whitehaven to Keswick

The official Sustrans route starts in Whitehaven, just a few miles north of St. Bees, but take the time to add the extra miles and take in pretty St. Bees and its fabulous red sandstone beaches and cliffs. Generations of locals have carved their names on the soft red rock and their labor remains to be seen in thousands of inscriptions, some over 300 years old. Remember to dip a wheel in the sea, then take the lanes that wind over the cliffs, skirting the old white lighthouse. This brings you into the old Roman port of Whitehaven, still bustling with harbor traffic. The C2C path is well marked through the town. Pick up the Whitehaven-to-Ennerdale railroad path and follow it toward Rowrah. The route has made use of old dismantled railroad lines, which are well surfaced and make perfect cycling paths. When the railroad path ends, a short road section takes you through the villages of Kirkland, Felldyke, and Lamplugh, then Waterend and down the shores of Loweswater. You have entered the Lake District National Park at this point—and you know it; the mountains and fells around Loweswater, Buttermere, and Crummock rise up out of the bedrock, enveloping the three lakes in this valley.

The signed route stays on the lanes and follows Low Lorton and High Lorton, with a long climb up Whinlatter Pass, but snicks off onto a well-surfaced forestry track halfway up. Riding off the road under the shade of the trees is a welcome relief. When you regain the road, it's at the Forestry Commission Visitor Centre, complete with café.

The fun continues off-road on a good bridle path down through Thornthwaite Forest to Thornthwaite itself. "Thwaite" is an old Cumbrian dialect word meaning "clearing in the woods," which is very appropriate here. Back on tarmac, the route takes quiet lanes to Keswick via Braithwaite, Ullock, and Portinscale. It's worth detouring very slightly through Keswick to go down to the shores of Derwent Water, by the ferry landing, and look out from →

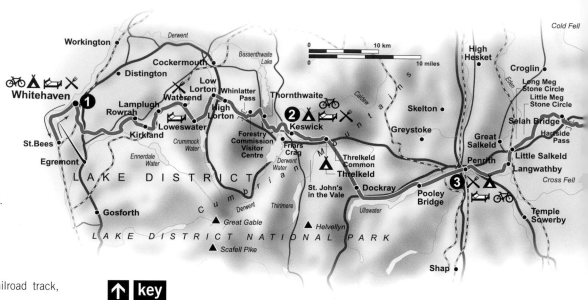

Friars Crag across the lake. This is one of the classic viewpoints in the Lake District. Keswick is a thriving little slate-built Lakeland town with all the conveniences, and makes a fine overnight stop.

•DAY 2   22 miles (35km)

Keswick to Penrith

Day 2 leaves Keswick via another old railroad track, beside the River Derwent. The Sustrans main route takes the lanes but the railroad ride is much, much better. At Threlkeld, a quick ride down St. Johns in the Vale gets you onto the Old Coach Road over Threlkeld Common. This is an off-road highlight, far away from roads, and pretty steep to begin with. Once the summit is gained, it's a fantastic rolling ride across moorland and fellside, with only the local Herdwick sheep and hill walkers for company. Again, the signed route takes you through the lanes, but a quick look at the map will show a variety of ways to get to Penrith. Drop down to Ullswater and try the scenic ride up the shoreline road. Take a last look at one of the biggest lakes in the park before heading out of Pooley Bridge for Penrith, leaving the Lake District behind you.

↑ key

▤	route of ride
▤	major road
▭	minor road
┅	railroad
▲	peak
⊔	pass
⚑	campground
🛏	hotel/guesthouse
✕	provisions
✈	airport
🚲	bike shop/repairs
M	museum

↑
Last stop of the Coast-to-Coast ride, the view of the lighthouse from Roker Beach, Sunderland is a sight worth waiting for.

←
The craggy, haunting moorlands of Garigill and the North Pennines.

→
The Whinlatter Pass forest path is an unforgettable ride through leafy woodlands and glades.

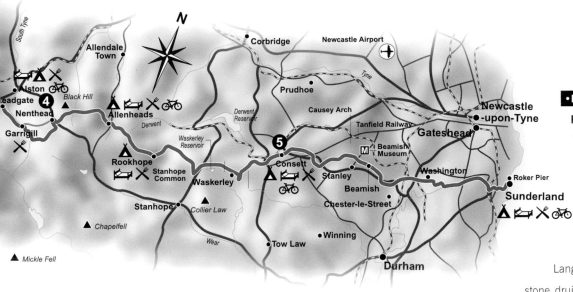

•DAY 3 27 miles (44km)

Penrith to Nenthead

The Northern Pennines has been described as "England's Last Wilderness," and in winter it's a harsh, barren environment, very different from the picture-postcard lakes and mountains of Cumbria. The route winds up into the backbone of England via Langwathby, Little Salkeld, and past the ancient stone druid circles of Long Meg and Little Meg in the Eden Valley. Following lanes toward Hartside Pass, you'll soon have an opportunity for an off-road excursion sign-posted for Selah Bridge, which continues up to the Hartside Summit Café. It's steep, but this is a fine viewpoint over East Cumbria, and a welcome tea break after climbing Hartside. The descent into the Alston Valley is a blast. At Leadgate, turn right for Nenthead, a relic of the old mining age with a heritage center.

•DAY 4 26 miles (42km)

Nenthead to Consett

Black Hill is the first hurdle of the day. The highest point on the C2C, it just tops Hartside, at 1,998 feet (609m), and so the route is, in principle, all downhill from here. There

↑

The ride on the Old Coach Road over Threlkeld Common anticipates the spectacular ride through solitary moorland that is to come.

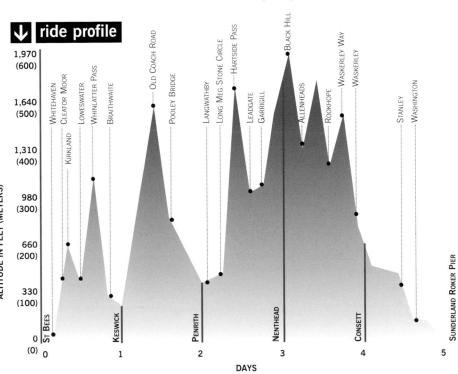

↓ **ride profile**

remains the steep-sided valley over to Allenheads to climb, but after that the way ahead is marked by a far-off horizon and a good deal of solitude.

Allenheads is a fascinating old mining village, with many relics still to be seen. The inn makes a great photograph, festooned with antique farm and mining tools. At Rookhope it's off-road across Stanhope Common, provided it's not closed for grouse shooting, which is usually between August and October. There is a dramatic change in the landscape now. The hills are without trees. Heather and gorse cover the empty horizons. The off-road section continues along another old narrow-gauge railroad track, crossing the fell road, past the Waskerley Reservoir, and on toward the village of Waskerley. The Waskerley Way has the advantage of staying fairly level for much of its length, being an old railroad track. It contours around the rolling moors, snaking a route as horizontal as possible all the way to Consett.

•DAY 5   25 miles (40km)

Consett to Sunderland

The route to Sunderland is an interesting and scenic meander along a disused railroad path once again. As you wind down toward the end of the Coast-to-Coast ride, the going gets easier—the landscape is at first more wooded and then increasingly urban; the way is marked with interesting

sculptures and monuments. Among these are the Causey Arch, a historic railroad bridge built in 1727; the Tanfield Railway, which is the world's oldest railroad still running; and the Beamish Museum, which houses a unique re-creation of past industrial and agricultural life in the northeast. The use of the old railroad line has enabled the route to sneak through towns and housing areas almost unnoticed. The path is hard-surfaced and retains that greenbelt atmosphere of all railroads that use embankments and cuttings to hide from their sprawling urban surroundings. Even the final miles to the North Sea through the center of Sunderland are filled with distractions; the railroad path continues through the town center, passing the Hetton Colliery Railway Monument, the Festival Park and Stadium of Light, and the National Glass Centre, and then into the Marina to finish by Roker Pier.

The beach at Roker Pier, Sunderland, is sandy and protected by the sweep of the harbor walls. It feels like a real finish to a long journey, gazing out over the gray North Sea, with the wind in your face and the tide surging up the beach toward you. You have traversed England from the Irish Sea to the North Sea, so remember to dip your wheel in the surf.

Take a break at Martindale Church to catch this marvelous view of Ullswater.

↓ factfile

OVERVIEW

The Coast-to-Coast is a very well-known, well-documented route. There are always riders along the way on any day of the year, taking up the challenge of traversing England's northernmost counties. The landscape starts with West Cumbria's old industrial towns, and continues into the lakes and mountains of the English Lake District—undoubtedly the most beautiful area in the country—and the bleak Pennine landscapes of Northumberland. The route is tough to start, with some fairly steep climbs to tackle, but eases off as it crosses into Weardale across the Pennines. The final days into Sunderland present easy riding on level ground.
Start: Whitehaven.
Finish: Sunderland.

ABOUT THE TRAIL

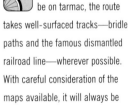
Although some riding will be on tarmac, the route takes well-surfaced tracks—bridle paths and the famous dismantled railroad line—wherever possible. With careful consideration of the maps available, it will always be possible to add more adventurous riding to the route if desired.
Major Climbs & Descents: All notable climbs are on tarmac, with off-road options if desired. Whinlatter Pass (820 feet/250m of ascent) and the Old Coach Road (985 feet/300m of ascent) in the Lake District are the first climbs. Then Hartside Pass (approximately 820 feet/250m of ascent), Garrigill to Nenthead (810 feet/248m of ascent), Black Hill and Allenheads to Waskerley (approximately 660 feet/200m of ascent).

Difficulty & Special Features: All the major obstacles are well described in the Sustrans map and guidebook for the route, which are indispensable. It's normal to complete this route west to east to take advantage of the prevailing wind and gradients. Take spare inner tubes; punctures are common and it's easier and faster to change tubes than fix holes.

ACCESS

Airports: the nearest international airport is Manchester (75 miles/120km south) which has good rail and road connections.
Transport: Whitehaven has good rail links from Carlisle, which links to the London–Glasgow line. By car it's a straightforward drive from Penrith over the A66 to the west coast. There is also a bus link to Carlisle and Penrith. Sunderland is also well connected by rail.
Passport & Visa Requirements: Passport with tourist visa for all non-Europeans.
Permits & Access Restrictions: Check the grouse-shooting seasonal restrictions over Stanhope Common.

LOCAL INFORMATION

Maps: The National Cycling Network's *C2C Cycle Route*.
Guidebooks: *A Coast to Coast Walk* by A. Wainwright (Michael Joseph).
Accommodation & Supplies: All the information that is required to complete this route, including accommodation, maps, and points of interest, is contained in *The Ultimate C2C Guide* by Richard Peace (Excellent Books).
Currency & Language: Pounds sterling; English.
Area Information: Sustrans, 35 King Street, Bristol, BS1 4DZ, England (tel.: 0117 929 0888).
Website: www.sustrans.org.uk will list any new or altered route information.

TIMING & SEASONALITY

Best Months to Visit: April to October.
Climate: The climate is influenced by the westerly airflow that prevails here. On the coast, the Gulf Stream gives a relatively damp and mild climate, with coastal areas experiencing warm summers and mild winters. The Lakeland hills get a very changeable weather pattern, with much rain, which turns to snow in the winter months. Winters in the Pennines are subject to easterly airflows, which are much colder, and make the Pennine moors very desolate and remote. The weather changes fast and snow is common even in spring and fall.

HEALTH & SAFETY

Vaccinations: None required.
General Health Risks: None.
Special Considerations: Watch out for irritating midges over the Lake District fells and on the moors of the Pennines from May through September. They come out in the evenings and love water and trees. The biggest danger on the moors is hypothermia, brought on by wind chill and dehydration. Always take windproofs, gloves, and lots of trail food and water. Leave word of your plans with a third party just in case.
Politics & Religion: No concerns.

Grasmere is a jewel in the heart of the Lake District; its eponymous village was the one-time home of poet William Wordsworth.

Crime Risk: Low.
Food & Drink: It is best to carry sufficient water with you. If you choose to drink from upland streams, check that there are no dwelling places or obvious sources of pollution above you.

HIGHLIGHTS

Scenic: The mining heritage of Allenheads and Nenthead is evident all around in countless abandoned workings and ruins. The grouse moors of Northumberland present a rolling, heather-covered prospect and then the route journeys through the fascinating post-industrial areas of Wearside into Sunderland, with many famous monuments, museums, and landmarks to take in.
Wildlife & Flora: The Lake District contains peregrines, ravens, buzzards, and even a pair of golden eagles at Haweswater. Red squirrels are common and there are wild red deer around Ullswater. St. Bees Head is an R.S.P.B. (Royal Society for the Protection of Birds) bird sanctuary, famous for breeding guillemots, razorbills, and fulmars. The Pennines are mostly grassland, heather moor, and blanket bog. Merlin, red grouse, and golden plover are found here. You may also spot an adder, Britain's only poisonous snake, if you're lucky!

↓ temperature and precipitation

	JAN	FEB	MAR	APR	MAY	JUN	JUL	AUG	SEP	OCT	NOV	DEC
°f	51	51	59	60	72	78	77	77	71	63	56	53
°c	11	11	15	16	22	26	25	25	22	17	13	11
°f	17	19	22	25	31	36	42	40	33	28	24	20
°c	−8	−7	−5	−4	−1	2	5	4	1	−2	−4	−6
ins	3.5	2.3	1.9	1.9	2.2	2.3	2.9	3.0	3.1	3.9	3.5	3.4
mm	89	60	49	50	57	59	74	76	81	100	90	88

HIGHLAND FLING

SCOTLAND, U.K.

Judy Armstrong

THIS CIRCULAR ROUTE WRAPS AROUND THE VERY HEART OF THE SCOTTISH HIGHLANDS. IT PASSES WITHIN TOUCHING DISTANCE OF BEN NEVIS, THE U.K.'S HIGHEST MOUNTAIN, CLIMBS TO THE WILD HEIGHTS OF THE CORRIEYAIRACK PASS, AND VISITS LOCH NESS, HOME OF "NESSIE," THE MYTHICAL MONSTER. IT INCLUDES TWISTING, SINGLE-TRACK, HISTORIC GRAVEL ROADS, HARD-PACKED TRACKS BESIDE THE CALEDONIAN CANAL, HAIRPIN BENDS THROUGH FORESTRY, AND THE CHANCE TO DANGLE FEET IN ICE-COLD LOCHS.

This is wild countryside, climbing around the southern flanks of Ben Nevis and along the shores of silent lochs, and the wondrous silence of the empty landscape and big skies of Rannoch Moor. There are exhilarating descents, long steep grinds, and superb technical riding, with views across the whole of western Scotland.

Described here as a three-day route, it could be extended to four by stopping for a night at Fort William; this creates a window for a foot ascent of "the Ben," or the chance to relax by the loch.

itinerary

•DAY 1 40 miles (64km)

Kinlochleven to Spean Bridge

The tranquil village of Kinlochleven sits at the head of a long sea loch, Loch Leven. Surrounded by mountains, it is a popular rest stop on the West Highland Way long-distance path, and the perfect launch pad for this three-day circuit.

The route initially follows the well-marked West Highland Way, climbing steadily toward the Mamore Lodge, with far-reaching views past the Pap of Glen Coe. When the West Highland Way veers left, our track pushes right (east)

A rough, stony track leads into the heart of remote Glen Roy on Day 2, from where the rest of the day's riding stretches before you for as far as the eye can see.

Riding rough cobbles below the Corrieyairack Pass is tiring, but the fantastic views of deep lochs and high mountains make it all worthwhile.

toward Loch Eilde Mòr, through the ancient, treeless Mamore Forest.

There is only one path, so navigation is simple, allowing plenty of time to enjoy the wild, open landscape. The gravel track rolls along the shores of Loch Eilde Mòr and Loch Eilde Beag, below the great hulks of Ben Nevis and Aonach Beag. The feeling of remoteness, of necessary self-reliance, becomes stronger the further you travel into these hills.

The deserted hunting lodge at Luibeilt, where the river runs so clear you can see fish sliding under stones, is a wonderful place for a lunch break. You'll need the energy—once you've hopped over the Abhainn Rath river, there's a long, tricky climb to a saddle between Meall a'Bhùirich and Meall Mòr.

From here, it's downhill all the way. This first section of descent toward Rannoch Moor is technical but fun, with rock slabs, sudden stone steps, and sliding gravel to contend with, on narrow single-track across a steep-sided hill.

Once on Rannoch Moor, at the Lairig Leacach (which means Slabby, or Granite, Pass), the route heads down the long, steep-sided valley toward Spean Bridge. It's a superb descent, with some really fast sections. The roller-coaster track is an old thieves' road that recrosses the river countless times until it enters forestry.

If you scout about in the forest, you'll find deep, inviting pools with natural slides and water chilled to spine-tingling levels. If you don't, you'll soon find the quiet road beside the River Spean, which leads into Spean Bridge. There are plenty of guesthouses and pubs here, with more at Roy Bridge, just up the A86 on Day 2's route.

•DAY 2 | **60 miles (97km)**

Spean Bridge to Fort Augustus

This is the big one—not in terms of distance, but in height gain. For today is Corrieyairack Day, when you'll climb the 13 switchbacks up a gravel road that was built in 1731 by General Wade and his soldiers.

Before that, though, is a gentle road ride—briefly up the busy A86, and soon branching off at Roy Bridge to follow an unfenced country lane deep into the heart of Glen Roy. A single-track road, it twists and climbs alongside the River Roy toward the Glen Roy National Nature Reserve. This has been created in recognition of the Parallel Roads—three level terraces carved into the hillsides that were once thought to have been built by the Romans, but are actually the shorelines of a lake formed during the last Ice Age, when the glacier blocking Glen Roy gradually melted and the lake spilled out into neighboring valleys, so lowering the level three times.

At Brae Roy Lodge, 20 miles (32km) from Spean Bridge, the road stops abruptly and you are faced with a dirt track vanishing into wilderness. Once over the picturesque single-arched Turret Bridge, where the rivers Roy and Turret meet, the track splits and you branch right to follow the Roy's left bank.

The river penetrates deep into the glen, surrounded by stream-spliced hills. The valley soon opens out to become a wide, grassy bowl, with the gravel track rising slowly upward toward a vast expanse of desolate moorland.

The sturdy Luib-chonnal bothy is a good spot to refuel the body before lifting bikes over a high stile in a deer fence, into little-trodden territory.

Locals may tell you that the track to Melgarve doesn't exist, but you'll be delighted to find it entirely ridable. A tiny path winds through rocks, across streams, and over moor-

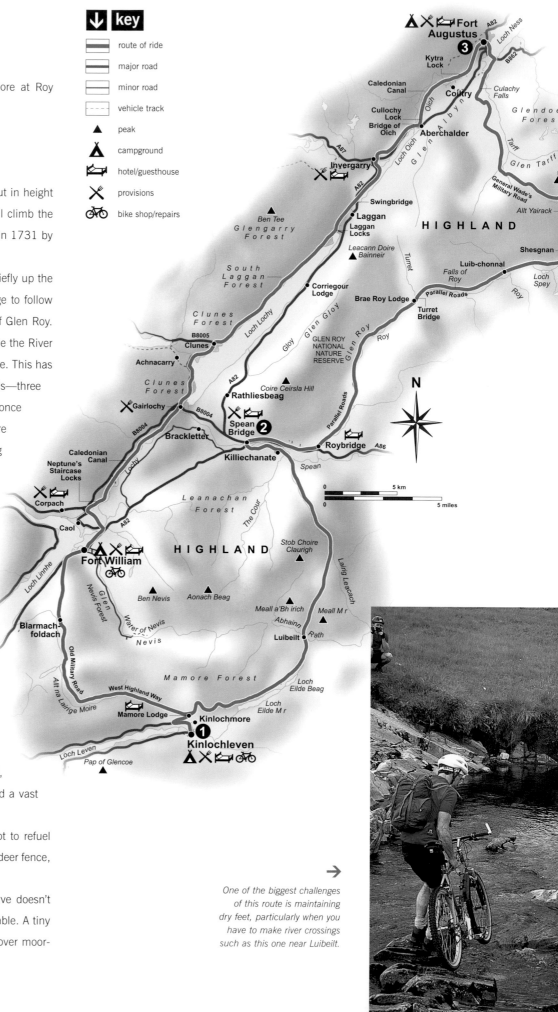

key

- route of ride
- major road
- minor road
- vehicle track
- ▲ peak
- ⛺ campground
- 🛏 hotel/guesthouse
- ✕ provisions
- 🚲 bike shop/repairs

→

One of the biggest challenges of this route is maintaining dry feet, particularly when you have to make river crossings such as this one near Luibeilt.

Stone walls, old hump-backed bridges, and ancient forests can cause you to lose all sense of time when biking in the Scottish Highlands.

land, with stunning views of lochs, mountains, and sky.

The track fails at the very end, on the boggy heather stretch to the ruined Shesgnan bothy. But relief is at hand—pick up a good track from Shesgnan to the tiny settlement of Melgarve, where you turn left to join General Wade's Military Road—in just one summer in 1731, 510 men built the 45-mile (72-km) road from Dalwhinnie to Fort Augustus, making it one of the greatest feats of engineering in the Highlands—and the start of the Corrieyairack Pass.

Start the long ascent over smooth cobbles (incredibly hard to ride), which soon give way to rough stones and hard-packed earth. Then suddenly the mighty zigzagged road is visible—the original 18 switchbacks have been reduced to 13 and make an awesome sight winding up to the pass.

The pass itself is wild and windswept, with distant pyramid mountains fading blue into the sky. Stop for breath, then rejoin the rocky track leading down, down into the view, on an exhilarating, neck-jarring drop of almost 2,630 vertical feet (800m) to Loch Ness and Fort Augustus.

On the last section the track splits; take the left-hand option to avoid being ensnared in the eroded depths beyond the Culachy Falls. Once on the road, turn right and follow your nose into town; a nice route is past the old burial ground and then right again down the main road into Fort Augustus.

•DAY 3 **80 miles (129km)**

Fort Augustus to Kinlochleven

It's worth pausing on your way out of town to watch ships navigate the Fort Augustus lock system before they sail up the Caledonian Canal. Follow them out, along the hard flat towpath toward the Aberchalder bridge—the fast riding is in marked contrast to yesterday's dusty efforts.

Joining tarmac at the bridge at Loch Oich's northern head, turn right and look immediately for a sign on your right, showing a cycle track leading into a forest. This skinny track, signposted to Invergarry, climbs and twists through the forest with views of the loch all the way. It →

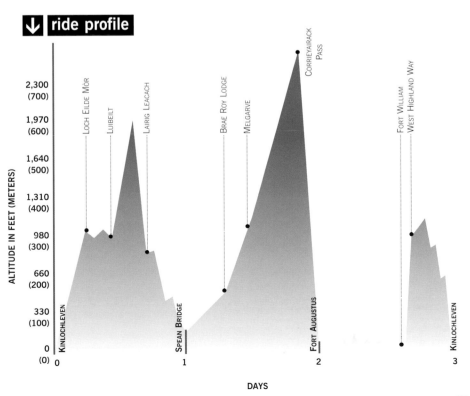

⬇ ride profile

ALTITUDE IN FEET (METERS)

2,300 (700)
1,970 (600)
1,640 (500)
1,310 (400)
980 (300)
660 (200)
330 (100)
0 (0)

KINLOCHLEVEN · LOCH EILDE MÒR · LUIBEILT · LAIRIG LEACACH · SPEAN BRIDGE · BRAE ROY LODGE · MELGARVE · CORRIEYAIRACK PASS · FORT AUGUSTUS · FORT WILLIAM · WEST HIGHLAND WAY · KINLOCHLEVEN

0   1   2   3

DAYS

drops you into Invergarry village; a quick left then right on the A82 leads to Laggan.

A narrow lane to the right takes you above the Caledonian Canal to Laggan Locks and on into the forest. This is a stretch of gentle climbing and descending, with views through the trees to tranquil Loch Lochy. The air smells of pine needles and the only sound comes from your tires on gravel—it's a treat just to be here.

Leaving the forestry at the settlement of Clunes, you'll follow a quiet country road to Gairlochy. Just by the locks is a hidden jewel: the Stable Tearoom, with outside picnic tables and fantastic views of Ben Nevis.

Back on the bike, stay on the left side of the Caledonian Canal for a fast section to Corpach at the head of Loch Linnhe. Turning left at the road will lead you soon to Fort William, with its cobbled main street and tartan-filled gift shops—and the end of the flat riding.

The steep climb out of town (turn left at the second major roundabout heading south) soon leaves suburbia and creeps skyward. A few gentle descents take the strain off the climbs, to a high point of 880 feet (270m) where the road bends sharply right.

Signposts, which you follow, point out the West Highland Way vanishing ahead into forestry. Another old Military Road dips and climbs through a steep-sided valley, following the line of the Allt na Lairige Moire stream. Isolated, remote, often windswept, this is a fitting final section to a wild ride. The rough rock and gravel track is hemmed in by mountains, with views of Loch Leven appearing only once the highest ground, at the watershed, is reached.

It's possible to follow the track back to the Mamore Lodge and down the track you rode up on Day 1, but a better descent is to branch right down a glorious single-track shortly before the lodge. Be warned: this has narrow drainage ditches edged with stone, which must be jumped if nipped tires and punctures are to be avoided.

Whichever route you choose, you'll land at Kinlochleven tired, happy, and thirsty. Luckily, the place is riddled with pubs and cafés. Go on, give way to hedonism. You deserve it.

factfile

You'll cross the River Roy several times, often on picturesque stone bridges.

OVERVIEW

This route takes in some of Highland Scotland's best scenery. It covers historical roads, gives close-up views of Ben Nevis, cruises gently between sea lochs along the Caledonian Canal, brushes against wild Rannoch Moor, and visits Loch Ness, home of the famous monster. This circular route takes 3 days (can be extended to 4), and covers 180 miles (290km).

Start/Finish: Kinlochleven.

ABOUT THE TRAIL

There is a healthy mix of single-track and double-track, with a minority of miles on

tarmac roads. The first day is almost entirely off-road, with a mix of double- and single-track. The second day has around 30 percent tarmac (on a quiet country road) followed by challenging single-track and double-track. The final day rolls easily down a path beside the Caledonian Canal, with forest tracks and some tarmac before the double-track section along the West Highland Way to the finish.

Major Climbs & Descents: On Day 1, the route starts with a steady climb of about 1,150 feet (350m) from Loch Leven (a sea loch) to Loch Eilde Mòr, on gravel tracks. After the lunch stop at Luibeilt, climb another 790 feet (240m) on

single-track to a high point of 1,930 feet (590m), before the sharp descent into Lairig Leacach on the edge of Rannoch Moor. The remaining descent to Spean Bridge (altitude 195 feet/60m) is on rough gravel tracks.

On Day 2, an easy 492-foot (150-m) height is gained over 12 miles on tarmac. The biggest climb of the route comes next—1,380 feet (420m) from Melgarve (1,150 feet/350m) to the Corrieyairack Pass (2,525 feet/770m), with a steep descent to Fort Augustus at sea level.

Lots of ups and downs on Day 3 through forestry, with the first real climb as you leave Fort William (sea level) for the start of the West Highland Way (885 feet/270m); luckily this is all on tarmac. The track then climbs to a high point of 1,115 feet (340m), with small climbs and descents, culminating in a 755-foot (230-m) drop-off on single-track to Kinlochleven, at sea level.

Difficulty & Special Features: The entire route is ridable, although only the strongest climbers will cycle all 13 hairpins to the Corrieyairack Pass. The only river crossing, at Luibeilt, is tackled with the help of judiciously placed stones. In wet conditions, the single-track from Luib-chonnal bothy to Melgarve can be difficult; there is always wet ground verging on bog near Shesgnan bothy. Front suspension is a tremendous asset for the descents from the Corrieyairack Pass to Fort Augustus, into Lairig Leacach, and down the West Highland Way to Kinlochleven.

ACCESS

Airports: Edinburgh and Glasgow are the nearest airports for international and domestic flights.

Transport: By train to Fort William (ScotRail: tel.: 0345 550033: you will need to book your bike onto the train). By bus to Fort William—Scottish CityLink Coaches (tel.: 0990 505050: they will not transport bicycles). There is a regular bus service between Fort William and Kinlochleven (Highland Country Buses, tel.: 01397 702373); they will transport bikes if luggage space allows. Failing that, organize a taxi for the 35-mile (56-km) trip. By car, use the safe, free Kinlochleven parking lot.

Passport & Visa Requirements: Citizens of the U.S., New Zealand, and Australia gain free visas on entry to the U.K.

The last leg of the journey follows the well-trodden West Highland Way, Scotland's most famous long-distance hiking trail.

Permits & Access Restrictions: None.

LOCAL INFORMATION

Maps: Ordnance Survey Landranger maps 34 and 41 (1:50,000 series).

Guidebooks: Most of the route is described, as separate day routes, in *Exploring Scottish Hill Tracks*, by Ralph Storer (David & Charles).

Accommodation & Supplies: Hotels, guesthouses, and independent hostels in Kinlochleven, Spean Bridge, Roy Bridge, and Fort Augustus. Snack food and bar meals are available at the towns along the route (Kinlochleven, Spean Bridge, Roy Bridge, Fort Augustus, Fort William). For cycle equipment, hire, and repair go to Off Beat Bikes, MacRaes Lane, Fort William PH33 6AB (tel.: 01397 704008. Bikes can be hired from Blackwater Hostel, Lab Road, Kinlochleven, Argyll PA40 1BT (tel.: 01855 831253; fax: 01855 831402).

Currency & Language: Scotland has its own bank notes, which are part of the British sterling system. The language is English—with a burr.

Area Information: Fort William Tourist Information Centre, Cameron Centre, Cameron Square, Fort William (tel.: 01397 703781; e-mail: fort.william@host.co.uk). Spean Bridge Tourist Information Centre, Woollen Mill Car Park, Spean Bridge PH34 4EP (tel.: 01397 712576; e-mail: spean-bridge@host.co.uk). Fort Augustus Tourist Information Centre, Car Park, Fort Augustus PH32 4DD

(tel.: 01320 366367; e-mail: fortaug@host.co.uk).

Websites: www.host.co.uk (accommodation); www.offbeatbikes.co.uk.

TIMING & SEASONALITY

Best Months to Visit: May to September, although midges can be irritating in July and August.

Climate: Expect a mixed climate—heat, rain, wind, and even snow are the norm.

HEALTH AND SAFETY

Vaccinations: None.

General Health Risks: Use sunscreen and carry warm clothing, including a lightweight breathable waterproof—the weather can change quickly in the Highlands.

Special Considerations: None.

Politics & Religion: No concerns.

Crime Risk: Low.

Food & Drink: Use a filtration or purifying system if you intend to drink from streams.

HIGHLIGHTS

Scenic: The Parallel Roads in Glen Roy are three level terraces carved into the hillsides of Glen Roy. Once thought to have been built by the Romans, they are actually the shorelines of a lake formed during the last Ice Age. As the glacier blocking Glen

Roy gradually melted, the lake spilled into neighboring valleys, lowering the level three times. The Parallel Roads are now protected as part of a national nature reserve. There's also Ben Nevis, Britain's highest mountain (4,406 feet/1,343m); there is a superb viewpoint of "the Ben" from Gairlochy. On Day 2 comes General Wade's Military Road. There were originally 18 switchbacks, now reduced to 13; for a century it was the highest-maintained public road in Britain, although it is now used to maintain the ugly pylons that follow the track.

Wildlife & Flora: Birds that may be spotted include the golden eagle and the ptarmigan. The golden eagle is the largest and most powerful of the true eagles, and magnificent in flight as it soars and glides around the mountains. The ptarmigan is a Scottish resident, famous for its plumage change—it becomes completely white in winter, except for its tail, which remains black. It is a very placid creature, yet can be difficult to spot on its mountain-top and rocky hillside habitat. Britain's largest deer, the red deer, is a common sight in the Scottish highlands. It is dark brown, rather than red, with a creamy patch on the rump. The stags bear impressive antlers and can be fairly vocal in the rutting season, which peaks in October.

⬇ temperature and precipitation

		JAN	FEB	MAR	APR	MAY	JUN	JUL	AUG	SEP	OCT	NOV	DEC	
▲	°f	53	52	58	61	71	75	74	73	68	62	57	54	°f
	°c	11	11	14	16	22	24	23	23	20	17	14	12	°c
▼	°f	22	22	26	29	32	38	42	41	36	32	27	24	°f
	°c	−6	−5	−3	2	0	3	5	5	2	0	−2	−4	°c
☁	ins	7.9	6.3	4.9	5.2	3.7	4.9	6.2	6.0	7.4	8.3	7.0	9.2	ins
	mm	203	162	127	133	94	125	160	154	190	214	181	236	mm

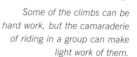

Some of the climbs can be
hard work, but the camaraderie
of riding in a group can make
light work of them.

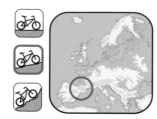

↓ itinerary

the HAUTES PYRÉNÉES

FRANCE & SPAIN

Steve Mead

THE PYRENEES ARE CLASSED AS THE LAST WILDERNESS MOUNTAIN RANGE IN EUROPE, AND OFFER A MAGNIFICENT BACKDROP TO THIS RIDE, WHICH PASSES OVER MANY FAMOUS COLS USED BY THE THE TOUR DE FRANCE, AND THROUGH VILLAGES THAT TIME SEEMS TO HAVE FORGOTTEN.

The snowcapped peaks of the Hautes Pyrénées will be your close companions over the seven days of this trip, but it is unlikely that you will tire of their beauty.

This ride starts on the edge of the Hautes (high) Pyrénées region at the Port de Balés and traverses westward across the mountain range, crossing the regions of the Hautes Pyrénées and the Pyrénées Atlantiques to the Basque country and the coastal town of Hendaye.

The route climbs mainly on road to give better coverage of ground and continuous off-road in the valleys and on the descents, thus enabling this trip to be ridable in just seven days. Time permitting, it is also possible to ride the whole of the Pyrenees range from the Mediterranean to the Atlantic, making a continuous ride lasting 18 days.

•DAY 1   35 miles (57km)

Port de Balés to St. Lary-Soulan

The ride starts at Col du Balés (5,760 feet/1,755m), which is accessed from the logging road in the Barousse Valley and the village of Ferrére. The col provides your first great view of the 9,800-foot (3,000-m) ridge line that forms the Spanish–French border and the Pic de Cecire (7,890 feet/2,403m). A descent of the old logging road to Bourg-d'Oueil follows, and then a crossing of the valley floor to reach a single-track descent past villages and on to the climb of Col De Peyresourde (5,150 feet/1,569m). At the ski station of Peyragudes on the west face, take an off-road descent through the village of Germ and down to the lakeside at Loudenvielle. This is a great place to take a lunch break or to enjoy the thermo spa center. From here, there are two options: you can take an off-road or a road climb up to Col d'Azet (5,330 feet/1,624m). The off-road option involves a steep but ridable gradient, while the road climb is one of the Tour de France's hardest challenges.

From the col, there is a decent start, with a traverse across open slopes and a gentle ride down into wooded tracks, finally ending up at the village of St. Lary-Soulan.

•DAY 2   51 miles (82km)

St. Lary-Soulan to Ste. Marie de Campan

The first main climb of the day is Col d'Aspin. This can be reached in two ways: by climbing the road that starts in Guchen—this follows a quiet single-track road that works its way up to Hourquette d'Ancizan, followed by a northward climb of a track and down to Col d'Aspin; or by the road climb of the D918, a great windy road climb also made famous by the Tour de France, but best avoided in the French holiday season.

There are many ways down through the pine forests to the lake and cross-country ski station of Payolle. Heading west out of the valley, the tracks climb up to a great viewpoint of the barren peaks of Pic de Monfaucon and then →

head north over Vallée de Campan, with its scattered thatched cottages lining the hillsides. The track finally rejoins the road at Ste. Marie de Campan, a nice village to spend the night in.

•DAY 3 27 miles (44km)

Ste. Marie de Campan to Luz-St. Sauveur

From Ste. Marie de Campan, take the 10½-mile (17-km) road climb to Col du Tourmalet. This must be the *most* famous of all the Tour de France cols in the Pyrenees, with its straight, steep road sections that lead up to the ski town of la Mongie. From la Mongie, you can take a cable car to the observatory on Pic du Midi De Bigorre—at 10,500 feet (3,200m), this is the highest accessed peak on the French side of the Pyrenees, and has magnificent panoramic views. After la Mongie, the road opens up and there are hairpin bends all the way to the col's summit at 6,940 feet (2,115m).

key

▬	route of ride
▭	major road
▭	minor road
- - -	country border
▲	peak
⊔	pass
⚑	campground
🛏	hotel/guesthouse
✕	provisions

←

This trip is organized so that you end each hard day of riding in a friendly town or village that will offer, at the very minimum, a guesthouse and a bar, so you can relax each night with a drink and a comfortable bed.

→ The occasional forest trail allows you to gain some shade, which will be particularly welcome if you choose to undertake this route in the height of summer.

challenging and potentially dangerous section must only be attempted with a local guide. Cutting across to the northern face and circling around to the south enables you to rejoin a single-track with 25 hairpin bends down to Barèges.

•DAY 4 | **68 miles (109km)**

Luz-St. Sauveur to Bedous

Head north on the road out of Luz to Argèles-Gazost. A westward climb to the village of Gez brings you to a forestry road that leads up the valley to the Gîte d'Étape Haugarou. Continue up the forest track to the cross-country ski station on Col de Couraduque, then head west to Col de la Serre. Follow the track past Col de Bazesand and continue to the road to Col du Soulor, from where you climb to Col d'Aubisque and great views of the Pic de Ger. A 10½-mile (17-km) windy descent through the ski town of Gourette brings you to a right turning at Eaux-Bonnes and on to Laruns. This is a good place to make an overnight stop.

If you prefer to press on, head northward down the valley and go over the short but steep climb of Col de Marie-Blanque. Head south up the Gave d'Aspe for an overnight stop at the town of Bedous.

VARIATION: An alternative off-road route that avoids the road section of the Col de Marie Blanque from the →

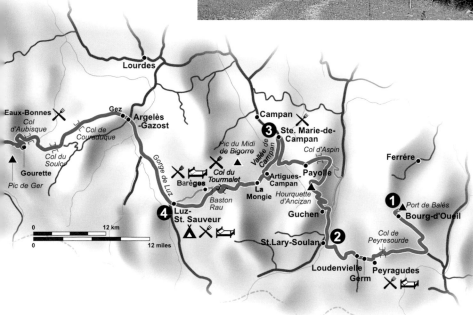

At the top of the col, join the many cyclists for a photo opportunity under the Tour de France monument to mark your personal conquest of the great climb. There is also a café there with galleries of newspaper clippings and photos.

From Col du Tourmalet, descend the road for about 1¼ miles (2km) to join a goat-track descent heading west on the northern slopes. This track joins the Bastan Rau River and crosses to the southern side of the valley to follow a westerly track to Artiguette. Climb this track to 4,720 feet (1,440m), and then head west through Soubralets. Eventually, you will descend into Luz-St. Sauveur.

VARIATION: An alternative route down the valley can be taken by climbing a dirt road to Capet and the snow barriers protecting the town of Barèges from snow avalanches. Avalanches nearly destroyed the town in 1897. On this route, the bike must be carried when traversing the steep mountainside through the barriers. This

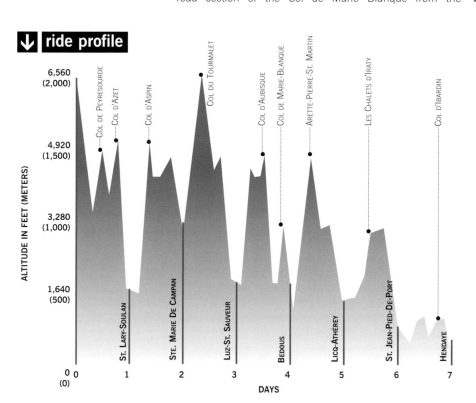

⬇ ride profile

ALTITUDE IN FEET (METERS)

6,560 (2,000)
4,920 (1,500)
3,280 (1,000)
1,640 (500)
0 (0)

COL DE PEYRESOURDE
COL D'AZET
COL D'ASPIN
COL DU TOURMALET
COL D'AUBISQUE
COL DE MARIE-BLANQUE
ARETTE-PIERRE-ST. MARTIN
LES CHALETS D'IRATY
COL D'IBARDIN

ST. LARY-SOULAN
STE. MARIE DE CAMPAN
LUZ-ST. SAUVEUR
BEDOUS
LICQ-ATHÉREY
ST. JEAN-PIED-DE-PORT
HENDAYE

0   1   2   3   4   5   6   7

DAYS

Laruns–Bedous crossing is via Col d'Arrioutort. The climb out of Laruns is steep and hard, so this short section would add another day to your itinerary.

•DAY 5 — 42 miles (67km)

Bedous to Licq-Athérey

Head out of Bedous to the village of Osse-en-Aspe, and climb the narrow road to Col de Houratate. Continue over Col de Bouezou and continue climbing to Col de Labays. Head south on the D132 to the Spanish border, passing the ski station of Arette-Pierre-St. Martin at 5,460 feet (1,666m). At the hairpin just before the border, take the westerly track up to the refuges. Follow the wide track cut into the hillside and into the forest. Technical single-track leads you on to a wider track that heads west to join the road at 2,770 feet (844m). Climb the road to Iratzordoky, and then take the forest track, which gives great views into the mouth of the Gorges de Kakouetta. Leave the trail on the spur above la Caserne, and descend the farm tracks to the road and onward down the valley to Licq-Athérey.

•DAY 6 — 38 miles (62km)

Licq-Athérey to St. Jean-Pied-de-Port

From Licq-Athérey, follow the road to Larrau and on to the ski station of les chalets d'Iraty. Join the GR10 route at the corner of Ireukatuturru and take the technical descent northwest to the main dirt road and continue on the GR10 to Esterençuby. Overnight in the Basque town of St. Jean-Pied-de-Port or continue to Bidarray.

•DAY 7 — 61 miles (98km)

St. Jean-Pied-de-Port to Hendaye

This is the final stage and probably the hardest. Leave the village and head west to the Spanish border at Bassassagar. Cross the bridge and head north to Col des Veaux. From the gîte, follow the ridge-line trail of the GR10 and descend into the village of Ainhoa.

Follow the GR10 through forests and lowlands to Sare. To make this stage ridable in one day take the road—at Col de Lizauniaga descend to Bera and then an enjoyable final road climb to Col d'Ibardin. From here, take the wider track that heads northwest to Lac de Poiriers, circle the lake up to Col des Poiriers, and rejoin the GR10 to Col d'Osin.

It is necessary to carry your bike on the next section as, although the path is descending, it is rocky and hard to ride. Descend the spur at the electricity pylons to the outskirts of Hendaye. From the buildup of houses follow the final few miles to the coast by road or by following the GR10. The seaside town of Hendaye is your final destination.

↓ factfile

OVERVIEW

The 324-mile (519-km), 7-day route takes in some of the best areas of the Pyrenees range. Climbs are mainly on the road, and lead to cols that open out into adjoining valleys, and off-road descents. It is possible to take longer off-road routes for the climbs, but the steepness of the valleys would mean that there would be many sections where the bike would have to be carried. The roads contour up the valleys, making them enjoyable, and provide the feel of following in the tracks of the Tour de France.
Start: Port De Balés.
Finish: Hendaye.

ABOUT THE TRAIL

This route covers most types of trail—single-track, double-track, and tarmac. The off-road surfaces on the first 5 days are well drained thanks to the local limestone, which can be slippery when wet; on the last 2 days the routes are drained by sandstone. The metaled sections follow narrow country roads.
Major Climbs & Descents: The road climbs of Col du Tourmalet and Col d'Aspin are busy in July and August. The maximum altitude reached is 6,940 feet (2,115m).
Difficulty & Special Features: Off-road tracks vary from single-track to wide jeep tracks; carrying is required on some sections. Although it is possible to ride this route independently, it is far more enjoyable if supported by a van.

ACCESS

Airports: Toulouse Blagnac, 78 miles

(125km) from the start; Biarritz, 19 miles (30km) from the finish.
Transport: There is no public transport available to the start of the route. There is a train station at Hendaye and a bus service to Biarritz.
Passport & Visa Requirements: Passports only are required by North American, Australasian, and U.K. visitors to France and Spain.
Permits & Access Restrictions: None.

LOCAL INFORMATION

Maps: Carte de Randonnées 1:5000, Numbers 1–6.
Guidebooks: The Rough Guides to an excellent *Pyrenees* guidebook.
Accommodation & Supplies: The route passes through major towns and villages with hotel and gîte accommodation (often closed in the months of April, May, and October). This route is planned to start and stop in villages and towns that have accommodation, shops, and supermarkets. Most small villages en route don't have shops, so buy provisions at the start of each day. There are no reliable bike shops along the way, so it is best to carry your own spares. In July and August, some ski shops hire out mountain bikes, sell a small range of supplies, and can make minor repairs.
Currency & Language: French francs and Spanish pesetas. Spanish, Basque, Catalan, and French are widely spoken; it is rare to find English-speaking locals.
Area Information: Tourist offices: Lourse Barouse (tel.: 562 99 21 30); St. Lary (tel.: 562 39 50 81); Bagnères de Bigorre (tel.: 562 95

50 71); Luz-St. Sauveur (tel.: 62 92 30 30); Vallée d'Aspe (tel.: 559 34 71 48); St. Jean-Pied-de-Port (tel.: 59 37 03 57); Hendaye (tel.: 59 20 00 34). This route, together with other trips and center-based mountain bike holidays, can be supported and guided by a U.K. company, Pyractif, based in the French Pyrenees (tel.: 562 99 26 38; e-mail: Pyractif@aol.com).
Website: www.pyractif.com

TIMING & SEASONALITY

Best Months to Visit: June, early July, September, October. The trail is best avoided during the busy French holiday season of July and August.

Climate: Expect snowfall on the higher passes from December through May.

HEALTH & SAFETY

Vaccinations: None required.
General Health Risks: Be aware of the possibility of hypothermia in cold, wet weather, and heat stroke in extremely hot conditions
Special Considerations: Keep campgrounds clean and dispose of rubbish in designated areas in towns and villages. Be polite to walkers.
Politics & Religion: No special concerns.
Crime Risk: Low.
Food & Drink: Filter surface water

←

What better way to spend a glorious summer's day in the Hautes Pyrénées than speeding along on a mountain bike, high above the pretty villages.

from lakes and streams. Water is available from village taps and bottled water can be bought from supermarkets in most main towns.

HIGHLIGHTS

There is an amazing backdrop to this ride— the Pyrenees mountain range is one of Europe's last wildernesses. You will find the trails empty most of the year, allowing you to appreciate fully its physical beauty and cultural variety.
Scenic: The ride begins in the height of the mountain range, with its backdrop of a 9,800-foot (3,000-m) ridgeline, and works its way west to the green and rolling mountains of the Basque region. Each day the scenery and culture change.
Wildlife & Flora: There is an abundance of wildlife with bears, stags, deer, wild boar, Griffin vultures, royal eagles, and bustards. However, many fragile species, such as the Pyrenees ibex and the brown bear, face extinction due to pollution and increasing urbanization. The timberline reaches 4,590–5,250 feet (1,400–1,600m), and the forests are mostly beech, oak, and pine.

↓ temperature and precipitation

	°f	JAN	FEB	MAR	APR	MAY	JUN	JUL	AUG	SEP	OCT	NOV	DEC	
▲	°f	43	45	54	57	63	73	79	75	72	61	50	43	°f
	°c	6	7	12	14	17	23	26	24	22	16	10	6	°c
▼	°f	30	30	36	39	43	50	54	54	50	43	36	30	°f
	°c	-1	-1	2	4	6	10	12	12	10	6	2	-1	°c
☁	ins	1.3	1.4	1.8	2.5	4.1	2.7	2.5	3.8	3.2	2.8	2.6	2.7	ins
	mm	34	37	46	63	105	69	65	98	81	73	68	69	mm
		JAN	FEB	MAR	APR	MAY	JUN	JUL	AUG	SEP	OCT	NOV	DEC	

→

*On the Tour du Mont Blanc,
the scenery is as dramatic
as the route is challenging.*

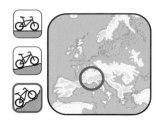

↓ **itinerary**

the TOUR du MONT BLANC

FRANCE, SWITZERLAND, AND ITALY

Seb Rogers

THE MONT BLANC MASSIF OCCUPIES A RELATIVELY SMALL PART OF THE ALPS, BUT IS UNEQUALED FOR DRAMATIC MOUNTAIN SCENERY. NESTLING IN A STEEP-SIDED VALLEY BENEATH THE TOWERING BULK OF MONT BLANC AND ITS SISTER PEAKS, CHAMONIX HAS BECOME A NATURAL HOME AND STOPOVER FOR OUTDOOR ADVENTURERS OF EVERY PER-SUASION. THE LURE OF THE MOUNTAIN, RISING 2 MILES (3KM) ABOVE THE VALLEY FLOOR, IS HARD TO RESIST.

The well-established Tour du Mont Blanc (TMB) hiking circuit forms the basis of this route, but it has been modified to mini-mize the necessity of carrying gear on steep and difficult sec-tions. Passing through France, Switzerland, and Italy, it takes in four major cols, over 23,000 vertical feet (7,000m) of climb-ing, and covers 132 miles (208km). Throughout the route, the views of Alpine villages, pine forests, lakes, and meadows are set against the dramatic backdrop of the Mont Blanc Massif. There is no other ride in Europe that compares.

←

*Snow may cover the higher
tracks throughout the year.*

• DAY 1   17 miles (27km)

Chamonix to Col de la Forclaz

Distances in this part of the Alps are deceptive. Hopping over the border at the Col de Balme into Switzerland for the first overnight stop may seem unadventurous, but there are longer days—and bigger climbs—to come. This is a good introduction to Alpine single-track. The quick and easy route out of Chamonix is to take the road—but the well-signposted Petit Balcon Nord walking route, although slower, is more rewarding. A bike-friendly cable car cuts out a nasty jeep-track climb halfway up to the col, from which the view back down the valley toward Chamonix opens up. The small refuge at the Col de Balme is usually open in summer, serving drinks and a limited range of food.

Clearly labeled signposts indicate that you've crossed the border from laissez-faire France into neat-and-tidy Switzerland. Even the grass seems neatly trimmed. The trail narrows to nearly a goat track, crossing a ridge, and traversing scree before dropping back toward the timberline. As late as June the path may be blocked by snow, but the descent into the Trient valley—a single-track plunge into the forest with the Trient glacier looming at the head of the valley—makes the effort worthwhile. A spin up the road to the gîte at the summit of the Col de la Forclaz heralds the end of the first day.

• DAY 2   21 miles (33km)

Col de la Forclaz to la Fouly

The second day's riding contrasts with the dramatic Alpine scenery of the first day, taking a diversion from the official TMB hiking route to avoid a long section of unridable trail. As you descend from the Col de la Forclaz to the village of le Brocard, the smoothness of Swiss roads provides an easy start to the day. A few miles of freewheeling brings you to the valley floor, winding through picturesque villages and terraced fields. If you need supplies, visit the small town of Martigny, which lies a short distance down the road—

otherwise, the next couple of hours are a steady uphill plod.

Le Brocard is the lowest point on the route at 1,800 feet (550m). The next opportunity for refreshment is at the lakeside tourist resort of Champex, 3,000 vertical feet (914m) and 7 miles (11km) up the road. The scenic climb is pleasantly narrow and winding, passing through pine forest, meadows, and clusters of neat Swiss houses and holiday homes. The touristy streets of Champex provide a choice of lakeside bars and restaurants for a break before the final leg of the day, up the Val Ferret. The path broadly follows the river along the valley floor, weaving in and out of pine forest, and clinging at one point to the side of a precipitous rock face, although there is a roped handrail at this point. The forest thins out as the valley climbs to the cluster of houses at la Fouly, where dormitory accommodation and an evening meal are available.

↑

The long climbs are made worthwhile by the equally long, technical, single-track descents.

•DAY 3 **18 miles (27km)**

La Fouly to Rifuge Monte Bianco

As you ride out of la Fouly, the mountain views are overwhelming, hinting at what's to come. The climb to the Grand Col Ferret is a major undertaking—around 3,000 verti-

The snowcapped Mont Blanc Massif is a constant companion along the route.

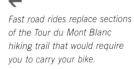

Fast road rides replace sections of the Tour du Mont Blanc hiking trail that would require you to carry your bike.

cal feet (914m) in as little as 6 miles (9.5km). One of the toughest climbs en route, the steep track is initially ridable, but beyond the cluster of shacks up from the valley floor it narrows and steepens, and you are forced to carry the bike.

The reward for all the pushing and carrying is the breathtaking view at the col. Straddling the border between Switzerland and Italy, it overlooks the narrow Val Ferret to the south, with the imposing bulk of the Glacier de Pré de Bard to the northwest. As you stand on the ridge at the top of the col, the drop into Italy appears precipitous. It is! The trail is steep, narrow, and often rutted. Soon you join a wide jeep track that descends the valley floor and becomes metaled. This is a popular spot for Italians to unwind in the shadow of the Massif. You're likely to find yourself trying not to barrel past clusters of picnickers as you gather speed toward Entrèves and Courmayeur, where the Mont Blanc road tunnel emerges from its 7½-mile (12-km) journey through solid rock. A short climb on the other side of the valley leads to the overnight stop at the Rifuge Monte Bianco, with stunning views of sheer rock faces.

•DAY 4   24 miles (38km)

Rifuge Monte Bianco to Beaufort

The fourth day features more dramatic high mountain riding. The Col de la Seigne—the second-highest col of the route—marks the border between Italy and France. From the Rifuge the route starts out on single-track for a while, then reverts to a jeep track climbing past a lake and a cluster of buildings toward the col. This part of the route is bleak, opening out onto a windswept plateau, marked with a cairn and often populated by hardened TMB hikers and bus tourists who've stumbled this far. The views are stunning. The descent into France, on a well-trodden and eroded trail, is fast and testing. Dirt yields to metaled road on the valley floor, with an opportunity for refreshment at les Chapieux.

The leg from les Chapieux to Beaufort is mainly on road, climbing over the Cormet de Roselend and descending for 8 miles (12km) past the Lac de Roselend, down hairpin bends with amazing scenery. Arrive in the picturesque town of Beaufort, ready for a well-deserved beer.

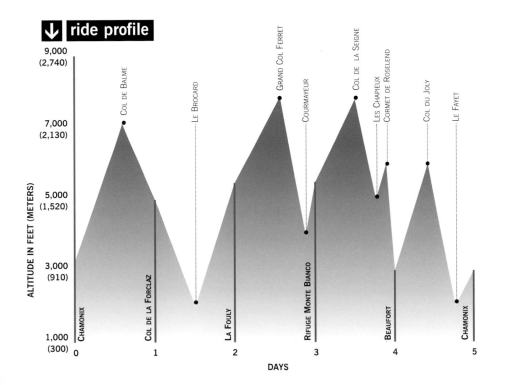

•DAY 5 52 miles (83km)

Beaufort to Chamonix

The final day is a long haul, beginning with a trudge up the road to the ski resort of les Saisies. From here, the route picks up a clear track and climbs past Mont Clocher to the Col de Véry, where it rejoins the official TMB route. Reverting to single-track, it traverses a steep hillside as it heads toward the final major col of the route. In places the trail is unridable, and farmers can place electric fences across the route without warning, so progress may be slow and interrupted. There is a skiers' restaurant and bar at the Col du Joly that is open sporadically during the summer.

The climb to the col is one of the longest and hardest, but the full-height descent is a highlight of the trip, traveling through pine forest, along a rocky trail, and on a track of natural slickrock. A mixture of streamside trails and wide, metaled road, brings you out into the ski resort of St. Gervais, then on to le Fayet. From here there are two options: ride back up the valley to Chamonix, or take the train; the latter option gives an opportunity to sit in a station bar and relive the last few days.

The Tour du Mont Blanc's combination of exciting trails and expansive mountain scenery is unmatched anywhere else in Europe.

Route finding in some areas can be tricky, so joining a guided tour is often wise.

factfile

OVERVIEW

This route borrows from the established Tour du Mont Blanc (TMB) hiking route, but departs from it in several places to avoid prolonged periods of pushing and carrying the bike. The emphasis is on maximizing ridability and making the best of the superb descents. It covers 132 miles (208km), split into 5 days with overnight stops at gîte or mountain refuge accommodation.

Start/Finish: Chamonix.

ABOUT THE TRAIL

The route has been altered to minimize carrying, so over 50 percent of the route is tarmac and jeep tracks. Wherever possible, the major climbs and descents are on single-track.

Major Climbs & Descents: Day 1: Chamonix climbing to Col de Balme—3,828 feet (1,167m) in 11 miles (18km); Col de Balme descending to Trient—2,965 feet (904m) in 4 miles (6km). Day 2: Col de la Forclaz descending to le Brocard—3,198 feet (975m) in 6 miles (9.6km); le Brocard climbing to Champex—3,004 feet (916m) in 8 miles (12km). Day 3: la Fouly climbing to Grand Col Ferret—3,073 feet (937m) in 6 miles (9.5km); Grand Col Ferret descending to Courmayeur—4,300 feet (1,311m) in 10 miles (16km). Day 4: Rifuge Monte Bianco climbing to Col de la Seigne—2,808 feet (856m) in 8 miles (12km); Col de la Seigne descending to les Chapieux—3,168 feet (966m) in 6 miles (9.5km); Cormet de Roselend descending to Beaufort—4,025 feet (1,227m) in 8 miles (12km).

Day 5: Beaufort climbing to Col du Joly—4,096 feet (1,249m) in 26 miles (42km); Col du Joly descending to le Fayet—4,622 feet (1,409m) in 13 miles (21km).

Difficulty & Special Features: Sections of the climbs to Col de Ferret and Col de la Seigne involve carrying the bike. The degree to which the descents are ridable depends on the rider's skill and technique. If the route is under-taken with a guide, van support is available. This is a tough route even for fit riders; the distance covered each day may be small, but the altitude and technical nature of the route mean it should not be underestimated.

ACCESS

 Airports: Geneva is the closest international airport to Chamonix.

Transport: Inexpensive transfers to Chamonix are available by taxi or minibus.

Passport & Visa Requirements: U.K., U.S., and New Zealand citizens do not require a visa. Australian citizens will need to obtain a visa for France.

Permits & Access Restrictions: No permits are required. Mountain bikes are permitted on all trails unless otherwise marked.

LOCAL INFORMATION

 Maps: Four maps cover the route, with the exception of the section between les Chapieux and Beaufort, which is easily navigable on the road—Institut Géographique National (IGN) 1:25000 series: 3630 O: Chamonix & Massif du Mont Blanc; 3531 E: St. Gervais-les-Bains;

↑
Chamonix's lively atmosphere and outdoor stores make it a good base for the trip.

3531 O: Megeve Col des Aravis. Carte National de la Suisse; 1:50000 series: 5003: Mont Blanc Grand Combin.

Guidebook: Andrew Harper's *Tour of Mont Blanc* (Cicerone Press) provides a description of the hiking route and useful background information.

Accommodation & Supplies: To enjoy this route fully, travel light and stay at gîtes or refuges in dormitory accommodation. Gîtes and refuges fill up in the summer, but you're unlikely to be turned away. Camping above timberline is permissible in Italy and France, but frowned upon in Switzerland. You can buy everything at Chamonix—bike spares, clothing, and food. Food supplies are available at most towns en route.

TIMING & SEASONALITY

 Best Months to Visit: Late June through

mid-September.

Climate: In the mountains anything can happen. Snow on the higher cols is possible into late June and any time from September onward. Be prepared for extremes of heat, cold, wind, and rain at any point during the route—particularly at altitude.

HEALTH & SAFETY

Vaccinations: None required.

General Health Risks: Be aware of the extremes of sunburn and heatstroke in hot weather and hypothermia in cold/wet conditions.

Special Considerations: Parts of the route include hazardous sections of exposed trail. Always use discretion and walk or carry the bike if in doubt.

Politics & Religion: No concerns.

Crime Risk: Low.

Food & Drink: Tap water is safe to drink unless labeled *"non potable."* It's advisable to filter stream water.

HIGHLIGHTS

Scenic: The Mont Blanc Massif is ever present on this route, dominating the horizon with an ever-changing array of craggy peaks and dramatic glaciers and snowfields.

Wildlife & Flora: The lower slopes are covered with pine forests, while the summer mead-ows are home to many species of wildflower and butterfly. The wild-life—mountain hares, marmots, foxes, lynxes—is more elusive.

Currency & Language: You'll need a combination of French francs, Swiss francs, and Italian lire. French is the first language in this part of Switzerland, and is widely spoken in Italy. English is not widely understood.

Area Information: Office de Tourisme, 85 Place du Triangle de l'Amiti, 74401 Chamonix (tel.: 04 50 53 00 24). This route was devised by Chamonix-based Mont Blanc Mountain Biking (MBMB), whose English-speaking guides know the local trails inside out and provide full guiding, complete with van support (tel.: 01705 233520 in the U.K.; e-mail: info@mbmb.co.uk).

Websites: www.chamonix.net is an excellent site; www.mbmb.co.uk.

temperature and precipitation

		JAN	FEB	MAR	APR	MAY	JUN	JUL	AUG	SEP	OCT	NOV	DEC	
	°f	36	37	45	52	61	68	72	70	63	54	45	37	°f
	°c	2	3	7	11	16	20	22	21	17	12	7	3	°c
	°f	21	25	30	36	43	48	50	50	46	39	32	25	°f
	°c	−6	−4	−1	2	6	9	10	10	8	4	0	−4	°c
	ins	3.1	2.9	2.3	2.5	3.1	3.5	2.7	3.7	3.9	3.7	3.7	3.1	ins
	mm	80	75	60	65	80	90	70	95	100	95	95	80	mm

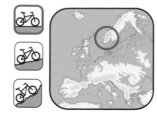

RALLARVEGEN

NORWAY

Nina Bjordal (Photography by Esben Haakenstad)

THE MOUNTAINS OF SOUTHERN NORWAY ARE HOME TO THE MOST POPULAR BIKE TREK IN THE COUNTRY—RALLARVEGEN. APPROXIMATELY 50 MILES (80KM) LONG, IT STRETCHES WESTBOUND OVER THE HARDANGERVIDDA, FROM HAUGASTØL IN THE COUNTY OF BUSKERUD TO FLÅM IN THE COUNTY OF SOGN AND FJORDANE. FROM HERE YOU CAN CONTINUE BY FERRY TO GUDVANGEN AND CYCLE ON TO VOSS.

The Rallarvegen ride provides a dramatic experience. The trail passes through fantastic high mountains, and offers the best of Norwegian history and open-air life. Rallarvegen is an adventure for both the body and the soul. The best thing about it is that the route starts at an altitude of about 3,280 feet (1,000m) above sea level and ends at 16 feet (5m). This means that people of all levels of fitness can enjoy the trip, and even children can experience a little piece of Norway from the bike seat.

Originally made as a construction and transportation track during the building of the Bergen Railway, which opened in 1909, Rallarvegen was carved by hand. The word "rallar" was used to describe the workmen on the Bergen Railway. In 1948, a man called Sigurd Stinessen, a member of a Norwegian bike association, suggested that the Rallarvegen should become a cycle path, but it wasn't until July 31, 1974 that it opened as a bikeway. Recently, it has become enormously popular, and some 20,000 people cycle the trail each year.

itinerary

•DAY 1 17 miles (27km)

Haugastøl to Finse

Rallarvegen starts at Haugastøl, 3,240 feet (988m) above sea level. If you don't have your own mountain bike, you can rent one at Haugastøl's tourist center. Cycle along the lake of Nygardsvatnet, along Ustekjveikja, to the old Storurdi keeper's house which is now a café. The road conditions up to Storurdi are good, but then some of poorer quality lead up a light climb to Finse. Enjoy the clean mountain air, experience the awe-inspiring silence of mighty nature, and watch the sheep along the route. You have a wonderful view to the Hardangerjøkulen, and to Blåisen, Norway's sixth largest glacier.

At Finse you can choose either to take a break or to stay overnight. Finse is 4,000 feet (1,222m) above sea level, and has a hotel, tourist cabin, shop, restaurant, and bike rental. You can take a walk in the mountains, or to the Blåisen glacier, and visit the Museum of Rallarvegen.

If you decide to stay overnight, the hotel offers simple but comfortable rooms and a good restaurant from where you can enjoy a panoramic view. The pub, where you sit in old train carriages, is well worth a visit. If you want more rustic accommodation, try the Norwegian Tourist Association's cabin or bring your own tent.

•DAY 2 22 miles (36km)

Finse to Vatnahalsen

There could be some snow between Finse and Hallingskeid, even in the middle of the summer, so be prepared. For about 6 miles (10km) westbound from Finse the road conditions are good, but then the quality deteriorates. Some parts can be difficult to cycle, and you must push your bike. But you can still admire the spectacular views, particularly the great one of the Hardangerjøkulen.

You pass the Nordnut keeper's house, from where it is a gentle ascent up to the highest point of Rallarvegen, Fagervatn at 4,400 feet (1,343m). Here you'll find Fagernut, the oldest and highest keeper's house, which was operational from 1904 to 1964. Today it's a café and exhibition area, and a good place to take a break.

You'll see several old keeper's houses along the Rallarvegen, and many of them operate as cafeterias providing opportune places to take a break along the ride.

To cycle the Rallarvegen is a worthwhile experience; all along the trail you'll observe architectural gems, such as historic stone bridges, and pass through beautiful landscapes.

The trek continues through fascinating landscapes and passes the lake of Tungevatn, through Kvina, and you get a great view over Moldå Valley. You pass Grøndalsvatnet and Klevavatnet, two lakes in beautiful surroundings. As you get to a lower altitude, the temperature rises and the vegetation becomes more green. The trek passes Kleva Stonebridge, and then arrives at the most dramatic part of the trek: Klevagjelet. The cycle path here is very narrow, and clings to a rocky wall. Down from the cycle path there is a cliff down to the Moldå waterfall. Here you must push your bike carefully because there is no fence. Take it easy through this part and enjoy the visual drama of the place.

Through Klevagjelet you pass two lakes, Seltuftvatnet and Regnungsvatnet. Here you find the Vatnahalsen Hotel situated by the famous Flåm Railway. You can stay overnight, eat a good meal, and relax with a swim in the outdoor pool or get into the outdoor Jacuzzi. Alternative accommodation can be found at Myrdal Mountain Lodge.

•DAY 3 11 miles (17 km)

Vatnahalsen to Flåm

From Vatnahalsen you can to go to Flåm, stay the night there, and then go on by ferry to Gudvangen and cycle to Voss. This route has a great view over the Flåm Valley and Flåm Railway, which is only about 12 miles (20km) long, but is an incredible train journey and has the steepest tracks in the world! This attracts people from all over the globe and it's one of Norway's major and most spectacular tourist attractions.

Before you bike from Vatnahalsen and down to Flåm, be very sure that your brakes work well! The Flåm Valley is very steep, and sometimes you need to push your bike. The trail turns 17 times, so make sure you're not in a hurry as it's a long haul to the top! Part of the road is in bad condition, and it is difficult for children. That said, however, you will experience a panoramic view over some of the wildest and most fascinating Norwegian terrain. You will see rivers

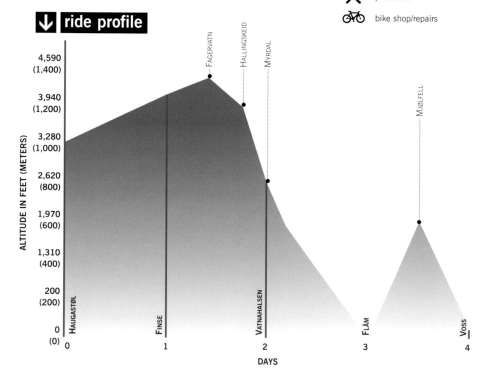

cutting through deep mountain passes, big waterfalls thrown out from steep rocky walls, snowy peaks, and small farms clinging to the steep mountains. You will pass Kårdal mountain hut, from where you can see the buildings in the Flåm Valley, the Kårdal waterfall, and the old transport road through the Ugjerd Valley. Take a rest in Berekvam—the station is midway between Flåm and Myrdal. From here you will see the Berekvam mountain pass, and the Flåm River goes deep down into the narrow landscape beneath you.

In Flåm you can either take a break or spend the night. Flåm is a small village in the Aurland Fjord, and has about 450 inhabitants. You will find a nice little center by Flåm station, with a souvenir shop, restaurants, and several hotels and other accommodation.

VARIATION: 27 miles (43km); Vatnahalsen to Voss

The day starts at Vatnahalsen and goes up to Myrdal station, which is the busy meeting point for bikers on the Rallarvegen. This is also the point where the Bergen Railway meets the Flåm Railway. At the station you'll find a

key

━━━	route of ride
▭▭▭	alternative route
‐ ‐ ‐	ferry journey
▭▭▭	major road
▭▭▭	minor road
‐‐‐‐‐	administrative border
‐‐‐‐‐	railroad
‐‐‐‐‐	seasonal river
▲	peak
⛺	campground
🛏	hotel/guesthouse
✕	provisions
🚲	bike shop/repairs

post office, telephone, toilets and coin-operated showers, a café, and a souvenir shop.

From Myrdal you take the local train, through the Gravhallstunnel, to Upsete. If you like, you can visit Upsete Mountain Lodge for lunch or dinner. After Upsete the trek goes comfortably downhill through the valley of Rounddalen, and passes by the lake Langevatn to Mjølfjell. By Mjølfjell Youth Hostel asphalt replaces the cycle path. You can spend the night at the youth hostel, or continue directly to Voss, which is a modern town with full services.

•DAY 4   30 miles (48km)

Flåm to Voss

You start from Flåm by ferry to Gudvangen. The ferry passes the Nærøy Fjord, the world's narrowest, at only 660 feet (200m) wide. From here you cycle to the Nærøy Valley, leaving the old route at Holten Bridge. Later, you arrive at the famous Stalheimskleivene, which has a rise of 1:5 and 13 turns. This is the hardest part, so take your time. On the way you see the great Stalheim and Sivle waterfalls. If you feel a little hot and uncomfortable after the hard ride up, why not take a "shower" by the waterfall? At the top you will reach Stalheim Tourist Hotel, where you can eat and visit the museum of Stalheim. There is a great view from the top of Stalheim, so don't forget your camera! The tour continues past the lake of Oppheimsvatnet, east to Loensvatnet, and on to Voss.

⬇ ride profile

Altitude in feet (meters) vs. Days

| 4,590 (1,400) |
| 3,940 (1,200) |
| 3,280 (1,000) |
| 2,620 (800) |
| 1,970 (600) |
| 1,310 (400) |
| 200 (200) |
| 0 (0) |

Labels: HAUGASTØL, FINSE, FAGERVATN, HALLINGSKEID, MYRDAL, VATNAHALSEN, FLÅM, MJØLFJELL, VOSS

DAYS: 0 1 2 3 4

There are some fast, steep sections down to Flåm, but it is worth stopping to enjoy the dramatic scenery.

↓ factfile

OVERVIEW

Rallarvegen can, if you are in a hurry and in great physical condition, be cycled in 1 to 2 days. However, 3 to 5 days are recommended to have time to enjoy the terrific views and surroundings and enjoy the attractions and activities along the way. Some parts of the route can be a physical challenge, although most of the cycle path is downhill from Finse to Flåm. Rallarvegen is a trek for everybody, but taking children younger than 10 years old over the Hardangervidda Plateau is not recommended.

Start: Haugastøl.
Finish: Voss.

ABOUT THE TRAIL

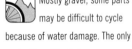

Mostly gravel, some parts may be difficult to cycle because of water damage. The only car traffic will be between Gudvangen and Voss and on the road down to Flåm. It is an asphalt lane down to Flåm and from Mjølfjell to Voss.

Major Climbs & Descents: There are some steep hills down the Klevagjelet and down to Flåm.

Difficulty & Special Features: You will need a good quality off-road bike with strong brakes, and with panniers for equipment.

ACCESS

Airports: Geilo Airport, Dagali (tel.: 32 09 51 00; website: www.geilo-lufthavn.no). On domestic flights you can bring your bike as luggage (but not on small planes).

Transport: If going by train, take the Bergen Railway (tel.: 815 00 888; website: www.nsb.no) from

Oslo or Bergen to Haugastøl. There is also a special "bike train" between Oslo and Voss from June 11 to September 17, on which you can make a reservation for both your bike and yourself. This train stops at Geilo, Haugastøl, Finse, Hallingskeid, and Myrdal. For local trains, tel.: 815 00 888. For Flåm Railway tickets and information, tel.: 57 63 14 00. If you want to go by bus, take the Nor-Way Bus Express (tel.: 81 54 44 44 or 23 00 24 40). Or you can take a taxi (tel.: 32 09 10 00).

Passport & Visa Requirements: U.K., U.S., Australia, and New Zealand citizens need a valid passport and an ordinary tourist visa to stay for up to 90 days.

Permits & Access Restrictions: Walking on the railway line is strictly prohibited. Stay on the path to avoid erosion—a wheel track does not disappear.

LOCAL INFORMATION

Maps: There are detailed maps in the official guidebook for the Rallarvegen (see below). You can buy maps that cover the Finse and Skarvheimen areas from local tourist offices.

Guidebooks: The official guidebook is Rallarvegen and the North Sea Route by Trond Bach and Johannes Gredaaker, and has detailed maps and information about accommodation, services, attractions, distances, communications, and so on. Cycle Treks Along the Bergen Railway is available free of charge from tourist offices.

Accommodation & Supplies: There are several places to stay overnight. Always book in advance, especially at weekends. There are

special zones and rules for campers, and don't pitch your tent anywhere that isn't specified. There is also "bike-friendly accommodation" detailed in the Norwegian Syklist Velkommen. This accommodation is especially for bikers, and it has its own bike garages, good conditions for drying clothes, and the means to fix bikes. Look for the sign "Syklist Velkommen." You can buy meals at Storurdi, Fagernut, and Finse. There are also restaurants at most of the hotels along the route. There are grocery stores at Haugastøl and at the Finse Hotel.

Currency & Language: Krone (plural: kroner), written as Nok. Most of the hotels accept credit cards. The official language is Norwegian; Norwegian is spoken in many different dialects. Most Norwegians speak very good English.

Area Information: Geilo

Turistinformation, Reiselivssenteret, 3581 Geilo (tel.: 32 09 59 00; fax: 32 09 59 01; e-mail: turistinfo@geilo.no). Haugastøl Turistsenter, 3593 Haugastøl (tel.: 32 08 75 80; fax: 32 08 76 74).

Websites: http://rallarmuseet.no; www.geilo.no

TIMING & SEASONALITY

Best Months to Visit: August and early September.

Climate: The biking season starts in mid-July if snow conditions are normal, but there may be snow between Finse and Hallingskeid. For road conditions and snow reports, please take a look at the on-line "Rallarveg Reports" before you go on http://rallarmuseet.no or www.slf.no. These are updated every 14 days from the end of May to the end of September. You can also call the hotel at Finse (tel.: 56

52 71 00) or Geilo Tourist Information (tel.: 32 09 59 00).

HEALTH & SAFETY

Vaccinations: None required.

General Health Risks: No concerns.

Special Considerations: The weather changes fast in the mountains, so even on short trips you need to bring rainwear, a thick sweater, a swimming costume, a fleece, gloves, bike pants, sunglasses, and sunscreen, and always wear a helmet.

Politics & Religion: No concerns.
Crime Risk: Minimal.

Food & Drink: You can drink most of the water from the brooks without boiling it. Don't eat berries or mushrooms found along the way unless you are absolutely sure that they aren't poisonous.

HIGHLIGHTS

Scenic: There are great mountains, the Hardangervidda Plateau (the biggest in northern Europe), and several waterfalls. You'll also find some lovely stone bridges and old houses.

Wildlife & Flora: Mountain flowers, birds, and sheep. The area around Rallarvegen is vulnerable, and it is most important to take care of the environment.

↓ temperature and precipitation

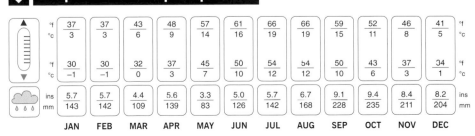

	JAN	FEB	MAR	APR	MAY	JUN	JUL	AUG	SEP	OCT	NOV	DEC
°f	37	37	43	48	57	61	66	66	59	52	46	41
°c	3	3	6	9	14	16	19	19	15	11	8	5
°f	30	30	32	37	45	50	54	54	50	43	37	34
°c	−1	−1	0	3	7	10	12	12	10	6	3	1
ins	5.7	5.7	4.4	5.6	3.3	5.0	5.7	6.7	9.1	9.4	8.4	8.2
mm	143	142	109	139	83	126	142	168	228	235	211	204

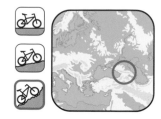

the CAUCASUS CHALLENGE

RUSSIA

Sue Webber (Additional photography by Trevor Creighton)

"EXTREME" IS THE ONLY WAY TO DESCRIBE THIS TRANS-CAUCASUS MOUNTAIN CROSSING. THIS RIDE IS FOR THE EXPERIENCED AND ADVENTUROUS ONLY. THE THREE-WEEK JOURNEY STARTS IN KISOLVODSK, A FASHIONABLE RUSSIAN SPA TOWN, AND ENDS ON THE BLACK SEA AT THE HOLIDAY RESORT OF ADLER. IN BETWEEN IS MOUNT ELBRUS, THE HIGHEST MOUNTAIN IN EUROPE AT 18,510 FEET (5,642M).

↑
The snowcapped peak of Mount Elbrus, the largest mountain in Europe, is a constant and imposing feature of this route.

The ride crosses remote high plateaux inhabited only by shepherds who bring their flocks up for summer grazing. It crosses the Caucasus mountain range that divides Russia from Abkhazia and Georgia and is described as the frontier of Europe and Asia. The rewards are some spectacular scenery, snowy mountain peaks, high grasslands, chance encounters with the people of the region, and an incredible sense of achievement when you reach the shores of the Black Sea.

⬇ **itinerary**

•DAYS 1–4 46 miles (74km)

Kisolvodsk to Mount Elbrus region

Kisolvodsk is a smart Russian spa town, a popular holiday spot for wealthy Russians and the last chance to eat café food for many days. The fashionable veneer vanishes as you ride south on the rough roads into the hills. The land becomes grazing country soon out of town and the foothills begin to rise. If there's been recent rain, expect to find the road turned to a muddy glue. After an ascent to 6,500 feet

The Caucasus Mountains form an impressive panorama as they rise above a high grassland plateau.

(1,950m), there's a descent to a bush camp by a river near to a hostel and holiday cabins.

Day 2 begins with a climb up to a ridge, along a rocky track, to a pass at 7,360 feet (2,240m). The high, grassy plateau provides summer grazing for sheep and horses and a vast, empty-looking, green landscape. Camp on the Kharbaz River. Two hours from the campground, Mount Elbrus appears over the horizon—twin, snowcapped peaks rising over the green plateau. The mountain dominates the rest of the day as you ride closer along the dirt tracks. Day 3's camp is another riverside site. There are many horses on the plateau and the shepherds use them for transport,

giving the area a "Wild East" feel. Day 4's camp is closer to the mountain, beside a spring that comes up through a creek to provide cool, refreshing mineral water.

•DAYS 5–7 55 miles (88km)

Mount Elbrus region to Karachayevsk

Turning north away from Mount Elbrus, retrace your wheel tracks over the pass of Day 4 and then head west. You will cross the same river three times; fortunately, although the water is cold and fast-flowing, these are all shallow crossings and easy to push through.

From the river, there is a climb back onto the Bechasyn →

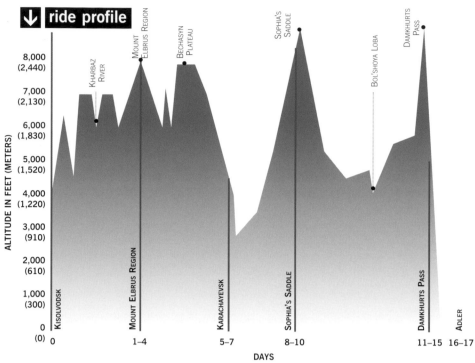

ride profile

ALTITUDE IN FEET (METERS)

8,000 (2,440)
7,000 (2,130)
6,000 (1,830)
5,000 (1,520)
4,000 (1,220)
3,000 (910)
2,000 (610)
1,000 (300)
0 (0)

KHARBAZ RIVER
MOUNT ELBRUS REGION
BECHASYN PLATEAU
SOPHIA'S SADDLE
BOL'SHOYA LOBA
DAMKHURTS PASS

KISOLVODSK
MOUNT ELBRUS REGION
KARACHAYEVSK
SOPHIA'S SADDLE
DAMKHURTS PASS
ADLER

0   1–4   5–7   8–10   11–15 16–17

DAYS

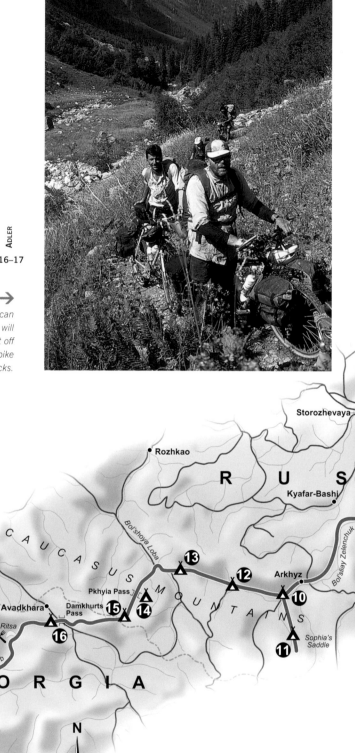

→

After riding as far as you can into the mountains, you will eventually be obliged to get off the saddle and push the bike up the rough mountain tracks.

plateau up a steep, grassy slope. The high track follows a line of telegraph poles; it's a hard-packed dirt surface and provides the fastest riding so far. A cistern to collect rainwater for animals provides a water supply for cyclists too.

The telegraph road leads to a little town—a headquarters for the summer grazing, with a small but well-stocked clothing and food shop. The road descends from the plateau into wooded alpine meadows, with masses of wildflowers in summer, where you will find quiet places to camp by the woods and mountain streams. From the camp, the road descends to the Kuban River and follows the river downstream, heading north through small villages toward Karachayevsk. As the road nears the town, there are trucks and cars once again, the first in any number since leaving Kisolvodsk.

•DAYS 8–10 81 miles (130km)

Karachayevsk to Sophia's Saddle

After leaving the camp outside Karachayevsk you will soon find yourself in a town with a post office and the possibility of food at shops and cafés. As you head north out of town with the trucks and buses, it's worth stopping to visit the memorial and museum for the people who fought against the Germans in the Caucasus during World War Two. The road leads through the towns of Sarytyuz, Kardonikskaya, and Zelenchukskaya

Storozhevaya

Rozhkao

R U S

Kyafar-Bashi

C A U C A S U S

Bol'shoya Loba

Borsilay Zelenchuk

⑬
⑫
Arkhyz
Pkhyia Pass ⑭
⑩
⑮
Damkhurts Pass
Avadkhara
M O U N T A I N S

Sophia's Saddle
⑪

Lake Ritsa
⑯

Bzyb

G E O R G I A

Adler
⑰

N

Gagra

Bzyb   Otkhara

Black Sea

0   15 km
0   15 miles

↑

Dark clouds looming over the Caucasus Mountains are an ominous albeit impressive sight for a cyclist riding along the high plateau.

and small villages where geese, ducks, sheep, cows, and chickens all provide moving obstacles along the road. Heading south toward the mountains once again, you'll find a place to camp away from the houses by a river. The road follows the Bol'sliay Zelenchuk River south and upstream toward Arkhyz. The river valley winds upward between steep pine-covered mountain sides and past a large, painted picture of Lenin with a quote that reads, "We can only win when we overcome our fear of admitting our mistakes and losses." Arkhyz is a popular base for walking holidays in the mountains. The national park requires passes to enter and, once you're inside, there are plenty of places to camp.

The detour up to Sophia's Saddle is a hard climb up a steep valley. It begins fairly well with a gradual uphill ride but the road ends and becomes a hiking trail up into the mountains. Cycling soon gives way to pushing up past a melting glacier to the saddle at 8,320 feet (2,530m) with views across the western Caucasus Mountains. →

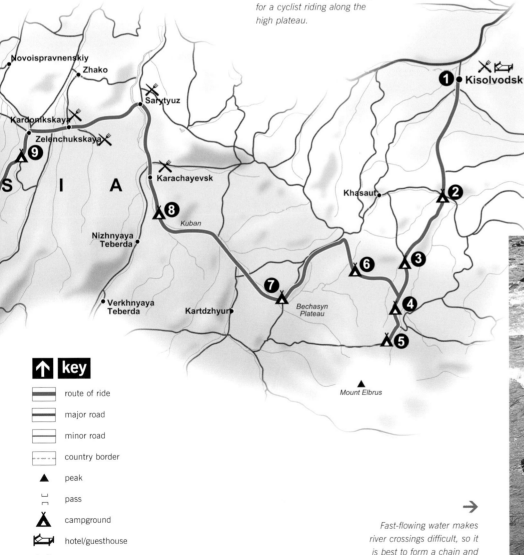

→

Fast-flowing water makes river crossings difficult, so it is best to form a chain and pass the bikes across.

↑ **key**

═══	route of ride
═══	major road
───	minor road
----	country border
▲	peak
⊔⊔	pass
Δ	campground
🛏	hotel/guesthouse
✕	provisions

↑

From the high plateau, the dirt track that is your onward route stretches away to the horizon on a seemingly easy level.

•DAYS 11–15 | 50 miles (80km)

Sophia's Saddle to Damkhurts Pass

There is a way through the mountains from Sophia's Saddle but it is easier to descend toward Arkhyz again and head further west for the crossing. Once down from the mountain the road is good through the park, but then follows a narrow, cross-country, hiking trail marked with red and white signs westward, and pushing will be the order of the day in some sections. Once over Pkhyia Pass, 6,720 feet (2,050m), the track descends again through the woods, becoming a wider rocky track further down and leading to a village. From the village there is a short stretch of sealed road before you turn off along a muddy logging track. A wide, fast-flowing river, the Bol'shoya Loba, is a challenge that may require several riders to form a line and pass bikes and panniers across through the deep water. From the river, the track heads up a valley toward the Damkhurts Pass.

The trail up to the pass is possibly the most demanding section of the trek with very few opportunities to ride up the rocky trail. Damkhurts Pass at 8,768 feet (2,670m) is the highest point of the trek and there is still ice at the top in midsummer. It's the border between Russia and Abkhazia. The descent is steep and rocky but ridable, and leads down to a fast river that requires care in crossing.

•DAYS 16–17 | 74 miles (119km)

Damkhurts Pass to Adler

The Caucasus crossing is over and it's all downhill to the Black Sea from here. The track soon joins a road leading down to the holiday resort of Lake Ritsa. There is a restaurant and a café here with coffee and ice creams for sale to the smart tourists up from the Black Sea for the day. The descent from Lake Ritsa is fast, easy, and a suitable reward for all that hard work in the mountains. It follows the Bzyb River down to the Black Sea, where vacationers sit on the stony beach and watch the water lap the shore. The road follows the coastline westward and over the border back into Russia to Adler and the railway back to Moscow.

factfile

OVERVIEW

Riders must be completely self-sufficient and Russian guides are a necessity in this region as good maps are hard to come by, so local knowledge can make or break the journey. There are few shops on the route and supplies are unpredictable. There are many rivers to cross and mountains to climb. Expect to push, pull, or carry your bike through sections. The daily distances look small but do not be deceived, 306 miles (490km) over 17 days may look easy on paper but it is hard traveling on the ground.

Start: Kisolvodsk.

Finish: Adler, on the Black Sea.

ABOUT THE TRAIL

Almost all of this trek is on dirt roads and tracks. Much of the double-track is poorly graded and hard going. There are some good hard-packed surfaces across the high plateau but these could easily turn to mud after rain. Most of the single-track is walking trails and sheep tracks; sometimes it's just too steep and rocky to ride with a laden bike.

Major Climbs & Descents: The most memorable climb is from Karachayevsk at 3,000 feet (915m) to Sophia's Saddle at 8,320 feet (2,530m) over 3 days, the last section is done on foot carrying the bike up. The incredible descent from Damkhurts Pass (8,768 feet/2,670m) down to the Black Sea at Gagra over 2 days is a fitting way to end the mountain crossing.

Difficulty & Special Features: The terrain is hard work; the Russian idea of cycle touring is to ride your bicycle as far as possible and, when cycling is impossible, to push the bike until pushing becomes impossible, then carry your bike, up and over mountain passes and across rivers. Your party must be completely self-sufficient as there are very few opportunities to buy new supplies or spares, or even get medical help. It is essential that someone in your party speaks good Russian and knows the region. It would be unwise to attempt this trek without a guide.

ACCESS

Airports: The nearest and most suitable international airport is Moscow.

Transport: From Moscow, it is possible to catch a train to Kisolvodsk to begin the ride. There is a railroad station at Adler, where trains leave for Moscow.

Passport & Visa Requirements: Full passports and tourist visas are required for all visitors to Russia.

Permits & Access Restrictions: Your Russian guide should organize all local permits.

LOCAL INFORMATION

Maps: Good maps of Russia are hard to find. Try the Tactical Pilotage chart TPC F4D ONC F-4.

Guidebooks: *Russia, Ukraine & Belarus* (Lonely Planet); *Trekking in Russia & Central Asia* by Frith Maier (The Mountaineers, U.S.A.; Cordée, U.K.).

Accommodation & Supplies: While there may be accommodation at some of the holiday places mentioned in this description, you should not rely on finding accommodation but be prepared to be completely self-sufficient and expect to camp throughout the trip. U.S. dollar shops allow visitors to buy luxury items but everyday essentials can be harder to find; you cannot rely on Russian shops to supply all your needs during the trip—your Russian guide will advise.

Currency & Language: Ruble; however, U.S. dollars may also be useful. The language is Russian.

Area Information: The local biking group is the Russian Cycle Touring Club, Krasina 24/28–20, Moscow 123056, Russia (tel.: 95 254 4521; fax: 95 956 6185; English-speaking president of biking group: Igor Nalima, tel.: 95 458 8365; e-mail: rctc@bigfoot.com).

Website: www.geocities.com/TheTropics/8640/

TIMING & SEASONALITY

Best Months to Visit: This is a summer trip—go between June and September to avoid the worst of the mountain weather.

Climate: Expect rain in the mountains during summer; snow is also possible.

HEALTH & SAFETY

Vaccinations: Tetanus, diphtheria, polio, typhoid, hepatitis A & B, cholera, encephalitis, tuberculosis.

General Health Risks: None.

Politics & Religion: Check with your Foreign Office for advice before your trip. The war in Chechnya means that the region may be disrupted.

Crime Risk: War-related crime may be a possibility (see above).

Food & Drink: The food at Russian cafés and restaurants may cause stomach upsets. Be careful about what you eat and consider the standards of hygiene before choosing where you eat. All water should be treated before drinking.

HIGHLIGHTS

Scenic: The first view of the twin snow-covered peaks of Mount Elbrus is a never-to-be-forgotten experience. Cycling across the high grassy plateau with a horizon filled with jagged mountains like a row of shark's teeth feels like riding your bicycle to the end of the world.

Wildlife & Flora: Marmots live in holes underground on the high plateau and occasionally pop up as cyclists go past. Look out for the many varieties of alpine flowers that grow in the region.

←
The grand scale of the mountainous landscape dwarfs mountain bikers.

temperature and precipitation

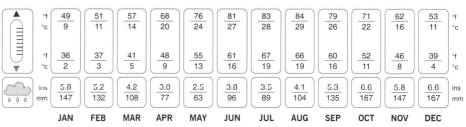

	JAN	FEB	MAR	APR	MAY	JUN	JUL	AUG	SEP	OCT	NOV	DEC
°f	49	51	57	68	76	81	83	84	79	71	62	53
°c	9	11	14	20	24	27	28	29	26	22	16	11
°f	36	37	41	48	55	61	67	66	60	52	46	39
°c	2	3	5	9	13	16	19	19	16	11	8	4
ins	5.8	5.2	4.2	3.0	2.5	3.8	3.5	4.1	5.3	6.6	5.8	6.6
mm	147	132	108	77	63	96	89	104	135	167	147	167

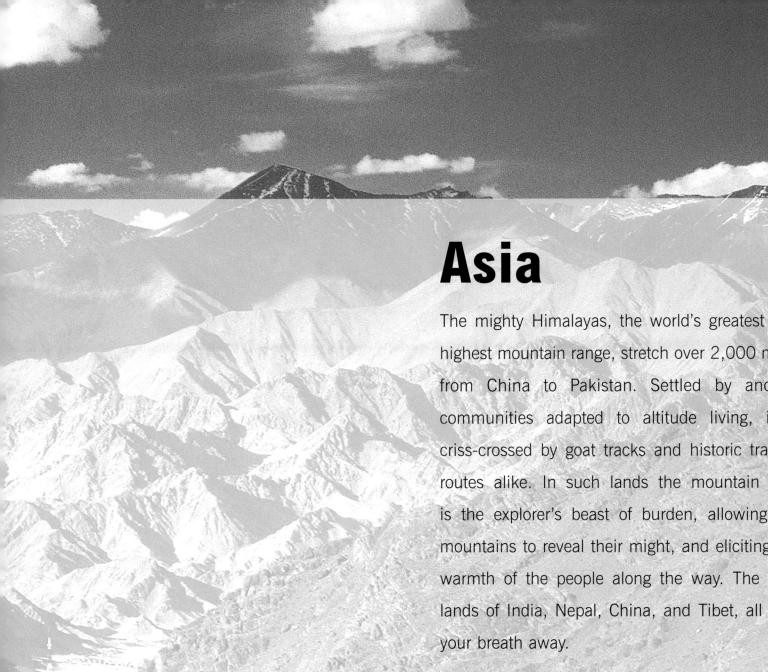

Asia

The mighty Himalayas, the world's greatest and highest mountain range, stretch over 2,000 miles from China to Pakistan. Settled by ancient communities adapted to altitude living, it is criss-crossed by goat tracks and historic trading routes alike. In such lands the mountain bike is the explorer's beast of burden, allowing the mountains to reveal their might, and eliciting the warmth of the people along the way. The high lands of India, Nepal, China, and Tibet, all take your breath away.

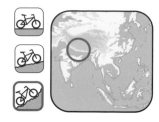

AROUND KATHMANDU

NEPAL

Jamie Carr

NEPAL IS A RELATIVELY SMALL COUNTRY. HOWEVER, IT RISES FROM 200 FEET (60M) ON THE INDIAN BORDER TO 29,000 FEET (8,840M) AT THE SUMMIT OF MOUNT EVEREST—SO THERE ARE PLENTY OF HILLSIDES TO RIDE DOWN. THIS PARTICULAR ROUTE GIVES YOU GREAT VIEWS OF THE MIGHTY HIMALAYAS BEYOND.

Nepal is easy and friendly to travel in, relatively simple to get to, and a big culture shock to the Western way of life. This route provides an enjoyable, thrilling, off-road circuit that can be easily fitted into a two-week holiday.

Durbar Square in Patan, just south of Kathmandu, is one of three such squares in the Kathmandu Valley, and is accessible only by foot or bike. This is where the provincial king used to greet and speak to his people; today there is only one king of Kathmandu.

↓ **itinerary**

•DAYS 1–2 **24 miles (38.5km)**

Kathmandu to Kakani

A test ride around the old town of Kathmandu and down the narrow streets crammed with Nepalis buying and selling is a great way to warm up for the ride ahead, and the sights and sounds are memorable. Day 2 of riding takes you directly north of Kathmandu up the road to Kakani, but first into the Queen's Forest, a private natural reserve that is very quiet and pollution-free, a sharp contrast to the main roads of Kathmandu. From here, it's a 19-mile (30-km) loop and a long climb, steep toward the end, on double-track to the top, then great single-track before you get onto the road again. Here, after crossing a small pass, the views open up down toward Trisuli Valley and there is a long but easy graded climb up to Kakani; you can either ride or, if you're too tired, take a bus. Camp, or stay in the hotel, and watch the sunset; in the clear early-morning air a fantastic panoramic view of the Himalayas will thrill you.

•DAYS 3–4 **28 miles (45km)**

Kakani to Chisopani

From Kakani, follow the old Himalayan mountain bike championship route up the ridge, with a short carry or push up to 6,950 feet (2,120m). There are good views again before psyching yourself up for an excellent single-track descent, with many ditches to hop and corners to contend with. A single-track ascent to test even the best rider's climbing skill comes next before joining a wide, fast double-track descent through the Shirapuri Watershed and Wildlife Preserve. A final short climb brings you to Nage Gompa, a Buddhist retreat, which the monks will sometimes show you around. It is possible to camp in the grounds and absorb the ambience and tranquillity. The next day follows the road around the Shirapuri Preserve, up and down some good tracks, to the trekking town of Chisopani. Enjoy more views of the Himalayas as you settle into the local teahouse.

•DAYS 5–6 **29 miles (46.5km)**

Chisopani to Nagarkot and Bhaktapur

An early start means good views before breakfast as you

backtrack for a few miles to a steep descent to a saddle en route to the hill town of Nagarkot. The trail is narrow and steep in some sections and requires careful riding; some may prefer to walk. The short climb at the end is rewarded by a warm welcome at the Nagarkot Vajra Farmhouse, where you can enjoy a couple of nights in the same bed. From here, there are a couple of options for day rides. A little more climbing up to the highest viewpoint gives maximum descent on some excellent single-track through small villages toward Nala and down a wide trail into Bhaktapur. An easier day for the less hard-nosed downhill biker is to visit the villages and the temple at Changu Narayan before crossing rice paddies into Bhaktapur. At Bhaktapur time has stood still since the king of Kathmandu defeated the Bhaktapur army; now the center is pedestrianised and easy to cycle around, while taking in the sights and sounds. The cool of the late afternoon provides some relief from the road climb back to the farmhouse, or you can take a bus.

•DAYS 7–8 34 miles (54.5km)

Nagarkot to Dhulikhel and Namo Buddha loop

From the farmhouse back down to the saddle passed the day before, is a single-track descent to rival any in the world. You drop off the back of the valley rim down into the Indrawati Valley, with a Himalayan backdrop staring you right in the face. A twisting single-track through villages leads onto a wide fast jeep track to Panchkhal. Lunch by the river gives you the chance to cool off before a good road climb up to the High View Resort in Dhulikhel, or you can hitch a ride once again on a bus. Another two nights in the same bed gives the opportunity to take a loop to the historical Namo Buddha, where a monk is said to have given his body as a sacrifice to a starving tigress. The trail is wide all the way with good views from the first ridge. There's an optional exploratory single-track via Panauti on the way back, where you can have a look around more temples before a short road ride back to Dhulikhel.

↑

Prayer flags mark the summit of Nagarjun and the "Queen's Forest," which you pass through on the way to Kakani. The Langtang Himalaya is visible in the distance.

→

•DAYS 9–10 40 miles (64.5km)

Dhulikhel to Pharping

A new road to Panauti and a ride through its charmed old streets take you to an unspoiled valley through which a gentle, wide, single-track climb goes up to the pass of Lakhure Banjyang at 6,330 feet (1,930m). This pass overlooks the whole of the Kathmandu Valley with peaks visible in the distance over the other side of the valley rim where you were just a few days earlier. A very steep and fast descent down a jeep track drops you onto the valley floor for a flat ride to Lubhu, from where you cross rice paddies and small fields to a typical Newari farmhouse run by the Appropriate Agricultural Alternative organization at Gomonea. This organization teaches Nepalese farmers better techniques of crop rotation and natural fertilizer to prevent them falling into the bad habits of Western quick-fix fertilizer and mutated genetic crops; the accommodation is simple but the food is worth it. From here, you cross the valley bottom and pass through several small communities to Chapagaon and Bungamati, then cross the Bagmati River near Chobar and join the road through Hatiban and on to Pharping.

↑ key

	route of ride
	alternative route
	major road
	minor road
▲	peak
⊐⊏	pass
⊿	campground
🛏	hotel/guesthouse
✕	provisions
✈	airport
🚲	bike shop/repairs

↓ ride profile

ALTITUDE IN FEET (METERS)

7,380 (2,250)
6,560 (2,000)
5,740 (1,750)
4,920 (1,500)
4,100 (1,250)
3,280 (1,000)
2,460 (750)
1,640 (500)

DAYS: 0   1–2   3–4   5–6   7–8   9–10   11–12

KATHMANDU   KAKANI   CHISOPANI   NAGARKOT   DHULIKHEL   PHARPING   KATHMANDU

NAGE GOMPA, NALA, BHAKTAPUR, INDRAWATI VALLEY, DHULIKHEL, LAKHURE BANJYANG, NEWARI FARMHOUSE, BAGMATI RIVER, DAMAN, SWAYAMBHUNATH STUPA

•DAYS 11–12 20 miles (32km)

Pharping to Markhu or Daman and Kathmandu

An ever-developing road-and-trail system around the populated valley area means a good trail is now followed over the southern valley rim at a much lower point than before. There's more twisting single-track and wider trails crossing a few small streams before coming to the hydro-power dam at Kulekhani. This dam, which looks like a natural lake, is very pleasant to cycle around toward the relocated town of Markhu overlooking the lake (the original village now lies under water). Camp here on lush green pasture, or ride/drive the climb up to Daman for a bit of comfort at the Everest Panorama Resort, where there is the longest uninterrupted view of the Himalayas. This is the highest point of the old Raj path, which was originally the only way into the Kathmandu Valley from the Indian plains over 6,560 feet (2,000m) below. From here, the ride is down a broken tarmac road, with some new smooth sections, to the junction where you joined from Markhu. Cross over a small pass before descending into Naubise on the main Pokhara/India-to-Kathmandu road; it is best to avoid the busy highway and jump onto a bus or local truck for the road climb to Thankot. Just a little way back down from Thankot is the last mountain bike trail around Dahachok to bring you out by Swayambhunath Stupa (commonly known as Monkey Temple). Carry on to make the quick blast into the Thamel district of Kathmandu for a hot shower and a beer to celebrate a great round trip of the unique Kathmandu Valley.

factfile

OVERVIEW

 This is an intricate route around the rim of the Kathmandu Valley on the best mountain bike trails that Nepal has to offer and visiting the best viewpoints. The days are short and mostly off-road; but there are a couple of long climbs that are best done on the road.

Start/Finish: Kathmandu.

ABOUT THE TRAIL

 Lots of single-track. There is no support possible on the off-road sections. It is a moderate to difficult route with easy options available along the way. A local guide is essential as route finding is difficult.

Major Climbs & Descents: Any climbs are relatively short considering that you are in the Himalayas, and any major climbs can be driven up in the support vehicle. There are excellent descents, all off-road and mostly on single-track.

Difficulty & Special Features: Generally, the days are short but mostly off-road and are quite tough in places. There are some harder days, a few big climbs, and some of the trails can be very rough just after monsoon. However, anyone who is reasonably fit and with a good level of bike skills can do this trip. Take specialist bike spares for any suspension units and spare brake blocks with a bottle of oil.

ACCESS

 Airports: Kathmandu is Nepal's only international airport, and flying into it is an experience in itself, with excellent views of the Himalayas.

Transport: Taxis are willing to take you and your bike anywhere. Support vehicles en route cannot follow on the off-road sections.

Passport & Visa Requirements: Just arrive with U.S. $25 cash, two passport photos, and a valid passport and you can buy a one-month visa on the spot.

Permits & Access Restrictions: No special permits needed.

LOCAL INFORMATION

Maps: Pilgrims Bookshop in Kathmandu sells a decent map that covers the Kathmandu Valley very well.

Guidebooks: The Lonely Planet *Nepal* guide is very comprehensive, but does not cater for cyclists; their phrasebook for *Nepalese* is very useful. There is a mountain biking section in the Insight Guide *Kathmandu Valley* guidebook, and the map is very good.

Accommodation & Supplies: Sleeping bags are necessary if you intend to camp or come in winter, as some guesthouses are quite simple. Local touring companies have all the necessary equipment, from tents to American-brand mountain bikes. Kathmandu has many well-stocked supermarkets.

Currency & Language: The Nepali rupee; U.S. dollars can be changed anywhere; traveler's checks can be changed in banks and at money-exchange counters; cash advances into local currency from credit cards are available in Kathmandu. There are many forms of Nepalese, but try to learn some basic greetings and thank-yous, as these are the same in all dialects. Most Nepalis working with tourists will speak good English.

Photography: Be courteous when taking photos of any local people, and you'll get a better photo as a result. Kathmandu is the only reliable source of camera film.

Area Information: This trip is best done with experienced local Nepali mountain biking guides from Kathmandu—contact Chhimi Gurung, chairman of the Nepalese Mountain Bike Association, at Dawn Till Dusk (fax: 01 412 619). If you want financial security and guaranteed departures when booking from your home country, and experienced and medically qualified Western and local mountain biking guides, contact KE Adventure (tel.: 1-800-497-9675 in the U.S.A. toll-free, or 01768 773966 in the U.K.).

Websites: www.keadventure.com; www.DTD@wlink.com.np

TIMING & SEASONALITY

 Best Months to Visit: October through April are good; December, January, and February are cooler; March and April are more humid and hot with some heavier showers as the monsoon builds.

Climate: The Kathmandu Valley is free of snow all year, but avoid the hot, humid, and wet summer months. Kathmandu has a very wet monsoon period, but you can still bike providing you get up early since the heavy showers usually come in the afternoon.

HEALTH & SAFETY

Vaccinations: See your doctor at least 3 months before you travel for currently recommended injections. Malaria is not present in the area.

General Health Risks: Avoid sunstroke and dehydration—cover up in the heat of the day, always wear a helmet and a good sunscreen.

Special Considerations: None.

Politics & Religion: Nepal is sandwiched between Buddhist Tibet and the Hindu population of India; as a result it has become a melting pot in which both customs and beliefs coexist. The Communist Party is in power, but politics are pretty low-key and tourists have very few restrictions on their movements.

Crime Risks: Low, but always keep an eye on your bike.

Food & Drink: Kathmandu has a multitude of restaurants with a huge variety of standards. Don't skimp and eat in a cheap, dirty place and ruin your holiday with diarrhea. Wash your hands before all meals and snacks; use iodine if water is not boiled, or consume bottled drinks.

HIGHLIGHTS

Scenic: The ride visits five of the best viewpoints of the Himalayas that the Kathmandu Valley has to offer. From Kakani, Chisopani, Nagarkot, Dhulikhel, and Daman, in clear weather, you can see up to 155 uninterrupted miles (250km) of the Himalayas.

Wildlife & Flora: There is an abundance of plants in the valleys of Nepal. Wildlife encountered will be mostly water buffalo and sacred cows, along with wild chickens and other farmyard animals left to wander around the villages.

←

Cyclists on the narrow trails must take care to give way to the hardworking Nepali farmers and their heavy loads.

↓ temperature and precipitation

		JAN	FEB	MAR	APR	MAY	JUN	JUL	AUG	SEP	OCT	NOV	DEC	
▲	°f	66	70	77	82	86	84	82	82	81	81	23	68	°f
	°c	19	21	25	28	30	29	28	28	27	27	−5.3	20	°c
▼	°f	36	37	45	50	57	64	66	66	63	54	45	36	°f
	°c	2	3	7	10	14	18	19	19	17	12	7	2	°c
	ins	0.7	0.4	1.3	2.1	3.3	10.6	15.1	13.3	6.3	2.4	0.3	0.1	ins
	mm	18	11	33	54	83	270	383	338	160	62	7	2	mm

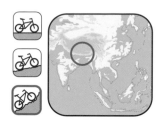

LHASA to KATHMANDU

TIBET & NEPAL

Jamie Carr

TIBET IS THE HIGHEST COUNTRY IN THE WORLD, AVERAGING CLOSE TO 13,000 FEET (4,000M). ITS HARSH ENVIRONMENT MEANS IT IS ACCESSIBLE BY LAND FOR ONLY A FEW MONTHS OF THE YEAR. THE ONCE FORBIDDEN CULTURAL CAPITAL OF CENTRAL ASIAN BUDDHISM, TIBET IS NOW OPEN TO ALL WHO WISH TO EXPERIENCE THE SIGHTS AND SOUNDS OF THIS FASCINATING COUNTRY.

Tibet has only been open to visitors since the early nineteenth century, at which time a few Western expeditions made the long trek in from Darjeeling. Tibet was slowly occupied by the Chinese from 1950 onward, and for the next twenty years was put through terrible atrocities. Now, however, the Chinese government has relaxed somewhat, and allows tourists to fly directly into Tibet as part of an organized tour. Once there, you can visit most places as long as you are accompanied by a Chinese or Tibetan guide and stick to the places on the itinerary. Bikes have their own permit and are checked in and out of the country. As you have to provide transport for your local guide, you can also use this transport to carry all your luggage, leaving you and your bike free to explore Tibet and Nepal with relative ease.

↓ itinerary

•DAYS 1–2 99 miles (160km)

Lhasa to Yamdrok Lake

Once you have finished sightseeing and acclimatizing in Lhasa, the first 44 miles (70km) down to Tsangpo Bridge at Quxu are easy. Make sure you turn left and cross the bridge here as the busy main road goes directly to Xigazê up the gorge alongside the river. A lot less traffic goes the long way past the lake, which is better for you, although your road does turn into a dirt track near the base of the climb. Here, there is a small village, slightly beyond which is a good camping spot ready for an early start the next day.

Day 2's climb is gradual but very long, and the altitude will slow you down—be prepared to climb for five hours, or more. The views back down the valley are stunning, but don't linger if you feel your head pounding; rather, descend quickly to the lake. There are many good campgrounds along the lakeside and a few small villages. However, there are no restaurants or guesthouses till you reach Nagarzê.

•DAYS 3–4 119 miles (191km)

Yamdrok Lake to Xigazê

Another pass, and the first one over 16,400 feet (5,000m) —the Karo La. It is much easier than Kamba La because you start much higher, and it has a longer run-out, past some mine workings and gradually down a long valley to Gyangzê. Here, there is a hilltop fortress that the early British explorer Sir Francis Younghusband and his troops occupied in 1904 on their way to Lhasa. There are many restaurants, but just one hotel that tourists are allowed to stay in, the Gyangzê Hotel. From Gyangzê it's a long, hot, flat road to Xigazê with an optional 12-mile (20-km) diversion to the seldom-visited Shallu monastery. Xigazê is a much bigger city with a good travelers' hotel—the Tenzing, near the old section of the Golden Temple—that has hot showers and cheap dormitory rooms.

The huge Tashilhunpo monastery is best seen early in the morning and has a well-worn "kora," or circuit, around

A panorama of never-ending mountains greets you as you reach the top of the Kardu La, the first of many passes traversed along this route.

Rains in the "Monsoon Zone" close to Nepal often cause landslides, and the roads can still be muddy and rocky as a result of these landslides for several months after the monsoon has subsided.

its perimeter that is used by the locals each day before the monastery opens at 9:30 A.M. Do remember to walk around all Buddhist koras in a clockwise direction—it is a universal one-way system and all the prayer wheels must always be spun in this direction. A day in Xigazê is well worth it, and the Xigazê Hotel has the last hot bathtubs until Kathmandu!

• DAYS 5–7 | 149 miles (240km)

Xigazê to Xêgar

Tibetans don't worry about which side of the road you cycle on; it's usually wherever is the smoothest. However, when a vehicle is overtaking you, you must stay on the side you are on—don't switch at the last minute. There is a good

road now for a short while to a small pass, then on to the bigger one, the Yulung La at 14,760 feet (4,500m). This pass gives the first views of the distant snowcapped Himalayas that you are heading toward. Either set up camp before this pass or push over to the town beyond the small junction road that comes from Sa'gyaxoi monastery. This area is even less visited, even though Sa'gyaxoi is one of the largest active monasteries in the area. The 16-mile (26-km) road to it from the highway is very rough and often washed out, so it can take over two hours to get there. Otherwise, it is a flat blast to Lhatze, where there are poor-standard hotels and cheap dodgy-looking restaurants.

It is better to camp on the nice grass close to the base of the next and highest pass on the road, the Jia Tsuco La at

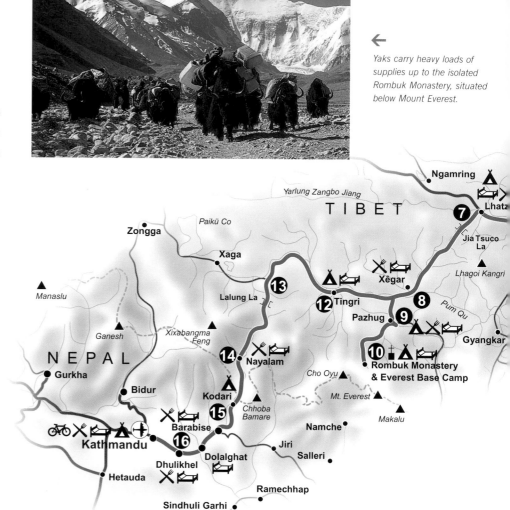

Yaks carry heavy loads of supplies up to the isolated Rombuk Monastery, situated below Mount Everest.

17,120 feet (5,220m). This is a very long climb that is steep in sections and has a very airy feel at the top, with good views of Everest and the Himalayas in the distance once you start descending the other side. An easy-angled valley takes you down to Xêgar and, again, cheap hotels on the roadside or more expensive ones in the main town that, sadly, offer little more. It is best to camp outside the town.

•DAYS 8–11 124 miles (200km)

Xêgar to Everest Base Camp and Tingri

This side trip up the Rombuk Valley to Everest Base Camp is one of the most memorable highlights of the trip. Leave the main highway after the checkpoint and go on to a small bridge that takes you left, up an unmarked dirt road, to another checkpoint. The pass is very rough on this side and many switchbacks lead up the Pang La to around 17,000 feet (5,200m)—nearly as high as yesterday's pass, but you should be more acclimatized for this one. At the top there is probably one of the best views of the Himalayas—Makalu, Everest, Llhotse, Cho Oyu, and Xixabangma Feng.

Prayer flags and paper blessings scatter everywhere as you line up to have photos taken with a backdrop that's sure to make all your friends at home envious. It is then a great descent down to Paro village, where you can visit a guesthouse that serves very strong *chang* (Tibetan rice beer). You can choose to stay either near here or further up the valley near Pazhug village, which has better views of Everest.

The ride up to Rombuk Monastery is sandy in places but otherwise a good track. The monks at the monastery have built a new guesthouse and a small restaurant. Two hours further up the valley the road ends at Everest Base Camp, where there are some buildings and a very smelly toilet block for expeditions to use. Throughout the summer you can usually see expedition base camps here, though most climbers are higher up at the Advance Base Camp, 13 miles (21km) up the glacier moraine. It's not worth trying to take your bikes up the moraine or any higher, but a walk up the nearby hillside gives a better view of Everest. Spending an extra day to explore the area is well worthwhile before making the ride back down, which is great in itself because

↑ key

▭	route of ride
▭	major road
▭	minor road
----	country border
▲	peak
⊔	pass
▲	campground
🛏	hotel/guesthouse
✗	provisions
✈	airport
🚲	bike shop/repairs
⌷	monastery

→ *Lush vegetation is abundant in the Bhote Khosi Valley, which you pass through on the descent from Tibet to Nepal.*

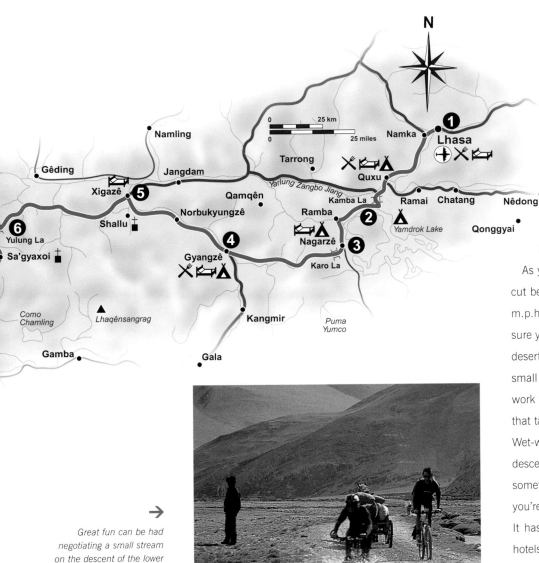

descent to a bridge where there's a small shop before a steep grind up to the final pass at 16,560 feet (5,050m) and a last look at the high plateau of Tibet.

Now you're faced with the last section of the journey, which starts with a 13,500-foot (4,110-m) descent over the next 100 miles (160km). As you descend the first section there's a tempting short-cut between the first two switchbacks and speeds over 50 m.p.h. (80 k.p.h.) have been reached quite easily, so make sure your brakes are working well! As you descend from the desert above to the lush valleys of Nepal below, you will see small bushes appear and streams fertilizing areas of patch-work fields. Then there's a short climb up to the descent that takes you past Nayalam, where good food is available. Wet-weather gear is now essential as you make your descent into the clouds. The road has been cut into, and sometimes through, the steep sidewalls of the valley. As you're descending, the town of Zhangmu comes into view. It has a checkpoint, many hotels, a road with shops and hotels, and a road of liquid mud that shows you the way to the Chinese customs barrier, and the end of Tibet.

You won't wish to hang around too long in Zhangmu, because the whole place looks as if it may slip down the →

→

Great fun can be had negotiating a small stream on the descent of the lower Everest Valley.

there are a few smaller trails one can always use instead of the main jeep track. After the Pang La has been climbed from the other side there are more shortcuts down the steep side, and riders often beat the support truck down to the main highway and over the next 28 miles (45km) to guesthouses at Tingri.

•DAYS 12–14 137 miles (220km)

Tingri to Kodari

The road winds around the back of a huge hill, and there are hot springs in a small hamlet along the way, but they are often in a pretty awful state. It is best to camp on a good grassy area after Gutsuo Army Camp in view of the base of your next pass, the Lalung La. This is a double pass and you will need plenty of time to cross both sections and get down the other side before being caught out in the dark. The first pass is 15,900 feet (4,850m) and a short steep

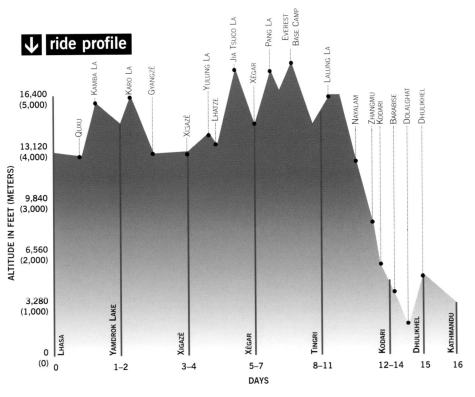

↓ ride profile

hillside into the river below. However, it does take time to get through passport controls and to move luggage. Continue down tight steep switchbacks, descending through no-man's-land for a further 7 miles (11km) until you reach the Friendship Bridge and the Nepalese border town of Kodari. A broad red line on the bridge marks the end of Tibet and you cross into a different world—the hustle and bustle of Nepal and laid-back customs officials who wave you in to stamp your passport or sell you a visa.

As you continue down, there's a choice of excellent riverside resorts near the border town run by the river-rafting companies. The first one is across a long suspension bridge from which you can bungee-jump down a 520-foot (160-m) narrow gorge toward the raging river below. You could always choose to raft the Bhote Khosi if your saddle sores are too much to cycle any further.

•DAY 15 50 miles (80km)

Kodari to Dhulikhel

From the resorts it's more downhill riding, crossing the river at Barabise, and a short climb before more descent on broken tarmac roads down to the base of the hill at Dolalghat. At only 1,800 feet (540m), this is the lowest point on the entire ride and 14,800 feet (4,500m) below the Lalung La, which you left two days ago. Unfortunately, from the lowest point, the only way is up, and it is an 18-mile (30-km) climb up to Dhulikhel on the very edge of the Kathmandu Valley rim.

•DAY 16 22–34 miles (35–55km)

Dhulikhel to Kathmandu

If the weather is bad, you can make a fast blast down the road in the morning to be in Kathmandu by lunch. However, if the weather is good, there are many options for biking in the valley. You can ride a loop around Namo Buddha to Panauti, then go back to the road at Banepa and along a dirt road to Nala and continue to Bhaktapur. From here, take the back road via Thimi to detour around the airport and through the Hindu temples of Pasupatinath and across the backstreets to Thamel. Check into your hotel and go downtown for a celebratory drink.

↑
Heavy snowdrifts often have to be cut through to clear the road that descends into Nepal from Tibet.

OVERVIEW

The entire trip is ridable in 16 days and covers approximately 70 miles (1,125km) on mostly good double dirt tracks and highway. However, the prudent will allow a couple of days extra, just in case. You should also allow an extra 5 days at the beginning for acclimatization and traveling from Kathmandu to Lhasa.
Start: Lhasa, Tibet.
Finish: Kathmandu, Nepal.

ABOUT THE TRAIL

It's mostly off-road; there's some single-track on the descents if you take the shortcuts between switchbacks. It is a challenging route but achievable. About 25 percent of the route is surfaced road of some description; off-road short-cuts, which can make the descents much more technical, can be made at your discretion.

Major Climbs & Descents: The highest point you cycle is over 17,120 feet (5,220m). There are some long climbs up to the passes, but with much bigger descents, especially the final 13,000-foot (3,960-m) descent off the plateau into Nepal.

Difficulty & Special Features: Altitude is the main difficulty. You should read up on altitude sickness and never run out of water during your ride. Be very aware of each other as altitude sickness can catch up with you at any time. However, with adequate time spent on acclimatization and innate determination, most reasonably fit mountain bikers can complete the route. If you choose to go with an organized cycle tour group you have the support of a bus in case you don't feel up to cycling one day. There is a good bike shop in Kathmandu where you can have repairs done with genuine Shimano products. Carry a few bike spares; a spare folding tire; spare spokes and brake blocks; inner tubes; and a basic tool kit with a bottle of oil.

ACCESS

Airports: Goggar Airport (58 miles/93km from Lhasa) is your best entry point; there are flights to here from Kathmandu, Nepal and Chengdu, China.

Transport: Transport is not a problem if you are with a group since all transport will be organized for you and there will be trucks for your bikes when needed. In Nepal, taxis are willing to take you and your bike to any hotel.

Passport & Visa Requirements: All foreign nationals require a visa to enter Tibet and Kathmandu.

Permits & Access Restrictions: To land in Goggar you are required to have an entry permit for the Tibetan Autonomous Region as well as a valid Chinese visa; this is only available to people in an organized tour of a minimum of five persons.

LOCAL INFORMATION

Maps: Pilgrims Bookshop in Kathmandu sells a map that covers the southern-central area of Tibet, and incorporates the trip from Lhasa to Kathmandu. These have no contours or grid lines but are accurate enough with the passes marked in the correct places.

Guidebooks: Lonely Planet's *Tibet* is huge and very comprehensive, but it does not cater for cyclists and is of little use outside the towns and the monasteries. However, the Lonely Planet Language Survival Kit Phrasebook for *Tibetan* is very useful.

Accommodation & Supplies: Accommodation is fine in the bigger towns but of a pretty poor standard elsewhere on the route. There are lots of restaurants and well-stocked supermarkets in Kathmandu.

Currency & Language: The yuan is the unit of currency throughout

all of China and Tibet; the Nepali rupee is the unit of currency in Nepal. U.S. dollars are easily changed anywhere; traveler's checks can be changed in banks and at money-exchange counters. Cash advances into local currency from Visa/MasterCard are available in Lhasa and Kathmandu. There are six different dialects of Tibetan, many forms of Nepalese, and a Sherpa language. Try to learn some basic greetings and thank-yous, as these are the same throughout all dialects. Some English is spoken in Lhasa and Xigazê, and lots of Nepalis in Kathmandu speak excellent English.

Photography: Be very courteous when taking photos of any Tibetan people and ask them first—you will get a better picture as a result. Carry plenty of film.

Area Information: A Chinese guide can be obtained from China International Travel Services, Xigazê, Tibet (fax: 891 6833515). However, joining an organized, customized mountain bike trip is the best way to have all the paperwork, yourself, and your bike in the right place with no problems. This can be done with experienced local Nepali and Tibetan-speaking guides from Kathmandu; contact Dawn Till Dusk (fax: 01 412 619 or e-mail dtd@wlink.com.np). However, if you want a company that will sort out all of the above, plus your flights and acclimatization program, and that employs experienced and medically qualified Western and local mountain bike guides, contact KE Adventure (tel.: 1-800-497-9675 in the U.S.A. toll-free, or 01768 773966 in the U.K.) or e-mail Jamie Carr on

→

Nomadic Tibetans analyze in amazement the detailed maps that are essential for visitors.

CrazeyMTBiker@yahoo.com.
Website: www.keadventure.com

TIMING & SEASONALITY

Best Months to Visit: July and August, although they can be busy. The monsoon in Nepal lasts until the middle of September. Snow and high winds rule out this trip for the winter months, but it is possible from April to October.

Climate: Dry, sunny, and arid in Tibet, but it can be very hot one minute and snowing the next. Be prepared for intense sunlight at very high altitude along with a high sunburn factor, but simultaneously carry waterproofs and some warm clothing—basically, be prepared for anything! Recommendations are glacier glasses and full gloves on top of the usual cool-weather gear.

HEALTH & SAFETY

Vaccinations: Typhoid, tetanus, diphtheria, polio,

hepatitis A and B, meningitis A and C, and cholera are all recommended; see your doctor at least 3 months before you travel to check current recommendations.

General Health Risks: Read up on altitude- *The High Altitude Medicine Handbook*, by Andrew J. Pollard and David R. Murdoch (Pilgrim), is very informative and handy to carry. Also, before you go, a dip through *Medicine for Mountaineering and Other Wilderness Activities* (Mountaineers Books) should prepare you for the higher regions. You will need to carry some Diamox and Ciprofloxin tablets. Beware of sunstroke and dehydration—carry plenty of dehydration sachets; always cover up in the sun, wear a helmet and good sunscreen.

Special Considerations: None.

Politics & Religion: Tibet underwent some of the worst human atrocities in recent history

when China occupied Tibet. Tibetans have a strong belief in the Buddhist way of life; their spiritual leader is the Dalai Lama.

Crime Risk: Low, but keep an eye on your bike, as if anything should happen to it, it would ruin your trip.

Food & Drink: Chinese food is available in Lhasa and Xigazê, which is better than some of the Tibetan food. Roadside cafés operate in some places along the route. Instant noodles are easy to buy and safe to eat with boiled water. Boiling water in lower altitudes is fine, but always use iodine at higher elevations. Freshly cooked and locally grown food is best: just look at what others are eating and point to that.

HIGHLIGHTS

The culture of Tibet; crossing the Himalayas; visiting Everest Base Camp, and descending the second biggest downhill in the world.

Scenic: The whole ride is scenic, from taking off from Kathmandu airport to around Lhasa and all the way back along the Himalayas.

Wildlife & Flora: There are plenty of yaks and huge guard dogs that protect the Tibetan compounds. There's not much vegetation on the higher levels where only the hardiest plants can survive the winters. The nomadic Tibetans and their yaks descend to lower levels in the winter to survive.

↓ temperature and precipitation

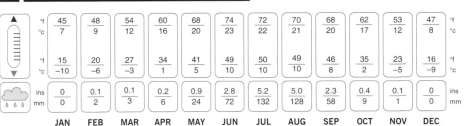

		JAN	FEB	MAR	APR	MAY	JUN	JUL	AUG	SEP	OCT	NOV	DEC	
▲	°f	45	48	54	60	68	74	72	70	68	62	53	47	°f
	°c	7	9	12	16	20	23	22	21	20	17	12	8	°c
▼	°f	15	20	27	34	41	49	50	49	46	35	23	16	°f
	°c	−10	−6	−3	1	5	10	10	10	8	2	−5	−9	°c
	ins	0	0.1	0.1	0.2	0.9	2.8	5.2	5.0	2.3	0.4	0.1	0	ins
	mm	0	2	3	6	24	72	132	128	58	9	1	0	mm

SOUTHERN CHINA

CHINA

Emma Barraclough

THE ROUTE FROM GUIYANG TO YANGSHUO PASSES THROUGH SOME OF THE MOST BEAUTIFUL SCENERY IN CHINA, FROM THE MOUNTAINS AND TERRACED VALLEYS OF SOUTH-EASTERN GUIZHOU TO THE AWE-INSPIRING KARST LANDSCAPE OF NORTHERN GUANGXI.

Along the route are scores of tiny villages perched upon hillsides populated by some of China's many ethnic minority groups, each of which has its own distinct culture and traditions. This part of China is often overlooked by travelers, largely due to its relative inaccessibility. But the dramatic scenery and winding mountain roads make it an ideal biking destination. The route is 500 miles (804km) long and, because it uses some of the main roads through Guizhou, it is relatively easy to navigate, but lack of traffic and poor road conditions en route ensure a sense of remoteness for much of the journey.

A local Yangshuo fisherman tries his luck on the Li River under the shadow of karst mountains. Yangshuo is the final destination of this trip.

↓ itinerary

•DAYS 1–2 74 miles (119km)

Guiyang to Machangping

The route leaves Guiyang, the industrial provincial capital of Guizhou, and heads southeast toward the multiethnic areas of Southern Guizhou. The city soon gives way to characteristic Guizhou scenery: mountains and terraced valleys. Over the centuries the Chinese have worked hard to make this beautiful but inhospitable land as productive as possible, and the result is carefully irrigated terraced strips of farmland high up on the hillsides. For the first two days the road meanders through the countryside, passing through the towns of Longli and Guiding before reaching Machangping.

•DAY 3 38 miles (61km)

Machangping to Duyun

The route heads deeper into the province, and many of the farmers on today's route are part of the Miao ethnic minority group, who have their own language, traditions, and costumes. Agricultural practices are still very labor-intensive in Guizhou, and you will pass people working in the fields and plowing the land with water buffalo. Many of the women work with their young children strapped to their backs in elaborately embroidered baby carriers.

•DAY 4 32 miles (51km)

Duyun to Danzhai

The road gains height as it winds out of Duyun and up through Miao villages where working methods haven't changed for centuries. Many of the villages have a weekly market and the chances are that you'll pass people streaming to neighboring villages in traditional costume carrying produce. You can be sure that, as you discreetly admire their colorful costumes, they will be equally intrigued by your bike setup. The road gradually gains height throughout the day, and there is a long, steady climb to Danzhai as the road snakes up to the head of the Duliu Valley.

•DAY 5 22 miles (35km)

Danzhai to Sanhe

The road begins a gradual descent from the town of Danzhai

as it follows the river for an easy day of cycling. The road has been cut into the side of the valley and mountains hug the valley tightly on either side. An early start will ensure that you catch the morning mists that hang over the hills to give stunning views of traditional Chinese landscapes. Throughout the day, tiny rafts carrying fishermen can be seen in the river far below the road.

•DAY 6 37 miles (59km)

Sanhe to Bajie

The dusty, unpaved road still hugs the valley sides and gently loses height, but the landscape opens up a little, allowing small villages to perch precariously on the hilltops. The houses in the villages are traditional, wooden stilt buildings and many of the villagers wear beautifully hand-woven and embroidered clothes, with patterns and styles that change from village to village.

•DAY 7 46 miles (74km)

Bajie to Tingdong

The route continues to follow the Duliu River and takes in the large, bustling town of Rongjiang before heading back into the countryside. The day ends in Tingdong, a tiny town with sporadic electricity supply and a basic guesthouse.

•DAY 8 31 miles (50km)

Tingdong to Congjiang

The route follows the river to the town of Xiajiang and then heads away, up a winding, unsealed road and over a pass to drop into Congjiang and rejoin the river. The climb is long but well graded, and from the top there is a stunning panoramic view of the terraced valley below. The sound of roosters crowing and people working in the fields echo up the valley as the road makes its final bone-shaking descent of the day into the town of Congjiang.

The terraced fields of this Miao ethnic village, on the road between Machanping and Duyun, are characteristic of the landscape in the Guizhou region.

→

•DAY 9 37 miles (60km)

Congjiang to Diping

The route to Diping follows the river along the valley bottom, making for easy riding although the road is stony, dusty, and slow. There are ethnic Dong villages along this stretch of the route, some of them with the beautifully carved and painted wooden drum towers and the wind and rain bridges for which the Dong people are famed. The road passes Fulu, a sleepy town on the banks of the river, where small cargo boats dock. The route leaves the main road near the end of the day and follows a minor road a few miles to Diping and its small guesthouse. Those wishing to extend their trip could take a 50-mile (80-km) round-trip detour by cycling up the mountainous and rough road to the village of Zhaoxing to marvel at the scenery and the spectacular drum towers and wind and rain bridges.

•DAY 10 40 miles (65km)

Diping to Sanjiang

The road remains rough and slow as the route heads toward Sanjiang, a town close to the boundary of the provinces of Hunan, Guangxi, and Guizhou. As you cycle, you will notice an interlocking network of bamboo poles running along the side of the road—this effectively irrigates the fields.

•DAYS 11–12 103 miles (166km)

Sanjiang to Guilin

The road is sealed for most of the rest of the route, which speeds up the cycling and makes the hills much less of a challenge. Not far out of Longsheng the road begins to climb and climb. Once you're at the top, a short detour takes you to a series of dramatic 2,620-foot (800-m) terraced peaks—the Dragon's Backbone. Back on the main route, the road eventually drops down into Miaoping village. From Miaoping, continue descending all the way to Guilin.

•DAY 13 40 miles (64km)

Guilin to Yangshuo

Guilin is famous for its beautiful karst scenery, an image evoked again and again in Chinese landscape art. The strange solitary hills are truly stunning as they stretch away into the distance, but it is in the area surrounding the Li River and the town of Yangshuo that the scenery is most beautiful. The road from Guilin to Yangshuo has been upgraded, so it is an easy ride to the backpacker mecca of Yangshuo, where you can relax and rediscover forgotten culinary luxuries.

↑ key

	route of ride
	major road
	minor road
	regional border
	railroad
▲	peak
	hotel/guesthouse
	provisions
	airport
	bike shop/repairs

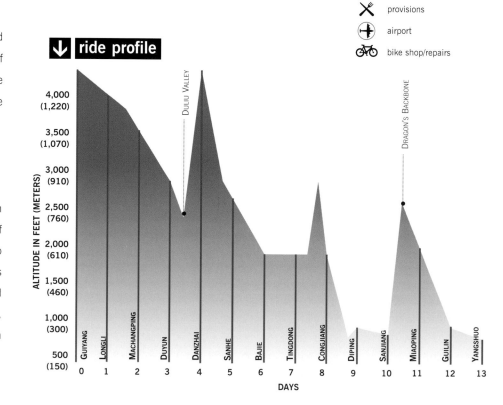

↓ ride profile

factfile

 The inhospitable, mountainous terrain of Guizhou has ensured that this region has remained one of the poorest in China.

OVERVIEW

 Most cyclists will be able to tackle this route, and they will be rewarded by stunning scenery and a glimpse of the lives and culture of some of China's ethnic-minority peoples. The distance covered is 500 miles (804km) in just under 2 weeks, and there is scope for extending the trip by exploring minor roads and tracks in Guizhou province.

Start: Guiyang, Guizhou Province.

Finish: Yangshuo, Guangxi Province.

ABOUT THE TRAIL

Poor infrastructure means that over half of the route is on unsealed roads.

Major Climbs & Descents:

Beginning the trip in the center of the mountainous province of Guizhou and heading southeast ensures that you gradually lose height throughout the trip to Yangshuo. However, the road gains 1,970 feet (600m) to the head of the Duliu Valley and 1,970 feet (600m) on the road climb out of Sanjiang.

Difficulty & Special Features:

Those choosing to leave the main route to explore side roads can expect steep climbs and moderate to difficult off-road conditions.

ACCESS

Airports: Guiyang has an airport with flights to and from major Chinese cities.

Transport: Both Guiyang and Guilin are on major train lines. Sleeper trains run from Guangzhou to Guiyang and take between 24 and 36 hours. Bikes can be carried on the same train if you are persistent

enough. Ticket sales can be unpredictable at Guangzhou Station, and it may be more convenient to arrange your train journey with a travel agent in Hong Kong. There are numerous travel agencies in Yangshuo that can arrange your onward travel.

Passport & Visa Requirements:

Visas are required for all foreigners visiting mainland China (these are usually granted for 30 days).

Permits & Access Restrictions:

The area is open to foreigners; mountain bikers may arouse the curiosity of the local police, but there shouldn't be any problems.

LOCAL INFORMATION

Maps: Non-Chinese speakers may experience difficulty with map reading and a combination of the following is recommended: the Nelles Southern China map shows main roads and has romanized place names; Chinese provincial maps (available in Guiyang) show a greater number of roads and show place names in Chinese characters.

Guidebooks: The Lonely Planet guide to *Southwest China* has useful travel advice.

Accommodation & Supplies:

Plentiful guesthouses along the route means that there is no need to carry camping supplies. Officially, guesthouses need a license to accommodate foreigners, but you are unlikely to experience any difficulty finding a bed in rural areas. However, in larger towns the rule is upheld and you will be firmly directed to the licensed (and more expensive) hotels. Be prepared for basic accommodation, with sporadic electricity and water.

Currency & Language: Chinese Renminbi (the yuan or "kuai"); Putonghua (Mandarin Chinese) is standard, although both Guizhou and Guangxi have strong regional dialects. Little English is spoken in the countryside; a phrasebook and dictionary are essential.

Photography: Be courteous and exercise discretion when taking portrait shots. Do not attract unwanted police attention by photographing anything that may have security or military sensitivity.

Area Information: China National Tourist Offices can be found in most major international cities: New York (tel.: 212-760-9700; London (tel.: 020 7935 9427); Sydney (tel.: 02 299 4057).

Website: www.lonelyplanet.com has up-to-date information on many areas in China.

TIMING & SEASONALITY

 Best Months to Visit: Fall, followed by spring.

Climate: The summers can be uncomfortably hot, and, although temperatures do not fall too low in winter, the high humidity in Southern China can make the place bone-chillingly damp.

HEALTH & SAFETY

 Vaccinations: Immunization against a number of diseases is highly recommended. Seek medical advice well before your trip.

General Health Risks: (See Food & Drink below.)

Special Considerations: Travel in China can be challenging—the government is becoming less wary of independent travelers, but be prepared for bureaucracy and form filling. Although there should be no practical difficulties in taking your own bike to China, Chinese officials may not be encouraging— be persistent and smile a lot.

Politics & Religion: Officially communist and atheist. Religion,

however, is growing in China, especially in the countryside. The government does not appreciate criticism of the one-party state.

Crime Risk: Petty theft is growing in the cities.

Food & Drink: Food hygiene can be an issue; carry your own chopsticks and take sensible precautions. The Chinese boil all drinking water and flasks of boiled water are available everywhere. Bottled mineral water is widely available.

HIGHLIGHTS

Scenic: The opportunity to visit ethnic villages, markets, and festivals is not to be missed. Rural Guizhou and Guangxi offer breathtaking scenery, including the wind and rain bridges of Dong villages in Guizhou and the karst scenery of Guilin and Yangshuo. The route travels along roads cut into mountains high above the Duliu River, passes through dramatic terraced valleys dotted with hillside villages, and eventually drops toward the magnificent hills of Yangshuo.

Wildlife & Flora: Sadly, extensive farming and logging has caused much habitat destruction, and you will find little wildlife. Likewise for flora—you will mostly see rice and other food plants, except on those parts of the mountains that are too steep to farm.

temperature and precipitation

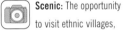

	JAN	FEB	MAR	APR	MAY	JUN	JUL	AUG	SEP	OCT	NOV	DEC	
°f	52	54	63	72	80	84	88	88	82	75	65	56	°f
°c	11	12	17	22	26	29	31	31	27	24	18	13	°c
°f	40	42	50	58	65	70	72	72	68	60	52	44	°f
°c	4	5	10	14	18	21	22	22	20	15	11	7	°c
ins	1.3	1.5	1.8	4.2	8.1	8.5	6.4	5.4	3.8	3.6	2.0	1.1	ins
mm	33	38	46	107	206	216	162	137	96	91	51	28	mm

SOUTHERN CHINA

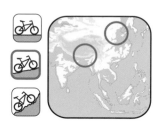

BEIJING to LHASA
CHINA & TIBET

Jamie Carr

THIS RIDE IS ABOUT DISCOVERING THE REAL CHINA. DURING WHAT IS A LONG JOURNEY ACROSS THE WIDTH OF THE NATION INTO TIBET, YOU WILL TRAVEL AS THE LOCALS DO, ON BIKES, AND PASS THROUGH AN AMAZINGLY DIVERSE AND CHANGING LANDSCAPE. AVOIDING THE CROWDED SOUTHEAST, THE ROUTE ROUGHLY FOLLOWS THE GREAT WALL FROM BEIJING IN A SOUTHWESTERLY DIRECTION, CLIMBING UP ONTO THE BACK OF THE TIBETAN PLATEAU AND CROSSING TO THE ANCIENT AND ONCE FORBIDDEN TIBETAN CAPITAL OF LHASA.

↓ itinerary

In Beijing your bike is by far the best transport—and you're in good company, for 8 million locals also move around by bike. The bike lanes in the city are bigger and more congested than the motor-vehicle lanes. However, the Chinese cycle slowly, so you feel super-charged as you pass hundreds of cyclists every mile. Things that you must do in Beijing are cycle across Tiananmen Square to visit the Forbidden City, attend a performance of Beijing Opera, see Mao Tse-tung in his tomb, and partake of Peking roast duck.

•DAYS 1–3 180 miles (290km)

Beijing to Laiyuan

As soon as you find your way out of the city the roads get less congested. Finding the way is hard at first because only the larger roads are signposted. Once in rural China the towns are much smaller and finding hotels and food is very easy. There's a 6,850-foot (2,090-m) pass as you cycle nearby the Great Wall. As you meander past, you will see different sections of the Wall in its true dilapidated state—the Wall has only been reconstructed near Beijing where most tourists go to take photographs of it.

The crossing of the Lhasa River in the Lhasa Valley is one of the last challenges of this trip; the best option is to take a makeshift, cowhide boat aross the wide waterway.

After crossing the valley in Gansu Province, there is a climb up the valley side, which, although strenuous, provides fantastic views from the top.

A surprisingly good tarmac road, reminiscent of long, lonely highways across the United States, runs for as far as the eye can see into Lhasa.

•DAYS 4–8 335 miles (540km)

Laiyuan to Taiyuan

Asking for directions can prove tricky because of pronunciation problems, and to ensure that you stay on the right route it is a good idea to carry cards with the name of the town written in Chinese characters on them. Heavy rain often washes away bridges in this area and turns some of the roads to sheets of mud. The Chinese do work hard to repair these and they are normally no trouble to get around. The people here are very inquisitive and keen to ask questions. Cycling past other cyclists makes them momentarily speed up, and you will occasionally get one who tries to keep up with you. You have to cross several high, off-road passes before turning south onto better roads toward the large town of Taiyuan.

•DAYS 9–12 233 miles (375km)

Taiyuan to Linfen

It is now easier and quicker riding along the riverside. If you engage in some hard bargaining you could manage to wangle a room in a posh hotel in Pingyao for a very reasonable sum! There are several busy roads in this industrial area, but you soon leave this and head for the hills.

•DAYS 13–18 460 miles (740km)

Linfen to Guyuan

Almost immediately after leaving Linfen you start climbing out of Shanxi Province on quieter roads into a large, intricately terraced, hillside landscape. Once at the top of the first hill, you will see some amazing views back across the valley that you have just climbed. As you wind your way through these hills, the road starts to deteriorate into a mixture of loose rock and gravel, before a sudden huge descent toward the mighty Huang He (Yellow River). After the summer rains, this river is more of a brown torrent as it is swollen with mud and silt. Climbing up the other side, you may have to try the locals' hospitality, as it is a fair way to the next town; if you are fortunate, you will be served good food and be given basic accommodation by friendly people. Yichuan town is in another new province, and the roads are better. Also, the crossings of low passes are easier in the large valleys. The land is so precious in this very fertile area that the locals live in houses dug underneath the terraced fields above. There are many watermelon stops to be had here and lots of towns for accommodation.

↑

A good surface for the last stretch of this incredibly long journey will be welcomed by all who get this far.

•DAYS 19–21 199 miles (320km)

Guyuan to Lanzhou

The good roads continue as you cross into Gansu Province. You will now use your tent for the first time and, if it's a clear night, you will experience an amazing sunset from your camp near the roadside on a high mountain top.

You can get great food in a nearby town, and then it is a 19-mile (30-km) downhill ride to meet the Huang He again and follow it into the welcoming city of Lanzhou. At 4,920 feet (1,500m), Lanzhou is cooler than the hot plains you have already crossed; it looks like a Chinese version of Denver, Colorado—it is on the cusp of a flat area, there are mountains nearby, and mountains behind the town. Good food can be had on the street here, and there is a reliable post office. Cheap rooms are available in a dormitory of the big Lanzhou Hotel.

•DAYS 22–25 276 miles (444km)

Lanzhou to Qinghai Hu

Now the climbing starts for real, but you should be well fed and well rested after your stay in Lanzhou. The road up to Xining is quite busy with trucks as it is the only route through to any towns further on and the Tibetan plateau beyond. You can stay in Huangyuan, and from there cross the Riyue Shankuo pass at 12,000 feet (3,660m). There is a slight downhill—the first after three days of climbing!

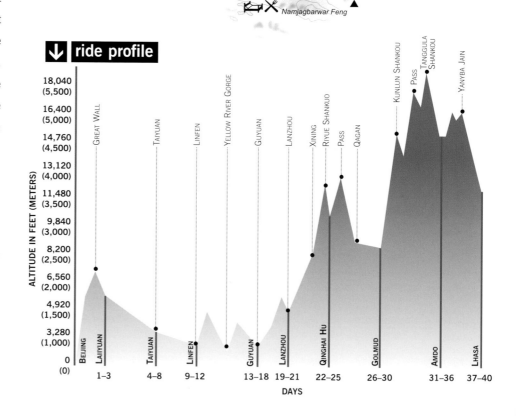

←

Rain can turn the dirt roads of Shanxi Province into pure mud.

You will also see your first snowcapped peak, and possibly a yak. The tent now becomes an essential piece of kit, and warm clothes are necessary to descend the pass. The lake of Qinghai Hu is massive, the biggest in China, and, at 10,000 feet (3,048m), it is high as well.

•DAYS 26–30 373 miles (600km)

Qinghai Hu to Golmud

All of a sudden the air is thinner and the distances between towns are much bigger, particularly as occasionally towns marked on the map just don't exist any more. This means that you must carry more food and emergency supplies. After the lake you must cross a 12,700-foot (3,870-m) pass to Caka Lake (saltwater), and then push on some more before making a camp. The next day your target is Qagan. The weather can be incredibly changeable at high altitudes and you can go from applying sunscreen to wearing all the clothes you have within half an hour. Use water (boiled) from the Qagan Us river to refuel ready for the long hot desert crossing, which can be particularly windy, to Golmud. Every 60 miles (96km) or so there are road builders' compounds that are manned to keep the road open all year round. From these, if you're brave enough to pass the huge guard dogs, you can get water. Golmud is a sprawling town surrounded by desert, where camels are more common than yaks. →

key

▬	route of ride
▭	alternative route
▭	major road
▭	minor road
┈	regional border
▲	peak
⊔	pass
▲	campground
🛏	hotel/guesthouse
✗	provisions
✈	airport

→

Open vistas of terraced hillsides and wide, deep valleys welcome you as you travel across Gansu Province in the depths of China.

•DAYS 31–36 | 432 miles (695km)

Golmud to Amdo

From here on it is all climbing until you get to Nepal on the other side of the Tibetan plateau. Turn south in Golmud to head for Lhasa and the first big pass. You can now see the Kunlun Shankou at 15,640 feet (4,767m), which will take you onto the plateau proper. Surreal landscape is all around and the natural light late on in the day gives an amazing effect. The valley stretches on as far as the eye can see. The road is still tarmac, but roadworks may force you to cycle on dirt and sandy tracks beside the road. You will now be cruising at a serious altitude of 14,760 feet (4,500m), and the next pass will be over 16,400 feet (5,000m). A long descent on the other side leads to a welcome town to resupply. A whole day of flat follows to prepare you for the highest pass on the road to Lhasa—the Tanggula Shankou. This climb is extremely hard, and once you have just crossed the path there is hardly any descent. Rather, the road turns to dirt, and you must be prepared to camp out if the weather turns bad. The road does eventually begin to drop and return to a good sealed surface. You will spin easily downhill, past a Tibetan camp, toward Amdo, where a welcome hotel bed will rest your weary body.

•DAYS 37–40 | 332 miles (535km)

Amdo to Lhasa

With the end in sight, the last two small passes just whiz by. Good sealed roads and a 50-mile (80-km) genteel downhill leads you into the fertile Lhasa valley. Trees and crops appear for the first time since Xining, and at 11,970 feet (3,650m) it will seem much easier to breathe here after the thin air higher up. Riding through Lhasa's main street is a joy, as the impressive Polata Palace dominates the skyline. Must-sees in Lhasa are the Norbulinka, Sera, Jolkhang, Barkor, and a Pujar—this is where the Tibetan monks chant the scriptures; the sound of their resonant voices and simple instruments will stay with you forever.

 factfile

The popularity of bicycles as a means of transport in China ensures that roadside repairs are widely available in towns.

OVERVIEW

The first part of the route roughly follows the Great Wall of China, traveling southwest through the northern provinces before climbing up onto the desolate northern edge of the Tibetan Plateau. From there, it passes the great Qinghai Hu to Golmud before heading southward, deeper and higher into Tibet. Total mileage is some 2,820 miles (4,539km), and it can be completed in 6 weeks.
Start: Beijing, China.
Finish: Lhasa, Tibet.

ABOUT THE TRAIL

No single-track, but all roads are in varying states of disrepair. It is a hard route if you decide to undertake the whole thing. Most of the roads are of dubious quality, and can degenerate to mud or rock.
Major Climbs & Descents: The highest point of the route is Tibet's Tanggula Shankou Pass at 16,700 feet (5,231m); the lowest is near the beginning, in Beijing, at about 1,000 feet (300m). There are numerous long climbs in China's northern hills crossing the Huang He gorge and then climbing into Tibet and ascending the plateau. As you are climbing toward Tibet, there are only a few descents.
Difficulty & Special Features: Except for the main cities, China is not set up for tourism and few people speak English in the villages. Bicycle maintenance is essential: look after the drive chain and wheels very carefully each night, and take a spare folding tire, spokes, brake blocks, and inner tubes, with a basic but comprehensive tool kit and a bottle of oil.

ACCESS

Airports: Beijing has a major international airport.
Transport: Foreign visitors have to use a separate ticket window in all bus and train stations. However, if you have your own transport (bikes), and are fit enough, you can

cycle everywhere. You could buy a mountain bike in China to do this route, but they are very heavy and of poor quality.

Passport & Visa Requirements: All foreign nationals require a visa to enter China. Thirty days is normally given, and longer stays are only likely to be permitted outside the summer months.

Permits & Access Restrictions: Permits are required for travel in all closed areas of China, and a Chinese guide is necessary for the Autonomous Region of Tibet. Information on these can be obtained from China International Travel Services, Xigazê, Tibet (fax: 891 6833515). If you try to enter China or Tibet without any of these papers you may have to pay a heavy fine, have your bike confiscated, or have to hire a guide and do all the necessary paperwork at the border. Entry into Tibet is by special permit only for travel on the roads with a guide and in organized groups of 5 people or more.

LOCAL INFORMATION

 Maps: Nelles Northern China (2) map and Bartholomew's Tibet and the Mountains of Central Asia both give good information, but some places on the maps have now disappeared; generally, the distances given between towns are fine, but they can be quite inaccurate for the more remote regions.

Guidebooks: The Lonely Planet guide to *China* is huge, so a tip is to rip it up and just take the relevant sections with you. However, it does not cater for cyclists, and is, therefore, not much use outside the big cities. However, The Lonely Planet Language Survival Kit Phrasebook for *Mandarin (Chinese)*, is invaluable.

Accommodation & Supplies:

Cafés are available everywhere on the roadsides. Instant noodles are easy to buy, but you will need a stove. Also, it is a good idea to keep extra rations as sometimes it's a long way between resupply points. In mainland China it's often hard to find a spare patch of ground to sit on, let alone pitch a tent, so you will have to use roadside guesthouses, which are mostly very cheap if a little shabby.

Currency & Language: Currency is the yuan. There are many different dialects of Mandarin so you will need a phrasebook. Some English is spoken in Beijing and large towns by teachers or officials. There is also an easy way of counting using the fingers of one hand, so it is possible to bargain for food or goods using this system. Sign language works very well and is much quicker than a book.

Area Information: China National Tourist Offices exist in most major international cities and provide advice for independent travelers: New York (tel.: 212-760-9700); London (tel.: 020 7935 9427); Sydney (tel.: 02 299 4057).

TIMING & SEASONALITY

 Best Months to Visit: May to late September is the best time for all areas covered, otherwise it is too cold on the high plateau. Avoid June and July in mainland China, as that is when most rain falls. Starting in May is ideal as you will hit the plateau in mid-June.

Climate: China is hot and humid with heavy showers at times. Tibet can be very hot one minute and snowing the next. Be prepared for intense sunlight at high altitude along with a very high burn factor, but also carry full waterproofs and warm clothing. Recommendations are glacier glasses and Gore-Tex

← *The friendly cosmopolitan town of Lanzhou means good food, some English spoken, a post office, and a chance to rest for a while.*

over-mitts on top of your usual cold-weather gear.

HEALTH & SAFETY

 Vaccinations: See your doctor before you travel, as you will probably need immunization against typhoid, tetanus, diphtheria, polio, hepatitis A and B, meningitis A and C, and cholera.

General Health Risks: Read up on altitude sickness, *The High Altitude Medicine Handbook* by Andrew J. Pollard and David R. Murdoch (Pilgrim), is very informative and handy to carry. Before you go, a dip through *Medicine for Mountaineering and Other Wilderness Activities* (Mountaineers Books) should prepare you well for the higher regions. You'll need to carry some Diamox and Ciprofloxin tablets. Avoid sunstroke and dehydration— carry plenty of dehydration sachets in addition to a normal first-aid kit;

watermelons are a good source of fluid. Cover up well and always wear a helmet and good sunscreen. Keep good levels of personal hygiene.

Special Considerations: None.

Politics & Religion: China experienced the Cultural Revolution so is devoid of any religious buildings. The Tibetans experienced some of the worst human rights atrocities in recent history when China occupied Tibet.

Crime Risk: Low, but try to keep your bikes in your room overnight and inside cafés and restaurants.

Food & Drink: Boiling water in lower altitudes is fine, but always use iodine in higher elevations. Ascorbic acid (vitamin C) tablets crushed and dropped into iodinated water will neutralize the effect and the taste of the iodine. Remember to time the boiling accurately to ensure it has worked, as the level of silt in the water and its

temperature have an effect on this. For instance, cold, gray water from the snout of a glacier will take twice as long to purify as water from a clear lowland stream. As for food, freshly cooked and locally grown is best: just look around the café when you go in to see what others are eating and point to that.

HIGHLIGHTS

 In Beijing try to see Mao Tse-tung preserved in his tomb and cycle across Tiananmen Square. Other highlights include meeting villagers in remote areas; climbing onto the Tibetan plateau and riding up the back of the Himalayas.

Scenic: The Great Wall of China is a handrail for the first section of this ride. The lesser-known large valleys and big panoramas of Northern China and the sheer gorge of the mighty Huang He are truly spectacular, as is the feeling of being alone in this vast land, when there are people all around.

Wildlife & Flora: The land is devoid of any flowers; as for wildlife, if an animal isn't pulling a plow or a cart, it is likely to be eaten! In Tibet there are wild camels that survive in the desert near Golmud, and plenty of yaks higher up.

↓ temperature and precipitation

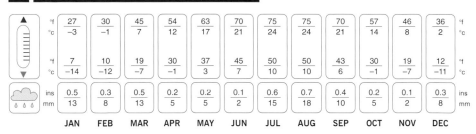

		JAN	FEB	MAR	APR	MAY	JUN	JUL	AUG	SEP	OCT	NOV	DEC	
▲	°f	27	30	45	54	63	70	75	75	70	57	46	36	°f
	°c	−3	−1	7	12	17	21	24	24	21	14	8	2	°c
▼	°f	7	10	19	30	37	45	50	50	43	30	19	12	°f
	°c	−14	−12	−7	−1	3	7	10	10	6	−1	−7	−11	°c
☁	ins	0.5	0.3	0.5	0.2	0.2	0.1	0.6	0.7	0.4	0.2	0.1	0.3	ins
	mm	13	8	13	5	5	2	15	18	10	5	2	8	mm

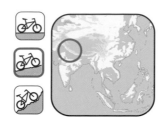

↓ **itinerary**

LEH to MANALI

LADAKH, INDIA

Jamie Carr

THE FLIGHT TO LEH IN LADAKH FROM DELHI OVER THE HIMALAYAS IS ABSOLUTELY SPECTACULAR—FANTASTIC VIEWS OF THE HIGHEST PEAKS IN THE WORLD STRETCH AWAY IN EITHER DIRECTION AND ON THE FINAL APPROACH DOWN THE LEH VALLEY, AT AROUND 13,000 FEET (4,000M), YOU ARE ONLY A FEW HUNDRED METERS ABOVE THE GROUND WITH MONASTERIES VISIBLE ON EITHER SIDE.

↑
Snow blocks the Baralacha La pass for nine months of the year, greatly reducing opportunities to make this trip.

This is a complete change to the city you have just left—Delhi in the summer heat is the closest you can get to visiting another planet, and a world apart from the clean and efficient West; good advice is to get out as quickly as possible, leaving the sights until later.

In Leh, orderly lines of taxis wait patiently to take you to whichever hotel you want—at a fixed price! Leh is the capital of Ladakh, high up in the northern Indian part of the Himalayas. At 12,000 feet (3,660m) some serious acclimatization is necessary before heading down to cross high passes and make some big descents. You will see the valleys change as you descend from an arid desert, past snow banks, and eventually into a lush, tropical Manali.

•DAYS 1–3   Variable distance

Around Leh

Once settled in your hotel in Leh take it easy: rest and hydration are the best ways to acclimatize. Be aware of how each member of your group is adjusting. Altitude sickness can affect you at any time and everyone is different. If sensible precautions are followed, you won't be affected. If necessary, you can call 560 in Leh for 24-hour medical help.

During the first few days in India gently take in the sights of Leh old town, sample a few of the many restaurants, and make some short rides around the environs.

A ride along the valley to Shey Monastery and on to Thikse, an even more impressive monastery, is a good distance to start with. A day rafting on the Indus or Zanskar river is also easy to arrange and a wonderful experience.

A more challenging ride after a couple of days is to visit Stok village, its gompa and old palace/museum. Return off-road, but beware of punctures, as off-road shortcuts are littered with thorny plants. Join the main road near the airport for a slow uphill back to Leh.

If you have time you may want to arrange a permit and a jeep to take you toward the restricted area of the Nuru Valley on the other side of the Khardong La (18,380 feet/5,600m). You need a police permit, but once you're past the checkpost they don't mind you riding the last 2,890 feet (880m), which can take some three hours! The sign at the top reads "THE HIGHEST ROAD PASS IN THE WORLD" (17,650 feet/5,380m), and it certainly feels like it. Dizziness and headaches will probably greet you; luckily, from there, there is only one way to go, and that's down!

After a couple of switchbacks you feel much better, as you quickly lose height on the wide jeep track you've just climbed. Soon after that, it's possible to start using the shortcuts between the loops (remember to spot them as you climb up). This stretch takes you down some of the highest, hardest single-track you're ever likely to encounter! A rock-strewn path will drop you over 6,500 feet (2,000m) of

all-out, arm-numbing, bone-shaking descent. (Good front shocks are a must; full suspension would be even better.) Eventually a wide, fast track leads you into Chaspa village and then Leh itself.

Other good options around Leh include driving out to Fotia La on the Srinagar road, and riding back from there after lunching in the monastery village of Lamyarum. You could ride to Walla village, continue to Alchi, stay overnight there, and return the next day.

Also, the area high above Tak-Tok monastery toward the Wari La makes for excellent mountain biking. It is best to get a jeep to drop you as high as it will go. Descend from here and then ride up to Hemis on the opposite side of this valley or back down the left side of the Indus to the bridge at Choklamgsar. From here, get a jeep back to Leh.

•DAYS 4–6 110 miles (178km)

Leh, via Tanggula La, to Pang

Pack up and leave Leh for a relatively short day after the Khardong La ride. Descend out of town and take the main highway to Manali until you reach the town of Choklamsar. Just after the main town, turn right and cross over the Indus and ride up the left bank on a much quieter road along the valley for 14 miles (23km). Remember to take plenty of water and sunscreen, as there is little shade on this side. Shey and Thikse, two impressive monasteries, are on the other side of the river. A 2½-mile (5-km) climb up to Hemis Monastery, one of the biggest and most important monasteries in Ladakh, reminds you how high you are. In the afternoon, look around and relax in the grounds; you can camp inside or out.

Torn and faded prayer flags are seen everywhere on the ride down to Manali.

→

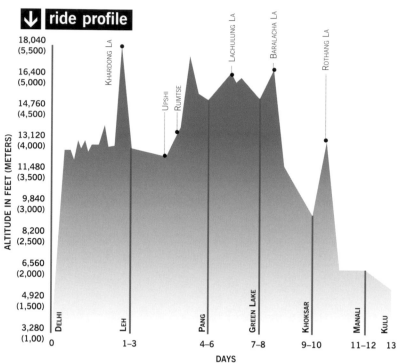

↓ **ride profile**

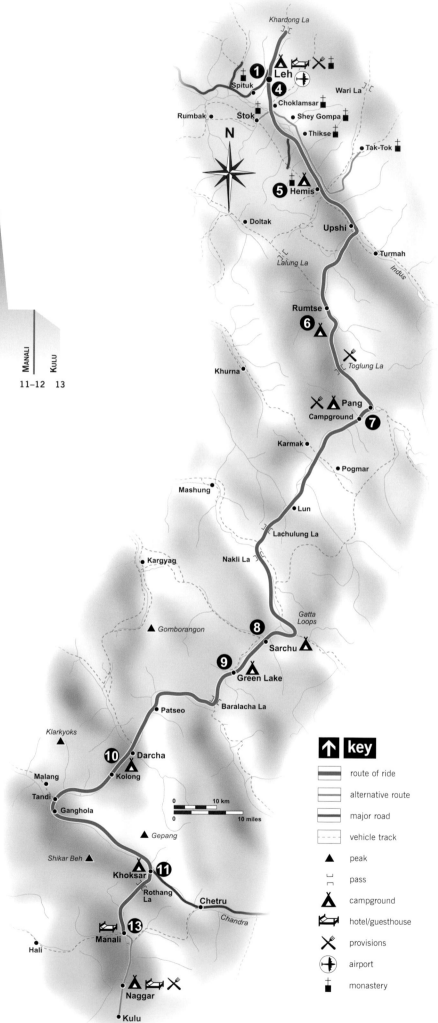

↑ **key**

	route of ride
	alternative route
	major road
	vehicle track
▲	peak
⊓	pass
⛺	campground
🛏	hotel/guesthouse
✕	provisions
✈	airport
✠	monastery

The next day is up the last bit of the valley to the check-point at the junction of the road at Upshi. Mount Kailash in Tibet, the source of the Indus, lies just ahead but this area is restricted; you turn right here and travel along a contributing valley toward the second highest pass in the world. There's a great campground 5 miles (8km) beyond Rumtse at 15,300 feet (4,670m) at the base of the pass.

From here, the road starts climbing in earnest and many switchbacks make the gradient a manageable 14 miles (22km) to the summit. There are always road gangs along the way rebuilding the road to keep it open and in good condition. At the summit there will be lots of food stalls and marveling bus tourists. It's 40 miles (65km) from here to Pang and no water in between, so get what you can before you leave. Fast and short descents drop you onto a weird landscape called the Moray Plains. Try to cross the plains behind your fittest pal, as there are often headwinds here in the afternoon. Just before you drop off the edge of the plains, take in the wonderful landscape across the valley, which opens up before you like a mini Grand Canyon. Descend to Pang, a small teahouse-tented village, for refreshments. If you're exhausted you can stop here, but there is a beautiful camping spot 5 miles (8km) further down the road, just below the third bridge, in a wonderful gorge by a lovely little river, still at around 14,700 feet (4,500m).

sometimes covered in ice if you're early in the season, or water if you're later. Banks of snow are near the top and you may have to carry your bike for a short section through deep snow, past snowplows stuck fast waiting for the snow to thaw. From the top, there is a 50-mile (80-km) descent down the main valley with a few small climbs. However, below this pass the road can be in a terrible condition as this side gets the worst of the rainfall, and at Darcha the bridge near the confluence is often damaged or washed away as another valley joins here. Darcha has a few guesthouses but they are not too nice, so it's better to stay in the Ibex Hotel in Jespa or at a pleasant camp nearby at a seemingly rich, oxygen-filled altitude of 11,000 feet (3,400m).

Day 10 is more downhill with a few climbs to the junction of two rivers at Tandi and then a surreal trip through an alpine-looking valley to ride up the Spiti River toward Khoksar; you could almost believe you were in Switzerland. However, the road is often rough and the presence of Tata trucks tells you you're still in India and close to civilization. Camp near the town of Khoksar in view of the Rothang La. →

•DAYS 7–8   65 miles (104km)

Pang to Green Lake

Another amazing day, one of the best on this route. There is a lovely ride through the gorge, with the road clinging to the side of the valley (it becomes apparent just how hard it must have been to build a road here), then it opens out again to show the way onward. There's another long gentle climb before a few switchbacks brings you to the summit of Lachulung La. There's a short descent (with a couple of decent shortcuts) to a small bridge with flowing water; this is a good lunch spot before another climb around a corner to Nakli La at 16,000 feet (4,870m), your second Himalayan pass of the day. After a short descent, you suddenly reach the Gatta Loops and, without any climbing, begin a 21-loop descent down the very steep valley side. There are a few steep and loose shortcuts for the foolhardy, but they're not recommended if you have luggage on your bike. In Sarchu there are a couple of checkposts and many tented overnight camps. Keep going along the valley on Day 8, to reach the Green Lake at the base of the last big pass.

A worthwhile side trip from Leh while acclimatizing is to the Stok Valley; the rugged landscape is mesmerizing.

The final descent into Manali is a smooth, fast ride—an exhilarating end to two weeks of fantastic biking.

•DAYS 9–10   99 miles (160km)

Green Lake to Khoksar

A 10-mile (16-km) windy road takes you up the Baralacha La, the last big pass and the main watershed for the monsoon rains of the tropical weather. Hence the road is

•DAYS 11–12　71 miles (114km)

Khoksar, via the Rothang La, to Manali

The tarmac climb to only 13,000 feet (3,990m) is relatively easy compared to the heights you've already covered, but the 12½ miles (20km) to the summit take an age, because the road is full of switchbacks and the gradient is easy. Once at the top you will feel supercharged. Here, you will meet Indian tourists who've come to see snow for the first time in their lives!

There's smooth tarmac now for about 32 miles (52km), and it's a 6,600-foot (2,000-m) downhill all the way to Manali. Be wary of the increase in traffic now with private jeeps, taxis, and mopeds all heading toward the snow. There are lush trees and bushes and it's really warm—no need for the big mittens and fleece, but keep your rain jacket handy, as you will descend into cloud and rain if the monsoon has not finished.

Once you cross the bridge into Manali you really have hit civilization. There is no need for tents now, since there are hotels for every budget and restaurants for every taste. A couple of nights are a must, even if just to get over the celebrations of finishing such an epic route over the Himalayas. The day off can be spent either shopping or cycling up (you could take a taxi) 3 miles (5km) to Vashist village to relax in the hot springs there—the communal one is free, and there's a covered one for women only, or you can hire a private, tiled, clean one nearby.

•DAY 13　28 miles (45km)

Alternative finish: Manali to Kulu

Depending on how much time you have and how little you fancy a long ride in a bus, you can spend another day riding down the other side of the Bias River to cover an easy ride to Kulu. Here, you can buy the famous Kulu shawl made from smooth soft yak hair (every grandmother loves them). Visit Nagar's wooden castle and even an art gallery en route. From here it's best to pack the bikes in boxes and prepare for the long journey back.

 factfile

↑
The descent from the Khardong La back to Leh involves 21 miles of off-roading.

OVERVIEW

The entire trip is ridable in 10 days and covers approximately 500 miles (805km) on mostly wide tracks and roads. However, if you have van support, there are plenty of off-road short-cuts between the switchbacks, which can be made at your discretion to make the descents much more technical.

Start: Leh, Ladakh.
Finish: Manali.

ABOUT THE TRAIL

The route is mainly on broken tarmac roads. There is dirt at the top of all the passes, and optional single-track

on the descents between switch-backs. The whole trail is ridable with a mountain bike with panniers or a trailer.

Major Climbs & Descents: This ride is full of them. It is best to start from Leh and ride down, so there are more descents than climbs by nearly 6,600 feet (2,000m). There are five climbs and six major descents along the way. The highest point you cycle to is 18,380 feet (5,600m).

Difficulty & Special Features: This is one of only three roads that cross the Himalayas and the only road within one country. It also claims to have the highest road passes in the world—the

Khardong La and Tanggula La. The main difficulty is the altitude, the actual riding is not so difficult. Read up on altitude sickness and never run out of water. However, if you follow adequate precautions and are with a reliable tour company, the guide will take care of any complications that may arise. With adequate time spent acclimatizing and a degree of determination, most reasonably fit mountain bikers can complete the route. Van/bus support is useful if you feel tired one day. Carry a few bike spares, a spare folding tire, spare spokes, brake blocks, and tubes, with a basic tool kit and bottle of oil.

ACCESS

Airports: Fly into New Delhi International Airport, and then take an internal flight to Leh. A flight to Leh on India Airlines must be booked well in advance.

Transport: Taxis are willing to carry you and your bike, at a small extra charge of course, around Delhi.

Passport & Visa Requirements: All foreign nationals need to arrange a visa from a consulate in their home country.

Permits & Access Restrictions: You will need a permit if you decide to go to the restricted area of the Nuru Valley on the other side of the Khardong La (see "Day 1" above).

LOCAL INFORMATION

Maps: There are very few junctions on this route, therefore a local map bought in Leh should be good enough.

Guidebooks: *Leh & Trekking in Ladakh* by Charlie Loram (Trailblazer Publications) is very useful for details of getting about Delhi, as well as providing all the information you'll need in Leh and places to stay in Manali as well. Cordée produce good guidebooks with maps for India and Nepal.

Accommodation & Supplies: Delhi has plenty of accommodation, as do Leh and Manali. However, in between there is not much to rely on. Taking a tent and a stove will assure you of many comfortable nights along the way. Leh has a few shops and local markets, but if you fly there before the road has opened there will be shortages of luxury food, and sometimes even vegetables, flour, and eggs.

Currency & Language: The Indian rupee is made up of 100 paisa. In Ladakh you can change cash and travelers' checks. There are many dialects of Hindi in India, and in Leh Ladakhi is spoken. The best

phrasebook for this is *Getting Started in Ladakhi* by Rebecca Norman. The Lonely Planet phrasebook for *Hindu/Urdu* is useful for all other areas. However, English is the most spoken language in India, and it is possible to get by with simple English conversations and some simple Ladakhi.

Photography: Be very courteous when taking photos of any Ladakhi people and ask them first. Carry plenty of film, and underexpose by a half to one stop on an SLR or just tell it a higher ISO rate than you are using.

Area Information: Rimo Expeditions in Delhi (tel.: 689-8734; e-mail: rimo@vsnl.com) can arrange a customized itinerary for small groups and provide all backup support. If you want the assurance of an experienced Western mountain bike guide, contact KE Adventure Travel (tel.: 1-800-497-9675 U.S.A. toll free; 017687 73966 in the U.K.).

Websites: www.atrav.com/rimo; www.keadventure.com

TIMING & SEASONALITY

Best Months to Visit: Snow closes the road for most of the year. Each year varies, but the road to India is rarely closed after late June and usually remains open until mid-September and sometimes into October.

Climate: Dry, sunny, and arid in Ladakh; but it can be very hot one minute and snowing the next. Be prepared for intense sunlight at high altitude, along with a high burn factor. Carry waterproofs, as you'll need them when crossing the high passes. Recommendations are good sunglasses, a thin hat

→ *If the weather is fine, clouds will sweep by above the Maria Plains, which you reach just before the Gatta Loops.*

for under your helmet, and full gloves on top of your usual cool-weather gear.

HEALTH & SAFETY

Vaccinations: See your doctor at least 3 months before you travel. The following are recommended: typhoid, tetanus, diphtheria, polio, hepatitis A and B, meningitis A and C, and cholera.

General Health Risks: Read up on altitude sickness. *The High Altitude Medicine Handbook*, by Andrew J. Pollard and David R. Murdoch (Pilgrim) is very informative and handy to carry. Also, before you go, a dip into *Medicine for Mountaineering & Other Wilderness Activities* (Mountaineers Books) would be useful. These should prepare you well for the higher regions. General advice is to avoid sunstroke and dehydration. Carry Diamox and Ciprofloxin as well as plenty of

dehydration sachets. Cover up from the sun; wear a helmet and good sunscreen; and try to keep good levels of personal hygiene.

Special Considerations: None.

Politics & Religion: Ladakh is often referred to as Little Tibet, as the Buddhist influence is easy to see in the many gompas and monasteries in the valley. There are also quite a few Muslims in Leh, and you may well be woken at 4:00 A.M. by the mosque's call to prayer. Once out of Leh, toward Manali, Hindu is the predominant religion. There is political unrest in nearby Kashmir, but this doesn't really affect Ladakh.

Crime Risk: Low.

Food & Drink: Boiling water at lower altitudes is fine, but always use iodine in higher elevations. Ascorbic acid (vitamin C) tablets crushed and dropped into iodinated water will neutralize the taste of the iodine and prevent a residue

building up in your liver if you use it a lot. As for food, freshly cooked and locally grown is best—just look around the café when you go in, see what others are eating, and point to that.

HIGHLIGHTS

Scenic: The whole ride is scenic from take-off in Delhi, around Leh, and all the way back to Manali over the Himalayas on the highest road in the world—an unforgettable experience. The influence of Buddhist culture—temples, prayer flags, and monasteries—is inescapable.

Wildlife & Flora: There are a few yaks still hard at work in Ladakh, though not much else in the way of wildlife. At high altitude only the hardiest plants can survive the winters, so vegetation is sparse. However, the lushness of the Manali Valley and Spiti Valley make up for the barren flora higher up.

↓ temperature and precipitation

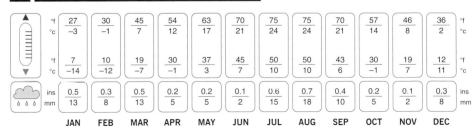

	JAN	FEB	MAR	APR	MAY	JUN	JUL	AUG	SEP	OCT	NOV	DEC
°f	27	30	45	54	63	70	75	75	70	57	46	36
°c	−3	−1	7	12	17	21	24	24	21	14	8	2
°f	7	10	19	30	37	45	50	50	43	30	19	12
°c	−14	−12	−7	−1	3	7	10	10	6	−1	7	11
ins	0.5	0.3	0.5	0.2	0.2	0.1	0.6	0.7	0.4	0.2	0.1	0.3
mm	13	8	13	5	5	2	15	18	10	5	2	8

Africa & the Middle East

Heat and dust, civilization and culture. In Africa, journeys across Ethiopia's Afro-alpine moorlands, over the peaks of Malawi, and through the Drakensberg range of South Africa deliver surprises that defy conventional thinking about the continent. To Africa's north, the Middle East is off the beaten mountain bike track, but Israel and Lebanon not only possess great beauty and history, but are easy to discover at pedaling pace.

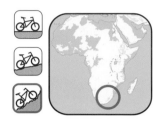

↓ itinerary

RIDING the DRAKENSBERG

SOUTH AFRICA

Johan Coetzee

RIDING YOUR BIKE IN PLACES WHERE MERE MORTALS MAY NEVER TREAD IS A PRIVILEGE ONLY TRUE MOUNTAIN BIKERS WILL EXPERIENCE. BUT TO FEEL AS IF YOU ARE RIDING ON TOP OF THE WORLD IS ONLY POSSIBLE FOR THOSE WHO ARE WILLING TO EXPERIENCE SOME HARD CLIMBS AND A LACK OF OXYGEN.

However, these seem minor conditions once you witness the wonder of creation unfolding before you in the Drakensberg, South Africa's highest and most awesome mountain range. Drakensberg is the Afrikaans word for "Dragon Mountains," and originated from the trekkers who moved inland a few hundred years ago and described this mountain range as looking just like the scales on the back of a huge slumbering dragon.

Beautiful sandstone rock formations surround you for almost the entire journey.

•DAYS 1–3 128 miles (205km)

Lady Grey to Mountain Shadows Hotel

The ride starts in the small, picturesque town of Lady Grey that nestles in the foothills of the Wittenberge (White Mountains). The town was founded in 1858 and named after the wife of Sir George Grey, the then governor of the Cape Colony.

A grueling climb up Joubert's Pass is repaid aplenty by the stunning view at the top. A good gravel track then winds up and down for 25 miles (40km) before reaching a tarmac road. A few miles along this, back toward Lady Grey, takes you to a turning onto a gravel track toward Dordrecht. From Clanville, a "town" with about three buildings, head toward Rossouw, but after some 13 miles (21km) turn left toward Barkly East, arguably the coldest town in South Africa.

A few hard climbs lie ahead. At Clifford, also just two or three buildings, turn right toward Elliot and the Otto du Plessis Pass. The road ascends slowly and you cross the Saalboom river several times; the river's crystal clear and ice cold water is safe to drink and an excellent remedy for aching legs and tired bodies.

At last the top of the Otto du Plessis Pass is reached, and an awesome view of the flowing grass hills at the foot of the Drakensberg is before you. Now, a serious downhill, down one of the steepest passes in South Africa, means speeds of up to 50 miles (80km) an hour. Riding on the edge at top speed should satisfy all adrenaline junkies.

The road meanders through the grass foothills of the Drakensberg. About 6 miles (9.5km) from the pass turn left toward Elliot and after innumerable ups and downs you reach the tarmac road again; this takes you along a few miles of "soft riding" to reach Elliot. This town was founded in 1885 and named after Sir Henry Elliot, a major in the British Navy who became a renowned peacemaker between the fighting Xhosa tribes in the region. The town is known for its cattle, sheep, and mushrooms. Indeed, the Xhosa name for Elliot is *eCowa*—mushroom.

Now you turn back on the tarmac road toward Barkly East and the Drakensberg. The breathtaking view of strange sandstone formations shooting bizarrely into the air awaits

you as you ascend the Barkly Pass and grind your way to the top. Just over the top of the pass, stop at the Mountain Shadows Hotel for a beer and a bed.

•DAYS 4–5 106 miles (170km)

Mountain Shadows Hotel to Maclear

Start off on a gravel road toward Sterkspruit and Rhodes. This track twists alongside the Sterkspruit river before reaching the Kraai river. Cross the bridge over the Kraai river, and turn right after a short climb. After a seemingly endless up-and-down road you will reach the small town of Rhodes. This town was originally named Rossville, but the locals later approached Cecil John Rhodes, then prime minister of the Cape Colony, for a donation toward development in return for naming the town after him. He complied and sent them a few small umbrella-pine trees. These trees have since grown into massive trees all along the main street of the town.

Follow a winding gravel road toward Naudesnek Pass, the highest vehicle pass in South Africa, past a few farmhouses that nestle in the beautiful slopes and valleys of the Drakensberg. Suddenly the pass is upon you—a long, hard slog for 9 miles (15km). By the time you get to the top you'll probably feel exhausted, because, at 8,990 feet (2,740m), the air is quite thin, but the view is just unbelievable; on a clear day you can see the Indian Ocean, some 156 miles (250km) to the east.

Again, it's downhill time and for most of the remaining 38 miles (60km) to Maclear the road descends along small river streams and beautiful valleys. The town was founded in 1876 as a military border post and named in 1881 after Sir Thomas Maclear, the royal astronomer stationed in the Cape Colony from 1834 to 1870. The town and surrounding area are known for their cattle farming and dairy products and the small streams and rivers are a fly fisherman's dream. Stay at the Royal Hotel.

→

→

You will cross the cool, clear waters of the Saalboom River several times on the first few days of this trail.

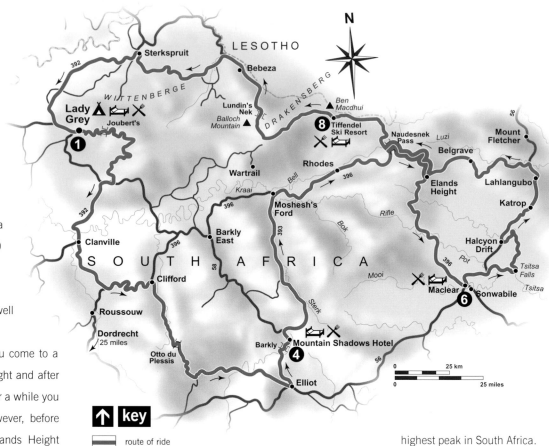

Maclear to Tiffendel Ski Resort

Continue along the gravel road to Mount Fletcher. Some 6 miles (9.5km) out of Maclear, turn right onto the road that leads to the Tsitsa Falls, a waterfall with a 100-foot (30-m) drop. The beauty of this waterfall is a small footpath that leads in behind a curtain of water; this will get you wet, so you might as well take a dip in the refreshing pool below.

Now it's back onto the same road until you come to a fork in the path at a farmhouse. There, turn right and after another mile (1.5km) or so turn left again. After a while you will join a track toward Mount Fletcher. However, before reaching Mount Fletcher, turn left toward Elands Height and the Drakensberg. Slowly grind your way up into the mountains again until you reach a junction where you turn right. What lies ahead is Naudesnek Pass, this time from the other side. At the top of Naudesnek, turn right and follow a jeep track. This is the route used for the annual Rhodes Mountain Bike Challenge, South Africa's premier mountain bike race. The air gets thinner as you ascend to an altitude of about 8,960 feet (2,730m) at Lesotho's View on the slopes of Ben Macdhui (10,000 feet/3,050m), the highest peak in South Africa.

On one of the plateaux is the only ski resort in South Africa, Tiffendel, where you can get refreshments and spend the night.

Tiffendel Ski Resort to Lady Grey

Back on track after a refreshing stay at the ski resort, keep following the jeep track from the resort. It's worth spending some time at the top of the mountains before an awesome descent into another beautiful valley. Ride along the Funny Stone Stream past a few farmhouses until you reach a road at Balloch Mountain, here turn right toward Lundin's Nek.

The road now winds its way up into the mountains and down into the valleys, but, all along, the splendid view is just unbelievable. Cruise along the border of Lesotho past a few "towns" before turning off to the left and following the snaking gravel track toward Sterkspruit.

Unfortunately, the route now runs out of gravel and from Sterkspruit to Lady Grey the ride is on tarmac. Maybe it's a blessing in disguise, because, after more than a week on the bike and riding one of the most grueling treks in Africa, your body may well be tired and aching. Reaching Lady Grey again means that an epic ride in the Drakensberg, the highest mountain range in South Africa, has been conquered. You will have seen great natural beauty and ridden in places where others may never tread.

key

- route of ride
- major road
- minor road
- country border
- administrative border
- ▲ peak
- ⊔ pass
- ▲ campground
- hotel/guesthouse
- ✗ provisions

ride profile

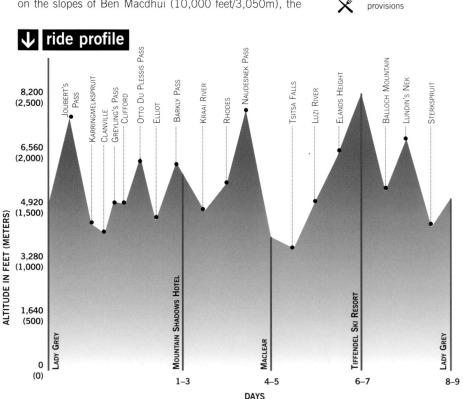

factfile

The awesome "scales of the slumbering dragon" near the Otto du Plessis Pass. A section of single-track is just visible against the backdrop of the steep incline of the mountain.

OVERVIEW

 This route is in a part of South Africa that is a paradise for hikers, fly fishermen, birdwatchers, four-wheel-drive enthusiasts, and mountain bikers. The crisp, clear mountain air and water will add to a memorable journey of some 440 miles (705km) in 9 days; but best of all are the unbelievable views that cover almost the entire distance.

Start/Finish: Lady Grey.

ABOUT THE TRAIL

About 8 percent of the route is on jeep track and 12 percent is on tarmac, while the remaining 80 percent is on fairly good gravel track.

Major Climbs & Descents: The route's low point of 3,753 feet (1,144m) is at Clanville while the highest point is at Lesotho's View on Ben Macdhui at 8,960 feet (2,730m). Joubert's Pass is at 7,707 feet (2,349m) and Lundin's Nek Pass is 7,304 feet (2,226m). The best climb is Otto du Plessis Pass at 6,900 feet (2,301m). The biggest climb is Naudesnek Pass, which has to be ascended twice.

Difficulty & Special Features: An individual carrying a full complement of camping and cooking gear will be able to tackle the route without any fear, while a fit rider will be able to ride the entire distance without once getting off the bike to push it. The route was designed to include drivable roads for four-wheel-drives, but there are numerous river and stream crossings. As 65 percent of the route is in the mountains, it will certainly present both a physical and mental challenge.

ACCESS

Airports: The nearest major airport is Bloemfontein Airport, some 156 miles (250km) from Lady Grey, while the nearest international airport is in Johannesburg, some 420 miles (675km) from Lady Grey.

Transport: Public transport is available from Johannesburg and Bloemfontein to Aliwal North, some 31 miles (50km) from Lady Grey. The best option, however, is to rent a car at the airport and drive to Lady Grey.

Passport & Visa Requirements: Citizens from the U.S., Europe, or Australia and New Zealand do not need visas to enter South Africa; passports will be sufficient.

Permits & Access Restrictions: The entire route is either on public land or on public-accessible roads that cross private property. No permits are needed.

LOCAL INFORMATION

Maps: Detailed navigational maps of the area, that include information on supplemental maps from the Automobile Association of South Africa, are available through Mountain Bike South Africa (MTBSA), P.O. Box 2289, Bloemfontein, 9300, Republic of South Africa (tel.: 012 7744838; fax: 051 4464127; e-mail: johanc@mtbsa.co.za).

Guidebooks: Mountain Bike South Africa is currently working on an extensive guide to all mountain bike trails in South Africa; however, a smaller and compact version is available now.

Accommodation & Supplies: This ride can be done as a camping trip, a trip with a backup vehicle accompanying the riders, or one that makes use of hotels and guesthouses. Most of the private farmers will be more than willing to provide a place to stay overnight if the group is not too large. There are grocery stores and other services available in Lady Grey, Elliot, and Maclear. Along the way there are a few small private stores that have the bare necessities.

Currency & Language: Rand; Afrikaans, English, Xhosa, and Southern Sesotho.

Area Information: Highlands Tourist & Information Centre, P.O. Box 138, Barkly East, 9786 (tel.: 082 8926998; fax: 045 9710722; e-mail: dave@lesoff.co.za). Mountain Bike South Africa plan to run organized tours in the future.

Website: www.mtbsa.co.za

TIMING & SEASONALITY

 Best Months to Visit: November to February.

Climate: Almost any type of weather imaginable is possible along this route. As this area is in the summer rainfall area, one can expect a rainstorm at least once a week even during the best months. Wind is also common, but usually the weather will be quite pleasant. It is, however, advisable not to ride this route during the winter months, because the extreme cold and snow make the roads inaccessible.

HEALTH & SAFETY

 Vaccinations: None required.

General Health Risks: Extreme weather conditions will certainly pose some health problems, but most of the time it is very pleasant to ride during the summer months.

Special Considerations: Beware of snakes, as some of the deadliest ones are common to this area.

Politics & Religion: Despite the the end of apartheid rule in 1991, tensions still exist between the African and Afrikaaner communities.

Crime Risk: Low, but beware of muggers in the towns. The only stretch in which you should be cautious of the locals is between Lundin's Nek and Sterkspruit; the people are usually very friendly, but a few can be aggressive.

Food & Drink: Water from the streams in the mountains is safe to drink.

HIGHLIGHTS

Scenic: There are amazing panoramic views from the top of each pass; the town of Rhodes is an official national monument; and there are fantastic rock formations in and around the town of Elliot.

Wildlife & Flora: Three types of flora dominate the area. First, there are the flowing grass fields covering most of the area. Then there are the protea-like bushes and a variety of indigenous and foreign trees in the valleys and ravines. The third type, alpine heath, can be found only in the highest parts of the mountains. Small wild animals are in abundance. One of the world's most impressive mountain hunters, the black eagle, is an unforgettable sight if you manage to spot it either gliding about or playing with another in the air.

temperature and precipitation

		JAN	FEB	MAR	APR	MAY	JUN	JUL	AUG	SEP	OCT	NOV	DEC	
	°f	86	82	79	72	66	60	61	66	73	77	81	84	°f
	°c	30	28	26	22	19	16	16	19	23	25	27	29	°c
	°f	51	49	45	37	27	20	20	24	32	39	40	48	°f
	°c	10	10	7	3	−3	−7	−7	−5	0	4	5	9	°c
	ins	3.0	4.0	3.5	2.8	1.4	1.0	1.0	1.9	2.0	2.9	3.3	2.4	ins
	mm	76	102	89	70	35	26	26	47	52	73	84	62	mm

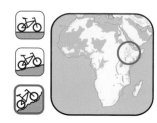

the ROOF of AFRICA

ETHIOPIA

Chris Ford

ETHIOPIA IS NOT WHAT MANY PEOPLE IMAGINE—WHERE YOU EXPECT TO FIND AN IMPOVERISHED NATION, YOU SEE A PEOPLE FULL OF PRIDE IN THEIR COUNTRY AND THEIR LONG AND COLORFUL HISTORY; YOU MIGHT EXPECT TO SEE DUSTY PLAINS, YET THE ETHIOPIAN PLATEAU IS THE LARGEST MOUNTAIN RANGE IN AFRICA, AND CONTAINS THE HIGHEST PEAK ON THE CONTINENT, NORTH OF THE EQUATOR. THIS IS A LAND FULL OF SURPRISES, AND THE WARM WELCOME YOU RECEIVE WILL MAKE YOU WANT TO EXPLORE IT.

This tour explores some of the greatest landscapes of North Africa. These include the rich variety of the Bale Mountains National Park, with its unique Afro-alpine moorlands, pristine forests, and rare species such as the Ethiopian wolf, Menelik's bushbuck, and the grand Mountain Nyala. Far below is the Rift Valley, with its volcanic formations, lush open fields, and bustling traditional villages. The dramatic biking takes in all of these sights, and includes the spectacular ride to the 14,000-foot (4,307-m) peak of Tullu Deemtu.

itinerary

•DAYS 1–2 110 miles (175km)

Addis Ababa to Asela

The first two days of the ride are a great warm-up, and take you through the northernmost reaches of the great African Rift Valley. This is fertile land and every plot is cultivated, with oxen plowing the fields as you roll past. You'll also see herds of camels being driven by their nomadic owners, the Oromo, and donkeys heavily laden with sacks of teff—the staple diet of Ethiopians. At Sodore, one of Ethiopia's hot-springs resorts, steaming water is tapped straight from the mountains to provide a great "al fresco" power shower at the end of your first day.

The route continues to follow tar roads up to Asela, and does not begin to climb the edges of the Rift Valley until the last 12 miles (20km), and gently even then.

•DAYS 3–4 164 miles (264km)

Asela to Goba

Leaving Asela, the road turns to gravel, and that's the last you'll see of a good surface for a long time. That's also the end of the warm-up, as today contains the first major climb—over the shoulder of 13,700-foot (4,180-m) Mount Kaka. The rich, grassy plains are dotted with small villages, with a great expanse of tilled fields stretching out to the rolling peaks. At Meraro, at 11,000 feet (3,400m), your work is done, and you can begin the long, steady descent to the Wabi Shebele river, 24 miles (38km) away.

After crossing the river, turn up the valley to Dodola; this is a good place to spend the night before heading on to the real mountains—the Bale Mountains. Dodola is a great place to mix with the locals. You'll possibly be the only cyclists they've seen for at least a year, and they'll have plenty of questions to ask you.

From Dodola, the going is level, as you ride the gravel road toward the base of the mountains. Then begins the steep climb up to the first ridge at 12,800 feet (3,900m), where the National Park begins. The scenery is totally

Riding into the Bale Mountains is like entering another world, far removed from anything you are likely to have seen before.

The descent from the peak of Tullu Deemtu is fast and exhilarating.

different now, you ride through juniper and hagenia woodlands, the light undergrowth allowing you to spot some of the wildlife. This is the Gaysay region, well known by nature lovers as the home of two of Ethiopia's most spectacular endemic mammals—Menelik's bushbuck, characterized by its deep chestnut-red color; and the Mountain Nyala, with its striking black and white markings, great size, and long horns.

Gaysay ends at the village of Dinsho, where the park headquarters is located. You have to visit here to pay your fees, but don't tell them you're cycling over the Sanetti Plateau as they sometimes insist on sending an "official guide" to make a bit of extra money. Riding on to Goba, you'll notice that the people here are very different, with a

tough but welcoming air, which comes from surviving the harsh conditions of the mountains.

Goba is the only town in Bale, but even then it has no more than a few hundred inhabitants. However, it does have one luxury that you'll be yearning for after two nights of basic village rest houses—the Wabi Shebele Hotel. Here, you can enjoy a traditional Ethiopian feast, with thick teff pancakes (known as *injera*) the size of your bike wheel and a huge variety of mild and spiced meat and vegetables to eat with them (known as *wat*, and spooned into the center of the *injera*). You have to use your hands, of course.

Goba is a good place for a rest day—if you feel the need—since, after this, you've got your toughest climb and really remote, wilderness biking.

•DAY 5 | 68 miles (110km)

Goba to Mena

Your challenge today is the third-highest peak in North Africa—Tullu Deemtu, at about 14,000 feet (4,307m)—which can be reached by a small dirt road from Goba. This is an opportunity for some amazing views over the Bale region, and a world-class downhill on the other side.

You climb out of Goba to the Sanetti Plateau, an area covered with bright alpine heathers and giant lobelias, peculiar-looking plants that only inhabit these rare Afro-alpine landscapes. Nowhere has such an abundance or variety of high-altitude plant life as the Bale Mountains National Park; this is also the place to see the world's rarest canid, the Ethiopian wolf.

Even the fittest riders will find the dirt trail across the Sanetti Plateau tiring in the thin air, so an early start is necessary if you want to make it down the other side before dark. As you descend the endless switchbacks you enter thick, untouched forests, and emerge onto the grassy flats of Mena.

•DAYS 6–9 | 230 miles (371km)

Mena to Wendo

The dirt road to Mena goes into some of the most remote wilderness you can find in southern Ethiopia. Winding

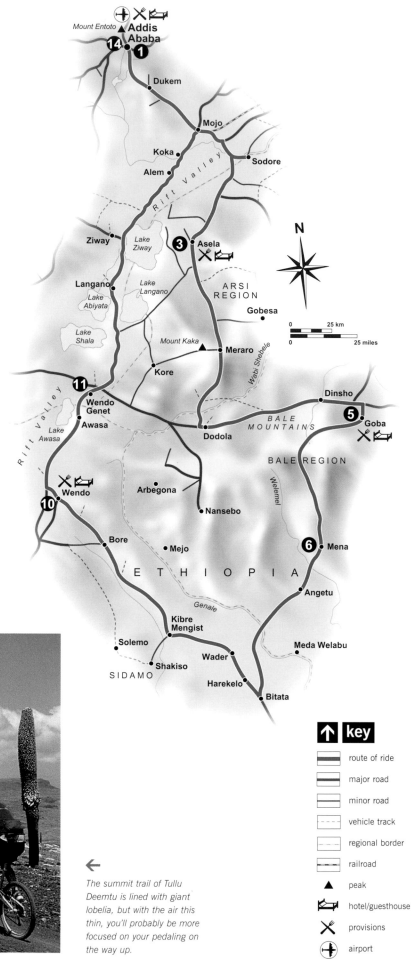

← *The summit trail of Tullu Deemtu is lined with giant lobelia, but with the air this thin, you'll probably be more focused on your pedaling on the way up.*

↑ key

▬▬	route of ride
	major road
	minor road
-----	vehicle track
	regional border
	railroad
▲	peak
🛏	hotel/guesthouse
✕	provisions
✈	airport

The Sanetti Plateau is covered in rare and beautiful heathers, which create a blur of color as you blast past.

southward, through tiny farming villages, you may well be the first non-Ethiopian seen by many of the children. The road crosses the Welemel and Genale rivers on its way to Bitata, where you finally join a busier route with a few more medium-sized villages along the way. Along the roadside you'll again see heavy cultivation, and the ingenious locals grow thick hedges of prickly cacti around their fields to keep the roaming goats away from precious crops.

•DAY 10 | 50 miles (80km)

Wendo to Wendo Genet

An hour on from Wendo and a tar road is reached once again, one of the main arteries joining Ethiopia to Kenya. Despite this, it's a quiet route, and brings you up through the Rift Valley into some breathtaking scenery.

Today, you'll wind through lush plantations of bananas and thick groves of tropical fruits, as well as acres of dark-green coffee fields. Coffee is Ethiopia's most important crop, and the country is among the world's biggest coffee exporters. During the U.K.'s recession in the 1970s, Ethiopia sent food aid in the form of tons of coffee; few people realize that aid flowed in that direction too!

Wendo Genet is another beautiful hot-springs resort, set in a forested grove on the edge of steep, untouched hills. You'll see the rare and serene colobus monkey swing →

The lush, grassy, flat ride to Mena is a welcome end to Day 5, during which you will have crossed the high Sanetti Plateau.

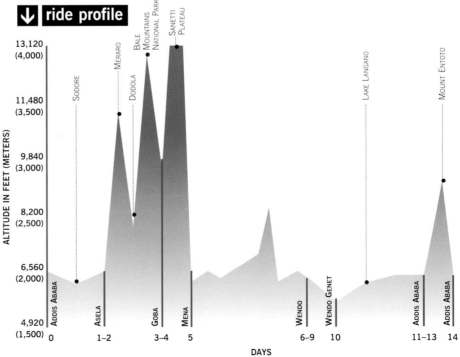

↓ ride profile

ALTITUDE IN FEET (METERS)

13,120 (4,000)
11,480 (3,500)
9,840 (3,000)
8,200 (2,500)
6,560 (2,000)
4,920 (1,500)

Labels: ADDIS ABABA, SODORE, MERARO, DODOLA, BALE MOUNTAINS NATIONAL PARK, SANETTI PLATEAU, LAKE LANGANO, MOUNT ENTOTO, ASELA, GOBA, MENA, WENDO, WENDO GENET, ADDIS ABABA, ADDIS ABABA

DAYS: 0   1–2   3–4   5   6–9   10   11–13   14

As you descend out of the mountains, you enter into rolling hills and lush valleys— an environment that is totally unexpected by most visitors to Ethiopia.

through the trees above you as you relax in the hot, therapeutic waters. There is another Wabi Shebele hotel here, providing a well-earned bit of luxury.

•DAYS 11–13 142 miles (229km)

Wendo Genet to Addis Ababa

Leaving Wendo Genet, you pass by three stunning and uniquely different lakes. First is Lake Shala, a deep volcanic crater speckled with the turrets of lava islands. Then, Lake Abiyata, which, in sharp contrast, is the country's most shallow lake, and strongly saline; as a result it attracts enormous flocks of flamingos. The third lake, Langano, is a great place to overnight; this is the only lake in the country that is clean and pure, so perfect for swimming. If you come at the weekend you'll even see a few jet-skis and water-skis out there, not what you'd expect in Ethiopia!

From Langano, the ride continues north to join the Addis-to-Asela road, which you headed out on at the start of your journey. From here it is plain sailing all the way back to the capital.

•DAY 14 25 miles (40km)

Mount Entoto

No cycle tour of Ethiopia would be complete without undertaking the best ride in Addis Ababa itself. Mount Entoto is the highest peak to tower over the city, and makes for a superb day ride. Climbing to the summit, you pass through dense groves of eucalyptus trees, which provide the wood to fuel the cooking fires of the city. Passing you on the slopes will be women and donkeys heavily laden with bundles of the wood, bound in part for their home and in part for market.

At the summit are two beautiful churches, and a breathtaking cityscape of Addis Ababa and the surrounding peaks. The capital was once at the top of this mountain. However, according to the history books, the emperor's wife didn't like the cold weather, and spent most of her time in the more temperate valley below. Eventually, the emperor, in a desire to see his wife more, moved the official center down to join her, and named his new city Addis Ababa, or "new flower."

factfile

OVERVIEW

This journey through southern Ethiopia explores the whole cross-section of African landscapes. From the lush plantations and sparkling crater lakes of the Rift Valley to the Afro-alpine moorlands over 13,000 feet (4,000m) above, you'll experience a wealth of natural beauty that few people know exists. The route described here covers some 790 miles (1,270km) in 2 weeks, but it is possible, and even advisable, to do it more slowly and take some rest days if you can.

Start/Finish: Addis Ababa.

ABOUT THE TRAIL

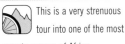

This is a very strenuous tour into one of the most remote corners of Africa.

Major Climbs & Descents: There are several major ascents at high altitude, up to 13,450 feet (4,100m), and there are long downhills.

Difficulty & Special Features: It involves long distances on rough roads. Riders need to be highly self-sufficient, carrying full camping and cooking gear, and space for 4 to 6 days' food. There are also no bike spares at all in Ethiopia, so you must come with all tools and spares, especially spokes.

ACCESS

Airports: Ethiopian Airlines fly to Addis Ababa from Washington and London. They are rapidly expanding their network of routes and are one of Africa's most well-run, profitable airlines.

Transport: Local transport is available everywhere, but in the mountains you may have to wait a few days to catch it. For a price, anyone will find a way to strap you and your bike to their vehicle.

Passport & Visa Requirements: All visitors need a tourist visa, obtainable from any Ethiopian embassy or high commission.

Permits & Access Restrictions: You have to pay a parking fee to enter the Bale Mountains National Park and the Lake Shala/Lake Abiyata National Park.

LOCAL INFORMATION

Maps: The Ethiopia tourist map shows altitudes and gradients, but is available only at booksellers in Addis Ababa or the airport.

Guidebooks: Excellent guidebooks are produced by Bradt and Spectrum, with good maps.

Accommodation & Supplies: Some places have government-run Wabi Shebele hotels—comfortable, simple places with en-suite rooms and hot water. Smaller towns have the simpler Bekele Molla hotels. Villages have local rest houses—basic rooms with just a bed, often thick with bugs. Rural villages have nothing, so you have to find a field and camp, or ask someone if you can stay in their hut for a small fee.

Currency & Language: The birr is the unit of currency. Amharic is the language, with English as a second language.

Area Information: Ethiopian Tourism Commission, Ras Mekonin Ave., P.O. Box 2183 (tel.: 44 74 70). CycleActive, an experienced U.K. mountain bike tour operator, runs guided, vehicle-supported trips to Ethiopia.

Website: www.cycleactive.co.uk.

On the streets of Asela the donkey cart rules.

TIMING & SEASONALITY

Best Months to Visit: November to April.

Climate: November through April are the dry months, which also coincide with winter time. Because Ethiopia is in the tropics, winters are mild, but at high altitudes it can still get cold at night, although rarely freezing. At lower altitudes it is hot all the year round.

HEALTH & SAFETY

Vaccinations: Meningitis, yellow fever, and tetanus.

General Health Risks: Malaria (in the valleys only); hypothermia and heat stroke when moving between blazing sun at low altitude and chilly nights higher up.

Special Considerations: Ethiopia is not set up for tourism, so you must be able to adapt to local ways of doing things.

Politics & Religion: Ethiopia is a stable nation with a mix of Muslims and orthodox Christians who coexist well. This is the only country in Africa that has never been colonized by the West.

Crime Risk: Low.

Food & Drink: Filter or boil all water, unless bottled and bought from a hotel. It is best to adapt to local food as soon as possible, as you may find it's all you can get in some places. In rural areas food is hard to come by, so be prepared to carry lots of provisions.

HIGHLIGHTS

The handful of explorers who dare to visit are rewarded daily by many treasures. They experience traditions and cultures totally untainted by western influence, and will almost certainly find themselves drawn back to Ethiopia again and again.

Scenic: Southern Ethiopia is a land that is stunningly beautiful, yet almost totally unvisited by western travelers. This is one of the few places where you have access to untouched unique cultures and giant mountains.

Wildlife & Flora: The huge geographical diversity of Ethiopia has allowed many unique plant and animal species to develop. The juniper and hagenia forests of the Gaysay region are home to the Mountain Nyala and Menelik's bushbuck. On the Sanetti Plateau are the extremely rare Ethiopian wolves and giant lobelia, while the lush, tropical Rift Valley has fruit and coffee plantations.

temperature and precipitation

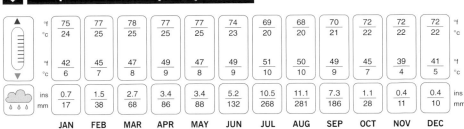

	JAN	FEB	MAR	APR	MAY	JUN	JUL	AUG	SEP	OCT	NOV	DEC
°f	75	77	78	77	77	74	69	68	70	72	72	72
°c	24	25	25	25	25	23	20	20	21	22	22	22
°f	42	45	47	49	47	49	51	50	49	45	39	41
°c	6	7	8	9	8	9	10	10	9	7	4	5
ins	0.7	1.5	2.7	3.4	3.4	5.2	10.5	11.1	7.3	1.1	0.4	0.4
mm	17	38	68	86	88	132	268	281	186	28	11	10

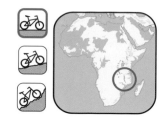

the GREAT RIFT VALLEY

MALAWI

Chris Ford

MALAWI IS ONE OF THE FEW AFRICAN COUNTRIES THAT RETAINS A TRUE SENSE OF UNEXPLORED AFRICA, AND THIS IS MOST EVIDENT AS YOU CYCLE THE DIRT TRACKS THROUGH ITS SMALL VILLAGES. HERE YOU WILL EXPERIENCE THE SIGHTS, SMELLS, SOUNDS, AND ATMOSPHERE OF RURAL LIFE AND RECEIVE THE WARMEST WELCOME YOU COULD EVER IMAGINE.

↑
Take a break from riding to catch up on your suntan or to take a cooling dip in a river swimming hole.

This tour takes you through an incredible variety of landscapes, thanks to Malawi's position in the great Rift Valley of Africa. There are the giant massifs and escarpments, with terraced fields, dense cloud forests, and foothills cultivated with tea, coffee, and cotton. Then, far below, lie the open plains, the wildlife rich Liwonde National Park, and the palm-fringed shores of Lake Malawi. What makes it the perfect African destination is that these areas are closely linked, so each day you'll find yourself pedaling past something new and exciting.

↓ **itinerary**

•DAYS 1–3   108 miles (175km)

Lilongwe to Cape Maclear

The well-surfaced road leading south out of Lilongwe follows the line of the great escarpment, with volcanic formations dotted all around it. The first day stays on this road, climbing steadily to a high point of the ridge at Dedza. An early start is needed from here on Day 2, to begin the stunning off-road descent to the base of the valley. The first views of Lake Malawi are breathtaking, and you're thrown into rural village life within seconds of leaving the main road—children run alongside, calling, "*wazungu*" (meaning "white man"), excited at the unusual event of your passing.

The dirt road twists through huts and farmlands, dropping all the time into ever denser tropical vegetation. Briefly ride along the main lakeshore road, then cut across it onto the seldom used Mtakataka road. This track was once a major route but has been left to disintegrate. The path cuts straight through the open forests and scattered villages of the southern lake shore, to the port of Monkey Bay.

The premier lakeside spot is at Cape Maclear, a few hours' ride away. Coming over the final rise of the headlands you'll see a line of golden sand, scattered with huts and small houses, opening out onto an endless expanse of blue-green water. Dotted along the horizon are islands, which you can kayak to for superb snorkeling.

•DAYS 4–5   56 miles (90km)

Cape Maclear to Liwonde National Park

Leaving Cape Maclear, retrace your steps over the forested headlands, then continue southward through the fishing villages of the southern lake shore. All along the roadside you'll see racks of tiny silver fish left out to bake in the sunlight, drying out ready to be bagged and sent to market.

There are many lakeshore resorts around, from luxury hotels to simple camps and chalets, so ride until you want to stop and swim in the cool water, then find a place to stay.

Day 5 takes you past the tip of the lake and into the bush at Liwonde National Park. The 10-mile (16-km) dirt road that accesses the park finishes at the wide and powerful Shire River, which flows out of Lake Malawi. A small boat

from the camp on the opposite bank will collect you and your bike in order for you to spend the night in this serene corner of African wilderness. From the camp you can enjoy game drives, boat safaris, and walking safaris. Alternatively, just relax and watch the hippos play and the elephants come to drink, right in front of you.

•DAYS 6–7   71 miles (115km)

Liwonde National Park to Zomba

The best way out of the park is to arrange a boat transfer south to the Liwonde Bridge, as from here it's an easy road ride to the town of Zomba. This is a fairly busy route by African standards, but nothing compared with the West, and it cuts through many lush plantations and banana groves. Zomba was once the capital of Malawi, but is now just a bustling provincial town, with one of the country's best markets.

The next day you can leave your bags at your hotel, as it's time to explore the Zomba Plateau. After the 7-mile

(11-km) climb to the "top" you'll be rewarded with stunning views across the plains from the luxurious Ku Chawe Inn, which sits perched on the plateau's edge. You'll also be subjected to more climbing, as you realize that the plateau is not even close to flat! The rough trail that leads right around the edge takes you though pine forests laced with waterfalls, suddenly opening into viewpoints to Lake Malawi, Mozambique, or the Mulanje Mountains, depending on which side you're on. From the high point at Chingwe's Hole, it's a stunning descent back to Ku Chawe and then onward down to Zomba Town.

•DAYS 8–9   100 miles (160km)

Zomba to Mulanje

The road south continues out of Zomba toward Malawi's biggest city—Blantyre. The center is a great place to explore, with thriving markets, interesting shops, and an excellent ice-cream parlor!

Leaving Blantyre the next morning you pass through →

The trail will take you past tea plantations as you ride along the edge of the Mulanje Mountains, Malawi's highest mountain range.

Limbe, its twin city, and then turn onto the old Mulanje road. On a clear day you can get your first glimpse of the giant Mulanje Massif from here. As you slowly descend from the escarpment onto the dusty plains, the sheer-sided granite walls of Mulanje will grow ever larger in your sights. At the base, lush, green tea plantations thrive, rising up to wild forests then finally to the sheer rock walls of Malawi's highest and most awe-inspiring mountain range. A few days' exploration on foot is well worthwhile.

Hidden behind this granite fortress is a pristine wilderness of ancient cedar groves, high meadows dotted with beautiful plants such as the stag's horn lily and everlasting sunflowers, and valleys with pure streams splashing through steaming tropical forests.

• DAYS 10–11   84 miles (135km)

Mulanje to Zomba

From Mulanje, take the quiet dirt road around the base of the massif northward toward Phalombe. This village is the main trading post on the northwestern corner of the mountains and the ride there passes through many smaller settlements. The views up into the mountains are ever changing, as you first pass the Likhubula Valley, then ride

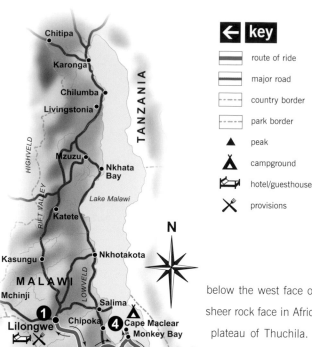

below the west face of Chambe Mountain—the highest sheer rock face in Africa—then, finally, high above is the plateau of Thuchila. At Phalombe you can find basic local lodgings and plenty of fresh food in the village market, but there is no electricity so be sure to arrive before 5:00 P.M. to get your shopping done and a candle lit before it's dark at 6:00 P.M.

From Phalombe, strike out across the wide open plains toward Zomba. The flat dirt track will speed by as the prevailing southwesterly winds blow at your back and help you through this barren landscape. It's a fascinating ride, stopping off at small trading centers, and seeing how people survive in the mountains' rain shadow.

• DAYS 12–14   140 miles (225km)

Zomba to Lilongwe

After a night in Zomba ride back to Lilongwe on the quiet main road, heading northward. The first section you have already ridden when coming from Liwonde Bridge, but after the bridge you turn onto a quieter section of the route that leads up toward the Mozambique border.

After a night in Ntcheu the border and the road become one, and you must pass through a customs post at either end of this section of the ride. At each village you'll see swarms of Mozambicans coming in to trade, some buying basic essentials such as sugar and flour, others selling the vast piles of clothing sent by aid agencies.

The road is studded with volcanic outcrops, which increase in size and number as you climb toward Dedza again, but this time from the other side. After a last night here, race down toward Lilongwe and the end of the tour.

↓ ride profile

Altitude profile with labels: DEDZA (8,200 ft / 2,500 m), ZOMBA PLATEAU, DEDZA; LAKE MALAWI, ZOMBA, BLANTYRE, PHALOMBE, NTCHEU; LIWONDE NATIONAL PARK; LILONGWE, CAPE MACLEAR, ZOMBA, MULANJE, ZOMBA, LILONGWE. Y-axis: ALTITUDE IN FEET (METERS) — 8,200 (2,500), 6,560 (2,000), 4,920 (1,500), 3,280 (1,000), 1,640 (500), 0 (0). X-axis: DAYS — 0, 1–3, 4–5, 6–7, 8–9, 10–11, 12–14.

↓ factfile

Elephants are easy to spot in the Liwonde National Park, particularly when they go down to the water to drink and wash.

OVERVIEW

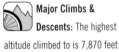 This journey captures the very essence of African exploration, traveling through one of its most undeveloped and seldom-visited lands. The beauty and variety of Malawi will astound any visitor. The journey takes in all of its highlights, covering most of the southern half of the country in 14 days of travel.

Start/Finish: Lilongwe.

ABOUT THE TRAIL

Major Climbs & Descents: The highest altitude climbed to is 7,870 feet (2,400m) at Dedza and also the top of Zomba; the lowest is just above zero on the sandy shores of Lake Malawi.

Difficulty & Special Features: This is not a difficult tour, as most dirt roads in Malawi are in good repair and there are only a few sections with strenuous climbs. What makes this a great destination for the novice African traveler is the ability to hitch with your bike. Just flag down the first passing truck or pickup and for a very small fee they'll take you and your bike to your next destination.

ACCESS

Airports: Several major carriers serve Lilongwe, including British Airways, KLM/Kenyan and Ethiopian Airlines.

Transport: Local transport is available everywhere, and you'll always be able to take your bike. If you intend to make a long journey, try to start early, as many buses leave around 6:00 or 7:00 A.M., but inquire locally first.

Passport & Visa Requirements: A full passport only is required for visitors to Malawi.

Permits & Access Restrictions: None.

LOCAL INFORMATION

Maps: These are few and far between for this region, although topographical maps are available from specialist map stores.

Guidebooks: Lonely Planet and Bradt both do excellent guidebooks for Malawi. Lonely Planet also feature Mulanje in *Trekking in East Africa*.

Accommodation & Supplies: In the main towns and cities there is a wide range of accommodation, from campgrounds and backpacker hostels through to budget or expensive hotels. In rural areas the main villages generally have simple rest house accommodation—a basic, small but clean room with bed and sheets, sharing a communal toilet/washing area. Camping is not easy. Supplies are easily picked up at village markets en route, and meals can be purchased at hotels.

Currency & Language: Malawi kwacha. The language is Chichewa, but English is a second language (less so in rural areas).

Area Information: Department of Tourism, P.O. Box 402, Blantyre (tel.: 620 300; fax: 620 947). CycleActive, one of the U.K.'s most experienced mountain bike tour operators, run guided, vehicle-supported trips to Malawi (tel.: 01768 881111; fax: 01768 881100; e-mail: sales@cycleactive.co.uk.)

Website: www.cycleactive.co.uk

TIMING & SEASONALITY

 Best Months to Visit: June to October.

Climate: May to early November are the dry months, but it's best to wait a month into the dry season before traveling to reduce the risk of getting caught in a shower. Traveling in the wet is not only dispiriting but can be dangerous—the roads become very slippery.

HEALTH & SAFETY

 Vaccinations: Meningitis, yellow fever, and tetanus.

General Health Risks: Malaria, especially during the rainy season, and sunstroke.

Special Considerations: None.

Politics & Religion: A stable political climate has existed in Malawi since independence in the 1960s. The transition to a multi-party democracy in 1994 also went smoothly and the country now has a fully democratic government. The dominant religion is Christianity, although there are also many Muslims in certain areas.

Crime Risk: Malawi is one of Africa's friendliest countries, with an astonishingly low crime rate. However, the gap between your apparent wealth and the poverty of the average Malawian means you should not flaunt your valuables as you may attract pickpockets.

Food & Drink: The rich plantations of the Rift Valley provide some of the most copious, tasty, and cheap fruit and vegetables you'll find anywhere in the world. Look out on the roadsides in Mulanje for fresh pineapples—picked from bushes just feet away, they're juicier and sweeter than any supermarket produce. Water in the cities is treated and doesn't need further filtration, but water from villages must be treated before being drunk.

HIGHLIGHTS

 Scenic: The geography of Malawi is dominated by the great Rift Valley, providing an amazing variety of landscapes in a relatively small area. The Mulanje and Zomba mountains rise up from the plains and are laced with streams, waterfalls, and pristine wilderness areas. Lake Malawi runs almost the length of the country—it's almost 370 miles (600km) long in total—and its palm-fringed shores, hidden coves, and remote treasure islands are serene and beautiful.

Wildlife & Flora: Malawi is home to all the big game—elephants, buffalo, impala, and waterbuck—as well as pools full of hippos and crocodiles. It is also one of the best bird-watching destinations in the African Rift Valley, while the mountain ranges of Mulanje and Zomba contain unique plant species, such as Mulanje cedar.

↓ temperature and precipitation

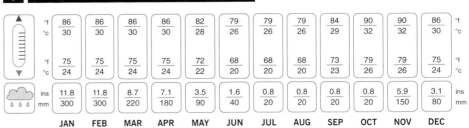

	JAN	FEB	MAR	APR	MAY	JUN	JUL	AUG	SEP	OCT	NOV	DEC	
°f	86	86	86	86	82	79	79	79	84	90	90	86	°f
°c	30	30	30	30	28	26	26	26	29	32	32	30	°c
°f	75	75	75	75	72	68	68	68	73	79	79	75	°f
°c	24	24	24	24	22	20	20	20	23	26	26	24	°c
ins	11.8	11.8	8.7	7.1	3.5	1.6	0.8	0.8	0.8	0.8	5.9	3.1	ins
mm	300	300	220	180	90	40	20	20	20	20	150	80	mm

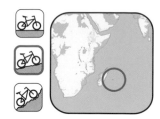

CANYONS and VOLCANOES

RÉUNION ISLAND

Chris Ford

RÉUNION ISLAND IS AN INCREDIBLE FEAT OF VOLCANIC GEOGRAPHY. FEW PLACES ON EARTH HAVE SUCH AN ARRAY OF LANDSCAPES AND ECOSYSTEMS IN SO SMALL AN AREA. WITH THIS COMES A VIBRANT MULTICULTURAL SOCIETY— ALTHOUGH THE ISLAND IS FRENCH, THE LOCAL CREOLE PEOPLE BRING THEIR OWN LANGUAGE, TRADITIONS, AND CUISINE INTO THE MELTING POT.

For mountain bikers this combination of landscapes and lifestyle is wonderful. After a ride across lava flows, or following the Galet riverbed (still half full of water!) into Cirque de Mafate, you can visit wonderful little Creole restaurants or relax at cafés on the beach.

This trip combines bike touring with serious off-road riding. You can load up the panniers to move around the island, then spend a few days at each location enjoying the great mountain biking without any baggage. For days off the bike there's an incredible variety of other adventure sports on offer too.

←

The rivers are a major form of access to the overgrown interior of Réunion for bikers.

↓ itinerary

•DAYS 1–2 31 miles (50km)

St. Denis to St. Gilles-les-Bains

Spend Day 1 exploring St. Denis, the island's capital. The next morning, ride west along the coast, and, after crossing the Rivière St. Denis, turn off into the mountains. The views down to the Indian Ocean are beautiful, and the hairpin bends up the lower slopes of Cap Noir are a good warm-up! The road drops to follow the coast into St. Gilles-les-Bains.

•DAY 3 47 miles (75km)

Cirque de Mafate

The Cirque de Mafate is the most inaccessible place on the island, with no roads reaching its sheer, hidden peaks and waterfalls. The only route into the cirque follows the bed of the Rivière du Galet during the dry season. This trail takes you through St. Gilles-les-Hauts, and down to Tours des Roches—a narrow, scenic road that winds through dense groves of coconuts, mangos, and bananas. You then rise up to the edge of the Galet river canyon at Sans Souci, before dropping onto a dirt trail. You're now on the riverbed, heading into the cirque. After 12 miles (20km) the valley opens up, and you ride through a tunnel to emerge at a clear pool, behind which is a canyon with swimming pools and dramatic *"plongées"* (12-foot-/4-meter-high jumps into a waterfall). The return along the river is no less exciting.

•DAY 4 40 miles (65km)

Piton Maido

About 7,900 feet (2,400m) above St. Gilles-les-Bains is Piton Maido, a sheer ridge that rises up from the ocean and drops into Mafate on the other side. Your aim is to climb the road to the ridge, then descend to the ocean on a stunning mix of single-track, fire roads, and plantation trails.

The climb takes at least four hours, and setting off early is essential to avoid the heat on the lower slopes. At Petit France there is a great Creole café that serves takeouts. Grab your lunch and take it to the top of Piton Maido, where you can enjoy it with views across the sea of peaks within the cirque. This will also be your first view of Piton des Neiges—the central summit of the island.

The descent begins on tarmac, then you'll see a board describing the nearby biking. You should take the left turn onto a waymarked forestry trail, with challenging shortcuts through steep, narrow forest single-track. Pass through high mountain heathers, then dense cloud forests, before meeting farmers tending their patches of flowers, sugar cane, and palm groves. Eventually you'll come out onto the road at St. Gilles-les-Hauts, for the last blast down to the beach.

•DAY 5   37 miles (60km)

St. Gilles-les-Bains to Cilaos

The first 22 miles (35km) of the day follow the coastal road past Réunion's most beautiful beaches. Heading inland, brace your legs for the hardest climb yet—nearly 6,000 feet (1,800m) with a fully loaded bike. As you twist and turn up the side of the St. Étienne river canyon, the road takes you through small villages, spaced by dense groves of bananas. The scenery gradually becomes more alpine—pine forests stretch from the road to the vertical cliff face that marks the east side of this rock amphitheater. At the village of Cilaos you will be surrounded by the giant rock walls of the cirque.

•DAY 6   34 miles (45km)

Cirque de Cilaos

Cilaos's tourist information center has a giant poster showing all the local mountain bike routes. A favorite morning option is to head out to the eastern edge of the cirque, right under the brow of Piton des Neiges, and return on forest trails to the road you rode in on yesterday. For the afternoon there are some great single-track routes that explore the region above the Hôtel des Thermes. The views from up here are fabulous. Some of these trails are black runs, so stick to the fire roads if you are unsure of your abilities. While in Cilaos, try canyoning—abseiling under waterfalls, jumping into pools, and whizzing down rock slides.

•DAYS 7–8   80 miles (130km)

Cilaos to St. Philippe

Leaving the mountains, you can enjoy the switchbacks and tunnels that you previously rode up, before continuing along the coast to St. Philippe. After the busy town of St. Pierre, the traffic disappears as you head toward the "Sud Sauvage"—the Wild South. This area sits right below Piton →

The barren Plaine des Cafres links the two volcanoes of Piton de la Fournaise and Piton des Neiges.

Bikes are the only vehicles that can access the stunning Cirque de Mafate, so you can rest assured there won't be any crowds.

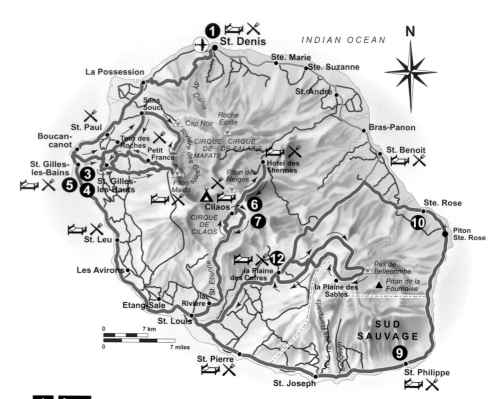

de la Fournaise, one of the most active volcanoes in the world. Looking up to the left you can see the giant canyon walls of the Rivière des Ramparts and Rivière Langevin, as the sea beats against the bleak, lava cliffs to your right. At St. Philippe, head for Hôtel Le Baril for the guide to local routes, all of which involve challenging climbs into the dense plantations and forests above.

•DAY 9   44 miles (70km)

St. Philippe to Ste. Rose

Today begins with a road ride through dramatic volcanic landscapes, following the coast along the "Grande Brulée," or great burnt lands. This is where the vast outer crater of Piton de la Fournaise widens out and slopes down to the coast. The lava flows have crossed the road and plunged into the ocean, enlarging the island and scouring a black line of destruction behind them. At Piton Ste. Rose you can see the miracle of Notre Dame de la Lave, the local church—the devastating 1977 lava flow stopped just 3 feet (1m) from its doors, split into two, and flowed around its sides before pouring into the ocean. There are some great lava trails to explore here, and the best ending is down the '77 flow.

•DAYS 10–11   28 miles (45km)

Ste. Rose to la Plaine des Cafres

Another road ride brings you into the central plains of Réunion, la Plaine des Cafres, which lie between dormant Piton des Neiges and active Piton de la Fournaise, on ground dotted with small cones from old, minor eruptions.

Early the next day, set off to explore the dramatic landscapes of la Fournaise. The road climb up to la Plaine des Sables is long and steady, but the views over the deep gorge of Rivière des Ramparts and back across la Plaine des Cafres are superb. Rainfall is more common here, so you'll ride through fields of lush green grass filled with cows. Then, suddenly, it all changes—the grass turns to colored heathers, sprouting out of volcanic rock; then the vegetation disappears, along with the surfaced road, as you descend into la Plaine des Sables proper. This outer region of the volcano is filled with bizarre rock formations, and stretches gently up toward the Pas de Bellecombe, on the rim of the main crater.

↑ key

▭	route of ride
▭	alternative route
▭	minor road
⛺	campground
🛏	hotel/guesthouse
✕	provisions
✈	airport
†	church
△	viewpoint

After you've returned across la Plaine des Sables the challenging riding begins. There are a variety of descents; the black runs offer the most varied scenery and best riding, but can be steep and strewn with chunks of volcanic debris.

•DAYS 12–13   68 miles (110km)

La Plaine des Cafres to St. Denis via St. Gilles-les-Bains

There are two routes out of the high plains: one goes direct to St. Denis via St. Benoit; the other is via St. Gilles-les-Bains and takes two days. Whichever you choose, after so much biking it's worth allowing yourself a day on the beach, and a night in the lively bars.

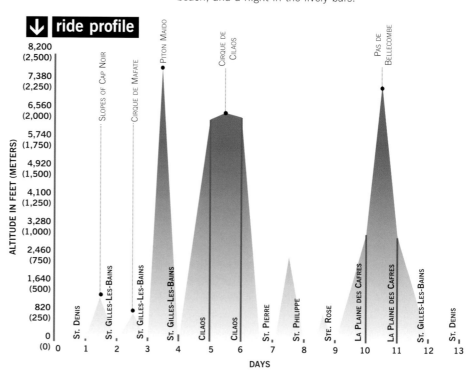

↓ factfile

The volcanic landscape of la Plaines des Sables makes for challenging mountain biking.

OVERVIEW

Réunion has adventure, beauty, culture, and fine cuisine, as well as clear waters and pristine beaches to enjoy after a day of biking. The island is crammed with so many different ecosystems and geographical regions that every day something totally new is encountered. Yet it's such a small place that you can see almost all of it in just 2 weeks.

Start/Finish: St. Denis.

ABOUT THE TRAIL

 This tour allows you to combine superb cycle touring with challenging mountain biking on the most fascinating island in the Indian Ocean.

Major Climbs & Descents: There are climbs from sea level to around 7,900 feet (2,400m). This route covers some severe climbs and equally challenging, superb descents. When riding the Piton Maido you bike from sea level to 7,220 feet (2,200m) on the road and then back down on a sometimes technical off-road route that will test the stamina of the very best riders.

Difficulty & Special Features: The trails on Réunion do require a good degree of fitness, and there is definitely a strong element of challenge to this trip. You can explore the island on easier trails, but you'll get more out of it if you are able to do the big rides.

ACCESS

 Airports: St. Denis is served by Air France, Corsair, and Air Liberté out of Paris, or Air Austral and Air Mauritius out of Johannesburg.

Transport: Local transport is available everywhere in the form of the Car Jaune (yellow bus) along the coast and the Car Pastel (minibus) in the interior; all will take bikes if they have space.

Passport & Visa Requirements: Réunion is part of France, so no visas are required for European, North American, Australian, or New Zealander visitors.

Permits & Access Restrictions: None.

LOCAL INFORMATION

 Maps: The tourist information desk at the airport has island maps, and boards illustrating local mountain bike routes can be found all over the island.

Guidebooks: Lonely Planet do an excellent guidebook to Réunion.

Accommodation & Supplies: Throughout the island there are hotels for most budgets, as well as some youth hostels and bunkhouse accommodation in the mountains. A good source of hotel information is through the Anthurium group, which represents many of the independent hotels on the island (see *Websites* below).

Currency & Language: French franc. French and Creole; you won't find many hotels or restaurants where English is spoken, so you should try to learn some French before you come; or bring a good phrasebook.

Area Information: The tourist information desk at the airport has the "RUN" guide, with full accommodation and activity listings by region; they will also call and make reservations for you. CycleActive, an experienced U.K. mountain bike

tour operator, run guided, vehicle-supported trips to Réunion. By teaming up with expert local guides, they have access to the island's best trails; they also offer other activities, such as canyoning, as part of their holidays.

Websites: www.anthurium.com; www.cycleactive.co.uk

TIMING & SEASONALITY

Best Months to Visit: May to December, but it is best to miss August which is busy due to it being the French holidays.

Climate: The west side of the island stays mostly dry right through this time, but over in Ste. Rose or up on Piton de la Fournaise there is the chance of rain at any time of year. The main season to miss is January to March, when

there is a high risk of hurricanes or powerful storms.

HEALTH & SAFETY

Vaccinations: None.
General Health Risks: None.

Special Considerations: None.

Politics & Religion: Réunion is mostly Catholic.

Crime Risk: Low.

Food & Drink: The great food on Réunion is a real highlight for many visitors. The island offers a combination of French cuisine and the traditional, spiced island dishes that have been developed by the Creoles. Food is taken seriously, with everything closing for 2 hours at lunchtime. The *boulangeries* serve superb pastries and filled baguettes.

HIGHLIGHTS

Scenic: The twin volcanic peaks of Réunion dominate the shape and ecology of the island. When the sides of Piton des Neiges collapsed many millions of years ago to form giant natural amphitheaters (or cirques), each one became a unique ecosystem, and their canyons, rivers, and forests took different forms at different altitudes, all surrounded by a wall of rock. Then, to the south, the Piton de la Fournaise, young and full of life, turned one end of the island into a dramatic lunar landscape of canyons, craters, fresh young forests, and cooled lava flows that touch the sea at the black beaches of Ste. Rose. When you pack in the fantastic beaches and warm waters of the Indian Ocean as well, you have a tropical island crammed so full of natural beauty you won't know what to see first.

Wildlife & Flora: All around the island are a mixture of tropical woodlands, palm sugar cane, and banana plantations, and on the eastern slopes of the island are the precious vanilla crops. The volcanic soil is so rich in minerals that once nature takes a grip the area can become a dense, tropical jungle. However, many of the fertile lower slopes have been cultivated to provide the island with much of its palm crop.

↓ temperature and precipitation

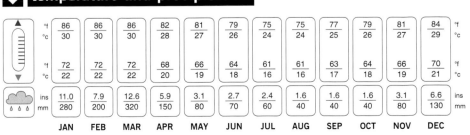

	JAN	FEB	MAR	APR	MAY	JUN	JUL	AUG	SEP	OCT	NOV	DEC	
°f	86	86	86	82	81	79	75	75	77	79	81	84	°f
°c	30	30	30	28	27	26	24	24	25	26	27	29	°c
°f	72	72	72	68	66	64	61	61	63	64	66	70	°f
°c	22	22	22	20	19	18	16	16	17	18	19	21	°c
ins	11.0	7.9	12.6	5.9	3.1	2.7	2.4	1.6	1.6	1.6	3.1	6.6	ins
mm	280	200	320	150	80	70	60	40	40	40	80	130	mm

ISRAEL BIKE TRAIL

ISRAEL

Carlton Reid

THE ISRAEL BIKE TRAIL (IBT) STARTS AT A SKI VILLAGE IN THE GOLAN HEIGHTS AND ENDS AT THE BUZZING RED SEA RESORT OF EILAT. THE TRAIL IS A WONDERFUL JOURNEY THAT GUIDES YOU THROUGH THE HISTORY OF ANCIENT ISRAEL AND THE COMPLEXITY THAT IS MODERN ISRAEL.

The 530-mile (850-km) route meanders through Israel's highlights: the sublime Mount Carmel fire roads, the biblical Judean hills, and the massive, genuinely unique craters of the Negev Desert. The IBT is the creation of enthusiasts from the Carmel Mountain Bike Club, based near Haifa in the north of the country. Half of it follows Shvil Yisrael, the Israel National Trail (INT), which is a meandering walking route. Israelis love their hiking and this route is marked in solid red on the brilliant 1:50,000 Israeli walking maps as well as being waymarked on the ground.

←

The Islamic Dome of the Rock in Jerusalem was built on the flattened Jewish Second Temple (from where Jesus evicted the market traders); the area is, therefore, of huge importance to Muslims, Jews, and Christians.

•DAYS 1–3 61 miles (97km)

Neve Ativ to Har Meron Field School

Start from Neve Ativ on Mount Hermon in the Golan Heights. You'll pass tank traps, bunkers, and minefields as every inch of land here was hard fought over in the 1967 Six Day War. A short climb to Birket Ram lake is followed by a descent into the lush Hula Valley. Spend the first night in Hagoshrim.

The next day starts with a testing climb up the escarpment next to Tel Hai and Kfar Giladi on undulating forest tracks. At the top, head to the border town of Kiryat Shemona, and overnight in Ramot Naftali.

Day 3 is physically challenging, with technical single-track, climbing Har Meron (the highest peak in Galilee), and a deep, fast-flowing stream that has to be crossed and re-crossed in Nahal Dishon. The going gets tough as the track enters the Mediterranean oak forest that covers the slopes of Har Meron; it becomes steep and eroded, and you must carry your bike to the road near the Har Meron Field School.

•DAYS 4–6 83 miles (133km)

Har Meron Field School to Kibbutz Harduf

Head for a mid-morning rest on the summit of Har Meron. Admire your first views of the Sea of Galilee (Kinneret Lake) as you descend the wide, fast tracks of the Har Meron Nature Reserve. Skirt the eastern side of Nahal Amud, a mighty gorge with craggy, cave-indented cliffs, and rejoin the INT at the Arbel cliff. Riding in Nahal Arbel, where Saladin once battled against the Crusaders, is made tricky by a rocky, dry riverbed. Stay at Moshava Kinneret.

From Yardenit, the route follows the River Jordan southward. After Menachamia, a big climb out of the Jordan Valley winds its way up to the Heights of Yavniel.

From Day 5's stopover at Dabburiya, it's less than a mile to the summit of Har Tavor; but there are 20 or so switchbacks on the steep road, which peters out to a dirt track.

Descend to Dabburiya, and then climb around the lower slopes of Har Devorah to Ein Mahil. Continue past Mashad and the mosque of Nebi Yunes, supposed burial place of Jonah—of whale fame. It's a long downhill into pine forest and a superb single-track into the valley below Hosha'ya.

Soon you arrive in the Tsipori National Park, with its extensive Roman remains. A short climb on a grassy trail takes you to the Ya'ar Hasollelim Nature Reserve. A stretch of tarmac leads you back onto dirt, meandering through pine forests and Bedouin farms. Stay at Kibbutz Harduf.

•DAYS 7–8 58 miles (93km)

Kibbutz Harduf to Zichron Ya'akov

Day 7 covers a wide variety of terrains—rocky single-track, streams, fast descents, and rough fields—as you cross the western extremities of the Galilean Mountains and ascend Mount Carmel. The descent into Nahal Tzipori is on dusty farm tracks, while the brief climb out passes by Bedouin farms, and then descends through the Kishon Valley to the orchards of Kfar Hasidim, a village of ultra-orthodox Jews. It's a short steep climb up the slopes of Mount Carmel to the Nof Carmel Panorama Track and then on to the Druze village of Isfiya. Stay at the kibbutz in Beit Oren.

A fantastic backdrop of sea, cliffs, hills, ancient river-beds, caves, and evergreen vegetation constitutes Day 8. Take the track next to the swimming pool of the kibbutz,

and then shoot down to the cliffs above Nahal Oren. From Ha Agam (the Lake), retrace some of your tire tracks from yesterday before beginning the tough ascent of Har Shokef.

Descend to the Druze town of Daliat El Carmel, and browse the souk before making the marvelous descent to the moshav of Kerem Maharal. Zichron Ya'akov is famous for its wine. But, first, head to a great beach at Nof Dor.

•DAYS 9–10 76 miles (122km)

Zichron Ya'akov to Nachshon

Skirt the Sharon coastal plain—almost wholly off-road and fairly hilly until Regavim. You're now in the central coastal strip, the agricultural heartland of Israel. You will hit tarmac at Kfar Saba, and eucalyptus-shaded springs at the Yarkon River crossing. End the day at Tel Afek in Rosh Ha'ayin.

Turn eastward at Moshav Mazor and climb through pines until you emerge on a ridge above the forest. Head south to Nahal Netuf and carry the bike across a rocky stream. A steep climb through olive groves to Tel Hadid, a Bronze Age mound, follows. Descend dusty tracks out of Ben Shemen forest to Nachshon.

Sunsets and sunrises in the Judean Desert are breathtaking.

The local, sticky snack foods sold on market stalls across Israel are excellent energy supplements for tired and hungry bikers.

147

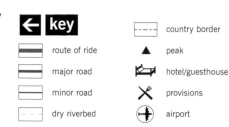

key

- route of ride
- major road
- minor road
- dry riverbed
- ------ country border
- ▲ peak
- hotel/guesthouse
- ✕ provisions
- ⊕ airport

LEBANON

Kfar Giladi
Neve Ativ **1**
Ramot Naftali **3**
GOLAN HEIGHTS
Har Meron ▲ **4**
Harduf **5**
Hula Valley
Lake Kinneret (Sea of Galilee)
Haifa
Beit Oren **7**
Zichron Ya'akov **8** **9** Ein Mahl
Kinneret
Kishon
Jordan

Mediterranean Sea

Kfar Saba
Tel Aviv-Yafo
Rosh Ha'ayin **10**
11 Nachshon
12 Jerusalem
Mevo Beitar
13 Beit Guvrin
Judean Desert
Dead Sea
14
Kramim
Arad
15
Dimona
16
17 Harvot Mamshit
Sde Boker
Tzin
18 Ein Be'erot
Machtesh Ramon

N E G E V

ISRAEL

EGYPT

Yotvata

Eilat
Red Sea

0 30 km
0 30 miles

• DAYS 11–13 89 miles (1,272km)

Nachshon to Kramim

Follow the Burma Road—a secret road constructed by Israel during the 1948 War of Independence—and then continue on forest tracks to Hamasrek. Take the fire road above Nahal Kisalon to Shoresh. A short, steep climb to Tzova leads to a fast descent into Nahal Zova. From Mevo Beitar, take a bus into Jerusalem.

On Day 12 descend to the spring of Ein Mata, then climb to the ruined Byzantine inn at Hirbet Hanot. Take care on the descent to Nahal Tsadsar and the valley of Emek HaElah, where David battled with Goliath. Continue through Park Britannia then climb away on technical single-track to the caves of Tel Goded. Stay in Beit Guvrin.

Follow the INT to Kramim.

• DAYS 14–15 57 miles (92km)

Kramim to Harvot Mamshit

Day 14 starts in a pine forest and ends in the rocky Judean Desert. Climb to the tabletop "peak" of Har Hiran, overlooking the valley of Estamoah. The summit of Har Amassa is the highest point on today's route, from where you drop down Ma'ale Dragot—1,000 feet (300m) of technically and physically challenging rock steps. Continue on the flat to Arad, said to have the cleanest and driest air in the world.

The next morning, head south on the Zohar Ridge overlooking the great Rift Valley. Stop for water at a quarry at the base of Har Yahel. In Nahal Dimona you will have to pick your way between tents and the animals tended by veiled Bedouin women. Today, you will have left the Judean Desert to seamlessly join the Negev Desert.

• DAYS 16–20 106 miles (170km)

Harvot Mamshit to Eilat

From Harvot Mamshit, follow a path around Har Rotem, then descend to single-tracks down to Machtesh Hagadol. *Machtesh* is Hebrew for "crater," and the trail passes through multicolored sands and rocks. Exit the crater by a daunting ascent: Ma'ale Avraham. Eventually you hit tarmac to freewheel down to Sde Boker, the final resting place of David Ben Gurion, a founding father of modern Israel.

Leave Sde Boker on Darb A-Sultana, the ancient Caravanserai route that once connected Arabia with Gaza. This leads to the stunning descent into Nahal Zin, one of the great dry riverbeds of the Negev. Head south into the Wilderness of Zin following the old oil pipeline road. From the spring of Ein Zik, there's the killer climb of Ma'ale Zik.

The rest of the trail follows the pipeline road, undulating over dried riverbeds to the edge of Machtesh Ramon, the largest crater of the Negev. Descend the crater, either by taking the red trail to Ma'ale Noah, from where there is a jeep trail, or by riding the hair-raising, crater rim to Mitzpeh Ramon. Spend the night at the Bedouin town of Ein Be'erot.

For the next three days, follow the waymarkings for the INT to Eilat, then jump into the Red Sea—you've earned it!

↓ ride profile

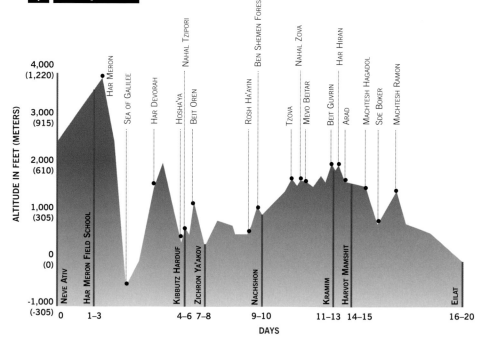

ALTITUDE IN FEET (METERS)

4,000 (1,220)
3,000 (915)
2,000 (610)
1,000 (305)
0 (0)
-1,000 (-305)

HAR MERON
SEA OF GALILEE
HAR DEVORAH
HOSHA'YA
NAHAL TZIPORI
BEIT OREN
ROSH HA'AYIN
BEN SHEMEN FOREST
TZOVA
NAHAL ZOVA
MEVO BEITAR
BEIT GUVRIN
HAR HIRAN
ARAD
MACHTESH HAGADOL
SDE BOKER
MACHTESH RAMON

NEVE ATIV
HAR MERON FIELD SCHOOL
KIBBUTZ HARDUF
ZICHRON YA'AKOV
NACHSHON
KRAMIM
HARVOT MAMSHIT
EILAT

0 1–3 4–6 7–8 9–10 11–13 14–15 16–20

DAYS

←

To explore the City of David, which sits outside of the ancient walls of Jerusalem, you must hire a Palestinian guide.

 factfile

OVERVIEW

It's tough terrain with extremes of weather, but it's beautiful. Israel has more tourist attractions per square mile, especially pilgrim attractions, than any other country. The IBT is a mountain biker's dream—530 miles (848km) of tough riding, including three truly phenomenal descents. This ride is almost totally off-road and rolls past locations that are important to three of the world's major religions. Twenty days is recommended for a relaxing trip integrated with sightseeing, but by rolling 2 of the suggested days into 1 it would be possible to do this route in a fortnight.

Start: Neve Ativ
Finish: Eilat.

ABOUT THE TRAIL

Unless you're very strong or traveling very light, you probably won't manage much more than 40 to 50 miles (64 to 80km) on a good day. Israeli hiking trails are generally waymarked with color-coded paint daubings on rocks. Not all of the INT is followed by the IBT. The Carmel Mountain Bike Club has mapped out its own route, and it hopes that, in time, this will be marked on the ground and published on official maps.

Major Climbs & Descents: There are hard climbs almost every day and even the lesser climbs will be hard if you attempt to do them in the heat of the Middle Eastern afternoon. There are some tricky, narrow descents. The high point of the trail is the starting point on Mount Hermon at 6,500 feet (1,980m) and the lowest point—if you make the detour—is the Dead Sea, the lowest point on Earth.

Difficulty & Special Features: There are many technical single-track sections. Pannier bags or a trailer are essential unless you have car support, but keep luggage to a minimum as bikes do have to be carried on some sections.

ACCESS

Airports: Ben-Gurion International Airport, 12 miles (19km) south of Tel Aviv.
Transport: To get to the trail head take a bus from Tel Aviv center. Bikes go in the voluminous luggage compartment of the bus.
Passport & Visa Requirements: Citizens of the U.K., U.S., Australia, and New Zealand need a valid passport. A visa will be stamped into it when you enter the country. Many Arab countries refuse entry to passport holders with Israeli stamps, so ask for the visa to be stamped on a loose piece of paper if you intend traveling elsewhere in the Middle East.
Permits & Access Restrictions: On those parts of the trail that take you through military areas, there will be warning signs to tell you if "live" artillery practice is in session. If in doubt about an area's safety, take a detour. Large-scale Israeli maps show "danger areas." Waymarked trails are safe.

LOCAL INFORMATION

Maps: Israel's Hiking and Touring Maps at 1:50,000, show waymarked trails, including the INT. Only one of them—#20, Eilat Mountains—is in English, so a crash course in the Hebrew alphabet would help.
Guidebooks: *The Rough Guide to Israel* has it all; dense with information, including political

briefings and Palestinian issues, it is indispensable.

Accommodation & Supplies: Wild camping is possible away from civilization, and in the Negev it may be your only option. Hotels can be found in the tourist spots, and kibbutz guesthouses are almost everywhere. There are 30 youth hostels in Israel. There are ample opportunities to restock with food and water except in the deserts.
Currency & Language: Shekels; Hebrew. English is widely spoken.
Area Information: Israel Government Tourist Offices have branches in most capital cities.
Websites: www.israelhotels.org.il; www.kibbutz.co.il

TIMING & SEASONALITY

 Best Months to Visit: Spring is best. Water will still be in many of the rivers, making the water splashes fun and guaranteeing a profusion of wild flowers. Midsummer in the Judean

and Negev deserts would require early mornings before it gets hot.
Climate: Israel's climate is Mediterranean in the north. In summer the entire area is dominated by a subtropical high that brings cloudless skies and no rain. In winter, the northern half is influenced by cyclonic depressions that bring moderate rainfall.

HEALTH & SAFETY

 Vaccinations: None.
General Health Risks: Sunstroke.
Special Considerations: The IBT takes you along tank trails, through firing ranges, and over manned dugouts. Off-road you'll often meet friendly Israeli soldiers who will be surprised to see you, so make a fair bit of noise when approaching!
Politics & Religion: Because of its historical importance to Judaism, Christianity, and Islam, Israel has long suffered from more than its fair share of wars and terrorism.

The trail avoids Israel's flash-points; but, at the time of writing, hostilities between the Israeli and Palestinian communities were making travel to Israel difficult.
Crime Risk: Pickpockets and snatch thieves in urban areas.
Food & Drink: Boil water when away from civilization; never drink from the black irrigation tubes that drip water into crops. South of Jerusalem, leave luggage space for extra water: you'll often need to carry up to 17 pints (8 liters).

HIGHLIGHTS

Israel packs a lot into a small space; you can ski in the morning and bask on a sun-drenched beach in the afternoon.
Scenic: Israel is a country of contrast, from the cool, pine-clad mountains of the far north to the incredible fertility of the Sharon Plain; the stark barren beauty of the desert, and the bizarre scenery of the Dead Sea area.
Wildlife & Flora: Thanks to its geographical location as a continental bridge, Israel has more than 3,000 different species of plants, 350 species of birds, 100 mammals, and 100 reptiles; but you'll be lucky to see any of them. Signs claim that panthers roam the Judean Desert, but few have ever seen them. There are wild dogs in the Carmel Mountains and Yael antelopes in the Judean hills.

↓ temperature and precipitation

		JAN	FEB	MAR	APR	MAY	JUN	JUL	AUG	SEP	OCT	NOV	DEC	
	°f	70	73	79	88	97	100	102	104	99	91	82	73	°f
	°c	21	23	26	31	36	38	39	40	37	33	28	23	°c
	°f	50	52	57	64	63	75	79	79	77	70	61	54	°f
	°c	10	11	14	18	17	24	26	26	25	21	16	12	°c
	ins	0	0.3	0.3	0.2	0	0	0	0	0	0	0	0.3	ins
	mm	0	8	8	5	0	0	0	0	0	0	0	8	mm

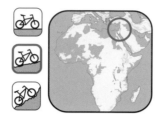

The chapel of St. Bernard is a
lonely Christian outpost found
at Cedars Ski Resort.

⬇ **itinerary**

BEIRUT BIKING

LEBANON

Carlton Reid

PURGE YOUR BRAIN OF IMAGES OF LEBANON AS A WAR-TORN COUNTRY AS IT'S NOT LIKE THAT ANY MORE. BEIRUT HAS BEEN REBUILT, THE CASINO DU LIBAN IS ONCE AGAIN THE MIDDLE EAST'S TOP ENTERTAINMENT AND GAMBLING HAVEN, AND THE HIGH MOUNTAINS NO LONGER WITNESS HEAVY ARTILLERY TRAINED ON DOWNTOWN.

It's not all plain sailing, however. Syrian soldiers still roam the streets; there's no escaping the obvious pockmarks in a lot of buildings; and tourists have yet to flock back to Lebanon despite the lack of fighting and the recent withdrawal of the Israeli army from southern Lebanon.

But Lebanon has a lot to offer: there are 300 days of sunshine; Mount Lebanon is a downhiller's paradise (use the ski lifts if you're feeling lazy), and you have the extra cachet of visiting a country that most people still think is a byword for terror and destruction.

The route is a series of climbs and descents on Lebanon's mountain ranges. There are two ranges, parallel to each other—the Mount Lebanon Range and the Anti-Lebanon Range. In between runs the Beqa'a Valley, a high, flat plateau. The Anti-Lebanon range borders on Syria and is mostly out of bounds.

→
It's worth spending a day in the tranquil port of Byblos, but if you only have time for lunch make sure you head for Pepe's.

•DAY 1 28 miles (45km)

Beirut to Beiteddine

Stay in town for a day or two before heading out to the hills. It will pay to watch the incredibly dangerous driving from a safe vantage point before risking life and limb on the roads with a machine—the bicycle—that is alien to the Lebanese.

You must take a wander around the downtown area—although reconstruction is still taking place, there's still plenty of evidence of the events that were so infamous in the 1980s.

Ride toward the airport and after about 12 miles ask a local if the Arabic road sign pointing left says "Beiteddine." If yes, turn left and start the climb up the Chouf Mountains, a Druze stronghold; if they say "No," ask for directions. Beiteddine, at 2,950 feet (899m), is a nineteenth-century palace now used by the president of Lebanon. There's a small museum here.

•DAY 2 29 miles (47km)

Beiteddine to Zahle

The mountain pass of Dahr al-Baidar is a strategic crossing that has been important for thousands of years. Today it's nondescript, except for the views down to the Beqa'a Valley—called Coele-Syria (Hollow Syria) by the ancients, and one of the great granaries of imperial Rome. The main road through the valley is pretty unpleasant, but there are no alternatives until you get past Chtaura, the main transport hub of the region. Chtaura is locally believed to be where Paul was converted to Christianity; nowadays it's a grim place. Stop for food but press on to the Greek Catholic town of Zahle, the epicenter of the arak trade—aniseed-flavored alcohol that packs a punch.

•DAY 3 52 miles (84km)

Zahle to Faqra

This is a long, tough day with some mighty climbs, but you've got to get to Faqra, because there are no hotels en →

route. Most of the day is on pockmarked tarmac, apart from the climb to Faqra, which is on smooth tarmac, but you have to breathe in diesel fumes from the lorries passing you at not much more than cycling speed.

From your Zahle hotel, head for the mountain behind the town. This is Mount Sannine. Just over a mile (1.5km) from Zahle you come to a large mausoleum built from Roman and Mameluke bricks known as Karak Noah, Noah's Tomb.

Five miles (8km) further on, take an off-road detour at the Christian village of Niha and ascend Hosn Niha (4,300 feet/1,310m), where there are two well-preserved Roman temples. There's an old fountain halfway up the track, from which the water is safe to drink. The better-preserved temple is dedicated to Hadaranis, an Eastern god, worshipped in part through ritual prostitution.

At Dhur ash-Shuwair, turn for Feitrun and the final, yet most punishing, climb of the day. Book your stay at l'Auberge de Faqra in advance.

As an alternative to this road route you could take the cross-country ski route over the Ouyoun el-Simane range of mountains (at the summit of Mount Sannine there's a lonely Syrian checkpoint), although it's best to

key

▬▬▬	route of ride
	major road
	minor road
- - -	country border
▲	peak
⊔	pass
⋀	campground
🛏	hotel/guesthouse
✕	provisions
⊕	airport

Unpredictable weather can sometimes hit the Beqa'a Valley, creating an awesome sight of black clouds suddenly overpowering blue skies.

The high mountains of Lebanon are almost totally populated by Christians.

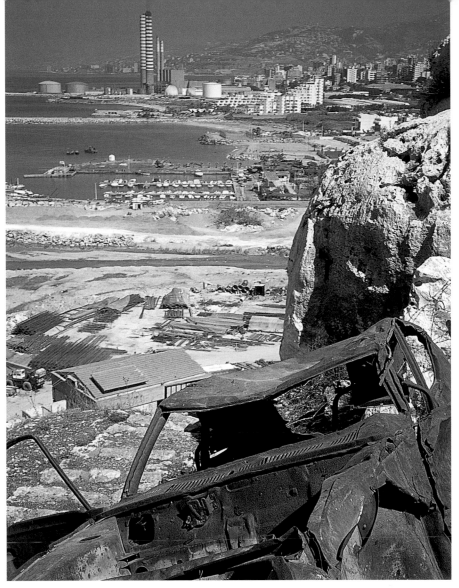

Lebanon is still full of relics from the "bad old days."

tackle this with a guide booked ahead of time. Ski instructors from Faraya know this route well and some double up as mountain bike guides in the summer.

•DAY 4   variable mileage

Faqra to Faraya to Faqra

It's playtime! Leave your luxury hotel and cycle uphill for a couple of miles until you reach the ski resort of Faraya. Pay for a lift pass and pick up your trails map. It's meant for the ski season, so use your imagination to work out the bikable routes. Faraya is Lebanon's biggest and most developed resort. There are 11 lifts that radiate to two major peaks: Jabal Dib (7,531 feet/2,295m) to the north, and Mzaar (8,085 feet/2,464m) to the south, from where you can enjoy a vertical drop of more than 2,000 feet (610m). The base of the lifts is at 6,068 feet (1,850m).

As well as plain downhilling and then hitching a lift back to the top, you could attempt the traverse from Jabal Dib to Mzaar via the Traversée vers Nabil and the Couloir vers Mzaar trails, both extremely tough rides.

Above the resort the views are stunning. To the north are the Anti-Lebanon Mountains; to the south you can make out Mount Hermon in Syria and Israel; below is the Beqa'a Valley; and to the west is the Mediterranean Sea, and—on →

 ride profile

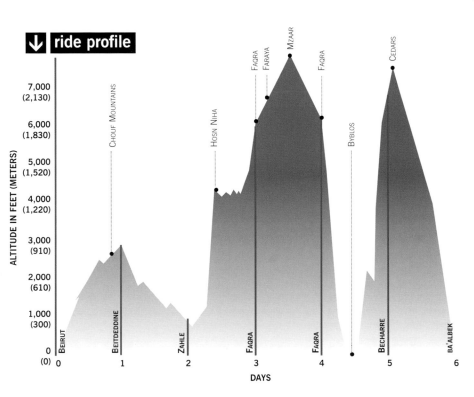

The medieval Arab fortress of Museilha, near Batrun, has dangerously thin walls, and would have been easily defeated in a siege; but as fairytale castles go, it's pretty hard to beat.

a good day—you can see as far as Cyprus. Even Beirut looks peaceful from up here.

•DAY 5 43 miles (69km)

Faqra to Becharre

In a perfect world you should stay the night at Byblos, which you'll reach mid-morning, but if you must press on at least have a meal at Pepe's Fishing Club. This was *the* restaurant in the 1950s, 1960s, and 1970s. Many of the world's top celebrities and borderline gangsters used to eat here when Lebanon was a top location for jet-setters.

Byblos is an ancient port, one of the oldest towns in the world, responsible for spreading the use of the earliest alphabet. The word "bible" comes from Byblos. There's plenty to see and do here, including visiting Roman and Crusader ruins.

It's a shame to rush away but, if you're on a tight schedule, head for Batrun. Here, the Koura Plain narrows to a gorge, the Kadisha Valley or Holy Valley (so called because of the many Maronite monasteries that line the gorge). Follow the rough, switchbacking tarmac road up the

punishing 30-mile (48-km) ascent to Becharre. Tease yourself by visualizing the swimming pool at the Chbat Hotel in Becharre.

•DAY 6 24 miles (39km)

Becharre to Ba'albek

Known as Beit el Chari—house of the sky goddess—by the Phoenicians, Becharre is the base for trips to the Cedars, Lebanon's highest and least-developed ski resort, too far away from Beirut to be used by the glitterati. Lebanon's most famous son Kahlil Gibran (author of the 1923 classic *The Prophet*) was born in Becharre (but spent most of his life in America); there's a Gibran museum in town.

The half-hour climb from Becharre to the Cedars is steep but scenic: the views back down to town keep getting prettier and prettier as you ascend. This, in part, is due to the fact you see less rubbish. Litter in Lebanon is endemic. The clump of trees that gives the Cedars its name—one of the few remaining cedar "groves" in Lebanon—is fronted by a scruffy, kitsch strip of souvenir shacks and cafés.

The ski lifts are closed in the summer, so there's not a lot to stop you completing your climbing for the day and beginning the stunning descent into the Beqa'a Valley, heading for the stunning ruins at Ba'albek. However, if you have time to spare, you could try the 25-mile (40-km), circular, cross-country, waymarked ski route starting and ending at the cedar grove, which can be pedaled when there's no snow. There's also a walking route to the peak of Lebanon's highest mountain, Qornet es Sawda, at 10,131 feet (309m), which could possibly be cycled.

Pass Chlifa and then take the long straight road to the bustling nerve center of Hizbollah at Ba'albek. Book into the Palmyra Hotel. This is a faded colonial hotel that has obviously seen much, much better days. Squint and you can imagine seeing characters from Agatha Christie's *Death on the Nile* around every corner.

The extensive ruins at Ba'albek—which boasts the largest acropolis in the world, bigger even than the one at Athens—are some of the best-preserved ruins in the whole of the Middle East, making an impressive end to an impressive ride.

The Temple of Jupiter in Ba'albek.

OVERVIEW

The peaks of the Mount Lebanon Range top out at 10,000 feet (3,000m), so this is a high-level route where mountain weather conditions prevail. It can take just 6 days if you're pushed for time, 9 days if you add in a day each at Beirut, Byblos, and Ba'albek.

Start: Beirut.
Finish: Ba'albek.

ABOUT THE TRAIL

Much of this route is on tarmac but, as many of the roads in the Lebanon are battle-scarred and in disrepair they can be considered off-road. Don't ride through "puddles": they could be 3 feet (about a meter) deep!

Major Climbs & Descents: The narrow coastal plain and the Beqa'a Valley are flat. Almost everywhere else in Lebanon is wall-to-wall mountains, and within minutes of turning off any coastal road, the climbs start. The climb to Beiteddine, at 2,950 feet (900m), is merely a taste of the gradients to come. The climbs to the Lebanese ski resorts are especially tough; but the downhills—all on chewed-up tarmac—are brilliant.

Difficulty & Special Features: The coastal road is busy and unpleasant to cycle; it may be worth taking "service" taxis to the start of the mountain climbs. There are also regular army roadblocks.

ACCESS

Airports: Beirut International Airport is a 45-minute cycle from downtown Beirut. M.E.A. (the national Lebanese airline), some European airlines, and most regional airlines fly into here.

Transport: A catamaran service links the seaport of Larnaca in Cyprus to Beirut. Return to Beirut from Ba'albek by taxi, as the road through the Beqa'a Valley is flat, boring, and full of traffic.

Passport & Visa Requirements: All visitors, except Syrians, need a valid passport and visa, available from Lebanese consulates around the world; in theory, visas should be available at your entry point to Lebanon from the Bureau de Change in the airport arrivals hall; however, this is all subject to change, so check before travel. Visitors with Israeli visas, stamps, or passport will be refused entry.

Permits & Access Restrictions: All of this route is accessible but, because of the country's violent history, it is advisable to check access with your embassy before planning your trip.

LOCAL INFORMATION

Maps: There are no reliable large-scale maps of Lebanon. The GeoProjects road map of the whole of Lebanon is the best, but is unreliable for off-road routes. Ask your hotel for any hiking trail maps or get hotel staff to draw you a rough map of the area. Chbat Hotel in Becharre and Hotel Douma in Douma specialize in hiking trips, and the maps they use can be easily adapted for biking.

Guidebooks: *Lebanon: A Travel Guide* by Carlton Reid (Kindlife Books) was researched from the saddle. Beirut changes almost weekly, so guidebooks date quickly.

Accommodation & Supplies: Hotels outside of Beirut are few and far between, so you will need to camp/bivouac when in out-of-the-way locations. There are a couple of faded colonial-type hotels in Ba'albek. Hotels are expensive in Lebanon, especially at the ski resort of Faraya. The hotels in less developed areas are much better value for money. Some, such as Chbat Hotel in Becharre, are keen to encourage out-of-season outdoor activities and produce hiking and biking route guides.

Currency & Language: Lebanese lira, but you can also use U.S. dollars. The main language is Arabic, but French and English are widely spoken.

Photography: Don't photograph military installations, ports, army roadblocks, or anything that's not of tourist interest.

Area Information: The Lebanese Tourist Board can send you basic leaflets and maps, many of which are pre-civil war. There's only one bike shop of note in Lebanon, and that's La Bicyclette, at Sin El Fil, Beirut, Lebanon (tel.: 499 846; e-mail: info@la-bicyclette.com).

TIMING & SEASONALITY

 Best Months to Visit: Any time from May through September avoids heavy snowfall. High summer can be very hot so err on the margins of this time slot.

Climate: Lebanon's climate is Mediterranean—summers are hot and dry; the country is rain-free between June and October; and the mountains are cold and snowy in winter. The heat at Ba'albek and in the Beqa'a Valley can be intense. The mountains are a lot cooler but beware of sunburn at altitude even in winter (on the Lebanon mountain ranges there is no shade above the timberline, which is at 3,500–4,000 feet/1,000–1,220m).

HEALTH & SAFETY

 Vaccinations: Polio, tetanus, and typhoid.

General Health Risks: Sunstroke.

Special Considerations: None.

Politics & Religion: Seventeen religious groups live side by side in Lebanon, and politics revolve around the differing needs and demands of these groups.

Crime Risk: There are no security guarantees; be aware of the dangers of terrorist crime.

Food & Drink: Stock up on Lebanon's famous sticky, nutty, sweet-cheesy pastries. The cheapest food is street food, such as falafel. Fruit and vegetables are widely available but are mostly imported, so they may not be that fresh. Buy bottled drinking water.

HIGHLIGHTS

Scenic: Beyond Beirut, Lebanon, dominated by the snowcapped Mount Lebanon Range, is a country of great beauty. Lebanon also has some of the largest cave systems in the world.

Wildlife & Flora: Lebanon has plenty of exotic birds because, like Israel, it is on a continental bridge that attracts birds migrating from Europe to Africa. The Beqa'a Valley is wall-to-wall grapes as it is now a wine-producing area, but during the civil war the area was infamous for producing hashish.

↓ temperature and precipitation

	JAN	FEB	MAR	APR	MAY	JUN	JUL	AUG	SEP	OCT	NOV	DEC	
°f	63	63	66	72	79	82	88	90	86	81	73	64	°f
°c	17	17	19	22	26	28	31	32	30	27	23	18	°c
°f	52	52	54	57	64	70	73	73	73	70	61	55	°f
°c	11	11	12	14	18	21	23	23	23	21	16	13	°c
ins	7.6	6.3	3.8	2.2	0.7	0.1	0	0	0.2	2.0	5.3	7.4	ins
mm	191	158	94	56	18	3	0	0	5	51	132	185	mm

Australasia

Outback Australia, there's nothing like it, specially when traveling by unmotorized vehicle. A vast land of extremes where an eight-day journey by bike is considered short and the animal life is wildly individualistic. Three routes here include a Tasmanian traverse, the Crocodile Trail through the tropical north, and a bold hack through the ruddy interior. A short hop away is New Zealand, which could have been created for the mountain bike whether touring or single-tracking, and where the pioneer spirit still lives in the trails.

the CROCODILE TRAIL

AUSTRALIA

Sue Webber

ONE OF THE GREAT MOUNTAIN BIKE ADVENTURES OF AUSTRALIA, THE CROCODILE TRAIL, HEADS OUT OF CAIRNS INTO THE REMOTE TROPICAL NORTH OF THE CONTINENT. IT FOLLOWS THE SPINE OF THE GREAT DIVIDING RANGE UP TO THE NORTHERNMOST TIP OF MAINLAND AUSTRALIA, EMERGING FROM THE INTERIOR TO THE BEAUTIFUL BUT TREACHEROUS WATERS OF THE TORRES STRAIT.

Along the way there are stunning National Parks that brim with wildlife, an awesome Aboriginal rock-art gallery, sparkling waterfalls, and perfect natural swimming pools, as well as the white sandy beaches and turquoise waters of the Tip. The route follows hard-packed dirt roads, sandy and corrugated tracks, and the exciting riding of the Old Telegraph Road with its many creek crossings. Cape York is famous for the saltwater or estuarine crocodiles that live in its many waterways. These crocs can grow up to 19 feet (6m) long and have been known to make a meal of passing people. The Cape also has some wonderful National Parks and a third of all the species of birds in Australia can be found here. You'll also see tropical butterflies, agile wallabies, dingoes, and a snake or two sunning themselves on the road. The 689-mile (1,108-km) journey is easily followed but maps and guidebooks are still recommended.

↓ itinerary

•DAYS 1–4   135 miles (217km)

Cairns to Helenvale

The Captain Cook Highway, heading north out of Cairns between sugarcane fields, is the only significant stretch of sealed road on the trip. From Mossman on the edge of Daintree National Park, the route follows an incredible coastline through Cape Tribulation National Park, where the tropical rain forest comes right down to the sea. There's a steep climb into the Alexandra Ranges and a good downhill

The wide, open view from Split Rock, near Laura, gives a lasting impression of Australia's vast landscape.

reward. The campground at Noah Beach is a great overnight spot.

After Cape Tribulation there are several steep hills to climb, and some are almost impossible to ride up with a heavily laden bike. You can ride or push through the shallow creek crossing but the tidal Bloomfield river is a bigger challenge. Cyclists should be extremely wary about crossing this, since the river is home to saltwater crocodiles. The safest option is to beg a lift across with a passing vehicle. From the Bloomfield, the route turns inland to Helenvale and the Lions' Den pub, a classic Australian bush pub with a campground at the back.

•DAYS 5–6 74 miles (119km)

Helenvale to Laura

The dirt Cooktown Development Road leads to the peanut-growing town of Lakeland and the Peninsula Developmental Road, the main road up Cape York. Split Rock Gallery, 12 miles (19km) south of Laura, is a wonderful showcase of Aboriginal rock paintings. Aboriginal people have been living in the area for at least 33,000 years and pieces of ocher several thousands of years old have been found nearby. If you can, allow yourself three hours to complete the longer walk around the top of the rock, where you'll see hand prints and paintings that have symbolic significance in the local Aboriginal tradition. Laura is a good spot for a rest day, and to do your washing and restock your panniers.

• DAYS 7–10 129 miles (208km)

Laura to Musgrave

From Laura, a sandy track leads into Lakefield National Park, the second largest national park in Queensland. There are extensive wetland areas and many crocodiles, so take heed of the warning signs and choose your camping areas with care. Lakefield provides some enjoyable cycling through stunning scenery—lily-filled water holes, giant termite mounds, and shallow river crossings—but it's worth taking some time to explore on foot. From Saltwater Crossing, the track deteriorates to a deep sandy track that leads to the Peninsula Developmental Road at Musgrave—camp by the airstrip and eat at the local pub.

• DAYS 11–12 67 miles (108km)

Musgrave to Coen

The road heads north through cattle properties to Coen. Water can be a problem on this section, so make sure you're carrying plenty. If there's no water at the Kendle

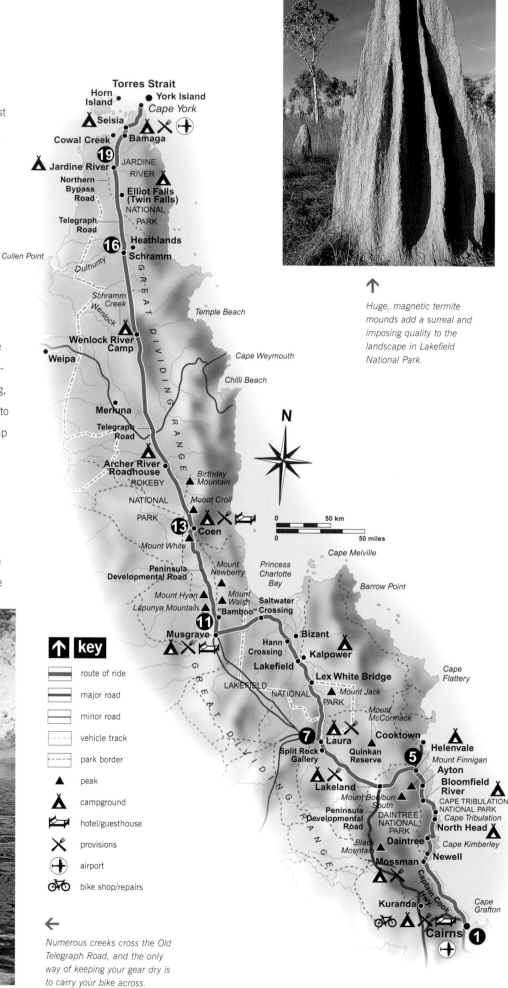

Huge, magnetic termite mounds add a surreal and imposing quality to the landscape in Lakefield National Park.

← *Numerous creeks cross the Old Telegraph Road, and the only way of keeping your gear dry is to carry your bike across.*

key

- route of ride
- major road
- minor road
- vehicle track
- park border
- ▲ peak
- ⛺ campground
- 🛏 hotel/guesthouse
- ✕ provisions
- ✈ airport
- 🚲 bike shop/repairs

While riding through Lakefield National Park, which is renowned for its wetlands and associated wildlife, it is important to watch out for crocodiles if you get near the water's edge.

↓

The area around Twin Falls has excellent camping and some great swimming holes.

river crossing, follow the creek bed until you find some. Coen is a major center with shops, a hospital, and a campground. Stock up here for the next eight days. Before you start this trip it's worth sending yourself a parcel to Coen Post Office with any special food items, films, and bike spares so that you know that they will be waiting for you when you arrive.

•DAYS 13–15 125 miles (201km)

Coen to Schramm Creek

The road heads north through Rokeby National Park and if you have sufficient food and time you could take a detour into the park. The Peninsula Developmental Road leads to the mining town of Weipa on the west coast, but you will follow the Telegraph Road north. You can camp at Archer River Roadhouse but don't expect to find much in the way of supplies here. There's also a great free camping spot down by Archer River itself. Before you leave, ask at the roadhouse about where to find water for the next few days and check if there is water in Rocky Creek on the Telegraph Road. The Wenlock is a major river and you'll need to carry your bike across. It's a popular camping spot, but Schramm Creek, 5 miles (8km) further on is quieter and cleaner.

•DAYS 16–18 111 miles (178km)

Schramm Creek to Jardine River

Most vehicles take the Bypass Roads around the Old Telegraph Road but cyclists can enjoy this rough, narrow track with its many creek crossings. This is some of the best cycling on the Cape York Peninsula and there is usually plenty of water in the creeks. Gunshot Creek is an extremely difficult crossing for vehicles so there's a bypass road via the Heathlands Ranger Station. Cyclists can ignore the detour and walk their bikes down the steep bank to the river →

↓ ride profile

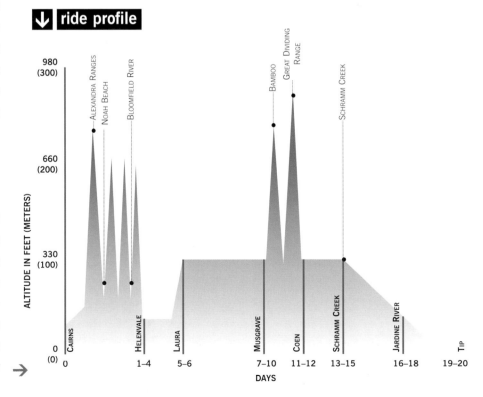

crossing. Elliot Falls is well worth a visit with lush tropical vegetation and beautiful swimming holes. If you have sufficient time and supplies, it's worth taking a rest day here before the ride to the top.

The Jardine river is well known for its crocodiles but the Aboriginal landowners run a ferry service that will take you and your bike safely to the other side, where there's a camping area, but choose a spot well back from the water.

▪DAYS 19–20 | 48 miles (77km)

Jardine River to the Tip

From Jardine River, ride into Bamaga, a major town with all the luxuries you've been missing. If you've time for another stop, take the road to Seisia. Seisia Beach has a relaxed campground with wonderful views out into the Torres Strait. For a good little mountain bike ride take the small track by the painted canoe at the entrance to Seisia and follow it east through the sandy woodlands for about 9 miles (15km) to the main road. The final section of the route takes you through the tropical rain forests to the Panjinka campground and lodge, just a short walk from the Tip.

↓ **factfile**

↑

It is worth taking an extra day to explore Elliot Falls, which are close to Twin Falls.

OVERVIEW

Although this is not a signed route, it's hard to go wrong if you take a reasonable map. Cyclists share the dirt roads with motorbikes and four-wheel-drive vehicles, but traffic is light and concentrated between 10:00 A.M. and 12:00 P.M., and 2:00 P.M. and 4:00 P.M. If you get going early it will be hours before you see a vehicle. There's about 620 miles (1,000km) of dirt road between Cairns and Cape York and you'll need to be ready for all conditions from corrugations to sand, gravel, and creek crossings. You'll also need to be able to carry up to 6 days' food and plenty of water: 2.6 U.S. gallons (10 liters) per person, minimum.

If you allow 3 weeks for the trip you'll have some time to stop and explore Split Rock, Lakefield National Park, and Elliot Falls. Cape York rewards those who travel slowly with subtle changes in landscape and environment and a full five-sense experience that's lost to most powered-vehicle users.

Start: Cairns, Queensland.
Finish: The Tip, Cape York, Queensland.

ABOUT THE TRAIL

Most of the route is on double-track dirt roads with some narrow sections along the old Telegraph Road, which, incidentally, provides the best riding. Expect everything from

hard-packed dirt to deep sand. Most creek crossings are shallow, although it may be better for your gear to carry your bike rather than ride or push through. the Bloomfield river crossing is the most difficult and dangerous and cyclists should beg a lift from passing vehicles to avoid close encounters with crocodiles.

Major Climbs & Descents: There are none of note, and once you're over the ranges of Cape Tribulation National Park and Cedar Bay National Park there are no real hills. Most of the hills are on the section between Mossman and Helenvale.

Difficulty & Special Features: The route is not technically difficult and could be ridden by anyone with reasonable fitness, good touring experience and mechanical ability, and excellent preparation. The challenge is to be self-sufficient in an environment where food and water are often in short supply. The route never rises above 1,928 feet (590m) and much of it is below 492 feet (150m). Watch out for crocodiles!

ACCESS

 Airports: There is an international and domestic airport at Cairns and a domestic airport at Bamaga with connections back to Cairns.

Transport: Greyhound Pioneer, McCafferty's, and Coral Coaches run to Cairns from Brisbane and Weipa. Trains run from Brisbane to Cairns. Jardine Shipping runs a barge service from Cairns to Bamaga that takes passengers once a week.

Passport and Visa Requirements: All visitors to Australia need a visa, except those holding a New Zealand passport.

Permits & Access Restrictions: The route follows public roads and no special permits are required. The fee for using the Jardine River ferry also includes payment for camping on Aboriginal land at designated campgrounds. If you plan to travel through other areas of Aboriginal land you will need a permit.

LOCAL INFORMATION

 Maps: The Hema map, Cape York From Cairns to the Tip, is excellent and provides all the detail you will need.

Guidebooks: Cape York, An Adventurer's Guide by Ron and Viv Moon (Kakirra Adventure Guides), is a very useful guide even though it is written for four-wheel-drive travelers rather than cyclists. Australia's Cape York Peninsula by

Clifford and Dawn Frith (Frith and Frith), is an excellent guide to the plants and animals of the Cape.

Accommodation & Supplies: This tour requires full self-sufficiency as many of the camping places have no facilities. You will find a full range of accommodation in Cairns. There are rooms at Musgrave Telegraph Station and Coen. At the Tip, Seisia Village Resort has rooms, and the Panjinka Wilderness Lodge, just 15 minutes' walk from the Tip, is a luxury resort with cabins. Stock up at Cairns, Lakeland, Laura, Coen, and Bamaga. It's well worth making up a food/spares parcel and mailing it to yourself to pick up along the way.

Currency & Language: Australian dollars; English.

Area Information: Queensland Travel and Tourism Corporation, 243 Edward Street, Brisbane, Queensland, Australia (fax: 07 3221 5320; e-mail: qldtravl@ozemail.com.au); Bicycle Queensland, P.O. Box 8321, Woolloongabba, Queensland, 4102 (tel./fax: 07 3844 1144; e-mail: enq@biq.org.au).

TIMING & SEASONALITY

 Best Months to Visit: Between June and September, although the later you go the harder it may be to find water in the creeks.

Climate: The wet or green season is between November and April. This is when most of the rain falls and many roads become impassable. Between June and September expect temperatures of 62–86°F (16–30°C), and the prevailing winds mean you're more likely to

→

Superb Quinkan Aboriginal art dating back 14,000 years circles the gallery at Split Rock, near Laura.

get a tailwind riding north. There is little rainfall between June and September.

HEALTH & SAFETY

 Vaccinations: None required.

General Health Risks: Take plenty of sun protection, including SPF 15-plus sunscreen, and wear long sleeves and head covering whenever possible. Mosquitoes are common on parts of Cape York and you should cover your skin at dusk and use a mosquito repellent. Dengue fever and Ross River fever are carried by mosquitoes in far North Queensland.

Special Considerations: Saltwater or estuarine crocodiles can grow up to 19 feet (6m) and live in both salt and fresh water. Don't swim, prepare food at the water's edge, or camp within 50 yards of deep-water areas. There are sharks in

the sea all around the Cape, so swimming isn't a very good idea, especially as there are also poisonous box jellyfish throughout the year. There are plenty of snakes on the Cape and you will probably see them sunning themselves on the road. Give them a wide berth as many are venomous: Taipan, King Brown, Brown Snake, and Death Adder. Be careful walking through long grass and by water.

Politics & Religion: No special concerns.

Crime Risk: Few. But keep an eye on your bike and spares. They may be hard to replace in a hurry, and then your trip could be ruined.

Food & Drink: Always purify creek water with iodine, Puritabs, or a filter. North of Musgrave, be prepared to carry as much water as you can—at least 2.6 U.S. gallons (10 liters) per person— and never miss an opportunity to

fill up. Ask the locals where to find water: if a creek is dry in one part there may still be water elsewhere. Once you reach the Old Telegraph Road your water worries will be over, since the track is crossed by many flowing creeks. The new DCS Bypass road, however, avoids all the creek crossings and is dry for much of the way.

HIGHLIGHTS

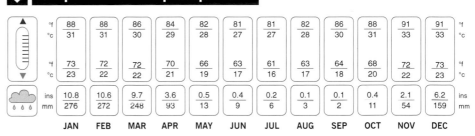 **Scenic:** The Aboriginal Art Gallery at Split Rock is a moving and eloquent experience. The Aboriginals' relationship with their land and all that lives and grows there is powerfully drawn and painted across this high outcrop, which overlooks the surrounding countryside; the interconnectedness of the land and the people is palpable. Lakefield National Park epitomizes the wild landscape of Cape York with its floodplains, water holes, and termite cities. Cycling here is like riding through a coffee-table book of magnificent images. Dawn and dusk are worth losing sleep for.

Wildlife & Flora: Crocodiles, snakes, wallabies, and more birds than a wildlife documentary. Many nocturnal marsupials live in the Cape, so take your torch and go for a nighttime walk to see what you can find. The flora changes as the landscape alters between mangrove swamps and tropical rain forest to wetlands, woodlands, and open grasslands.

⬇ temperature and precipitation

	°f	JAN	FEB	MAR	APR	MAY	JUN	JUL	AUG	SEP	OCT	NOV	DEC	
▲	°f	88	88	86	84	82	81	81	82	86	88	91	91	°f
	°c	31	31	30	29	28	27	27	28	30	31	33	33	°c
▼	°f	73	72	72	70	66	63	61	63	64	68	72	73	°f
	°c	23	22	22	21	19	17	16	17	18	20	22	23	°c
☁	ins	10.8	10.6	9.7	3.6	0.5	0.4	0.2	0.1	0.1	0.4	2.1	6.2	ins
	mm	276	272	248	93	13	9	6	3	2	11	54	159	mm
		JAN	FEB	MAR	APR	MAY	JUN	JUL	AUG	SEP	OCT	NOV	DEC	

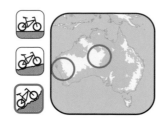

to the RED CENTER

AUSTRALIA

Jamie Carr

AUSTRALIA'S OUTBACK IS THE COMPLETE OPPOSITE TO MOUNTAINOUS—TO THE RED CENTER IS A FLAT RIDE FOR HUNDREDS OF MILES ACROSS DESERTS AND SAND, SO WHY GO THERE? FOR JUST THAT REASON, AND TO SEE ONE OF THE GREAT NATURAL WONDERS OF THE WORLD WHEN YOU REACH THE MIDDLE—ULURU, OTHERWISE KNOWN AS AYERS ROCK.

The Outback is steeped in history, going right back to Len Beadell's first crossing and his building of the Gunbarrel Highway, which links wells across one of the greatest deserts in the world. The first part of the route, crossing the Gibson Desert, is the most dramatic. The area around the World Heritage Site of Shark Bay is one of Australia's best-kept secrets; at nearby Monkey Mia you can feed wild dolphins and, if you're lucky, even swim with them. However, access to Steep Point is through a restricted salt-mining area and access can be difficult to obtain; so an alternative start is also given.

↓ itinerary

•DAYS 1–9 435 miles (696km)

Steep Point to Wiluna

After looking over the Indian Ocean and swimming with wild dolphins at Monkey Mia in Shark Bay, you leave the small solar-powered lighthouse and coast behind, point your tires toward the east, and set off down sandy dunes at the start of the longest off-road ride of your life. Cross Highway 1, the circular coast road, and enter into the sandy tracks of the Outback. Making camp at 5:30 P.M. each evening is easy as there will always be an area of sandy bush available. Official campgrounds in towns aren't very common, but then you pass through Meekatharra and Wiluna, and find two in a row. Both these towns are very small mining towns, though they do have the obligatory pub, shop, and gas station. Either is good for a night stopover. These are the last services till Warburton.

VARIATION: If you can't get permission to start off from Steep Point, a good alternative is Geraldton, below Steep Point. The terrain and the tracks are very similar and pass through Mullewa, Mount Magnet, and Sandstone en route to Wiluna. The route travels up the rarely used Murchison River valley, which is full of kangaroos to watch out for. A 300-pound male bull kangaroo can cause serious damage at the speed they travel through the bush, and you definitely give way to them—that's if you can see them coming! If time is a limiting factor, a good way to experience Outback life is to cycle to Kalgoorlie in mid-September, when there is a huge horse-racing festival. You can start cycling from there, or from Laverton, on the Great Central Road to Warburton. The latter route is along more frequently traveled sandy dirt tracks that are easier to navigate; you might even see a couple of other vehicles if you go this way!

•DAYS 10–14 400 miles (640km)

Wiluna to Warburton

Soft sand and heavy rain could make these days very hard going. The rain can be unpredictable in June, July, and August, making the sand combine with red dust to form a glue-like consistency that sticks to everything you own. Extra-wide tires (3 V-Claws) make cycling over this sand

"Graders" (sand equivalents of snowplows) clear the dirt roads of corrugations and provide smooth paths. Eventually you will be able to appreciate a rare view from these smooth, but lonely, roads when you reach the impressive monoliths known as the Olgas.

If the rains come, the Gunbarrel Highway bursts into life with flora and fauna. If you happen to experience this rare occurrence, make sure you fully appreciate it as these may be the last gum trees you see for hundreds of miles.

much easier. Desert riders have also successfully used Alaskan Snow Cat rims, which, at 45 millimeters wide, were developed for winter races—strange as it sounds, soft sand and fresh, cold, powdered snow have very similar quilts and need the same riding techniques. Make sure, however, that your bike can cope with the huge tire clearances necessary to run these monsters. Passing through Lake Carnige and a small oasis is a change from the open deserts, and there are actually a few corners to negotiate, making for some interesting riding! A sign marks the official start to the Old Gunbarrel Highway, about 220 miles (354km), from Wiluna, but, other than that, the trail looks the same.

There are many trails in this area, and after Wiluna it is quite easy to get lost and local guidance is needed. Fortunately, Warburton is an important outstation and most tracks in this area pass through it. At Warburton the Great Central Road joins the Gunbarrel Highway.

•DAYS 15–18 | 330 miles (528km)

Warburton to Uluru/Ayers Rock

Now you should be in a good routine of riding and camping wherever you drop at the end of a day in the saddle. Having a set start and end time to a day, or a specific point to aim for, is a good idea when crossing the Gibson Desert, since long sections without towns can be offputting. A support truck can get ahead and set up a camp for you to ride into—and it feels as if you have arrived somewhere. However, on this section, those long rides will eventually get you somewhere official, as you will cross into the Northern Territories from Western Australia, and a welcome signpost tells you this. In the distance on the fourth day of cycling from Warburton, something begins to appear on the horizon and stays there for a long time, slowly getting bigger—for the first time in ages you actually have a view of something, albeit a multitude of lumps. A look at the map

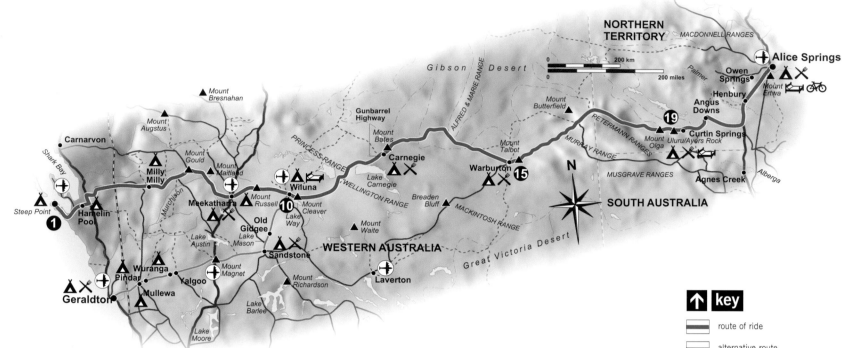

soon reveals that this is the Olgas—a collection of monoliths, nowhere near as famous as Ayers Rock, but much taller and some believe more beautiful. There is a canyon through them that contains a cycle route. From here you can make out Ayers Rock, only 40 miles (64km) away, and you are in the middle of Australia's red center. Camping is prohibited around Ayers Rock—called Uluru in the aboriginal language—so you have to stay at the nearby town of Yarala, where there is a hotel and a few restaurants that serve the tourists who come to see and climb the rock.

smooth and sealed with good tarmac, so narrow high-pressure slicks and big chain-rings are the order of the day. It's easy cycling and a dream come true when you see shops, pizza houses, and bars materialize in Alice Springs. There's a choice of places to stay and eat, a swimming pool, and the all-important ice cream! Alice has a nice feel about it and, as the only town of any size in the center, it has many facilities that no other town has in the Outback. There's also a well-serviced airport and car rental returns.

•DAYS 19–21 286 miles (458km)

Up Uluru and down to Alice Springs

Watching the sun set and the colors of the red Outback change to orange while sitting on top of a rock in the middle of Australia is amazing in itself. But also knowing that you have ridden from the very coast of this massive country, some 1,165 miles (1,864km) away, gives an immense feeling of satisfaction and personal achievement—a feeling that very few people can say they have experienced, and one that will stay with you forever. The Aboriginals hold Uluru as a most sacred place and do not climb it. However, there is a path and a chain to pull yourself up the rock. Be careful, though, as many people have died falling off the rock in strong winds or from slipping on a steep section.

Once you're safely down you will need some well-deserved comforts. It's a half-day drive or two to three days' cycling to the metropolis of Alice from here, but the road is

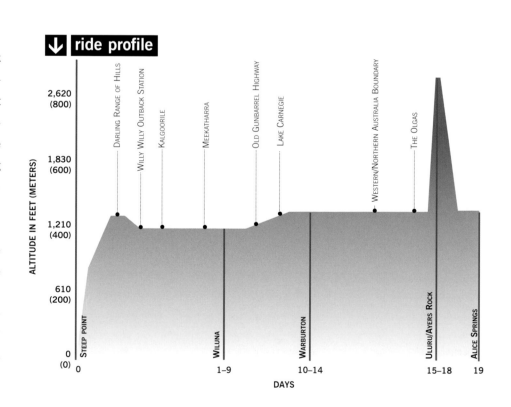

166

 factfile

OVERVIEW

 This is a long, hot desert route on which you will experience the vastness of the Australian Outback, the massive sky, and absolute darkness with amazing stars. You can also, if it rains, witness the desert in bloom, before reaching the amazing sight of Uluru, Ayers Rock.

Start: Steep Point, Australia's most westerly point, or, alternatively, Geraldton, near Perth.

Finish: Alice Springs.

ABOUT THE TRAIL

 All wide, sandy jeep trails or hard-packed dirt roads. Those sections with a hard-packed surface are very fast; others are harder work.

Major Climbs & Descents: None of any significance.

Difficulty & Special Features: The severity totally depends on how long you ride for each day. There are no fixed days, rather you just camp wherever you stop. The trails can be quite rough, and a good soft saddle is essential and some suspension is recommended. Take specialist bike spares for any suspension units your bike has, since the corrugations on the sandy tracks wear out suspension units very fast. Carry a spare chain and the usual basic repair and tool kit.

ACCESS

Airports: Perth has an international airport; Alice Springs has a good internal service from anywhere in Australia.

Transport: A four-wheel-drive support van will be necessary to carry supplies through the long, deserted areas. Britz:Australia hire four-wheel-drives fitted as campers. One-way self-drive is possible to Alice Springs or any other large city.

Passport & Visa Requirements: All North Americans and Europeans need a visa in advance. Thisy can be obtained from Australian embassies, and lasts 6 months.

Permits & Access Restrictions: Aboriginal permits for passing through an Aboriginal reserve area are necessary; these are free and available from the Aboriginal Reserves office in Perth.

LOCAL INFORMATION

 Maps: Large-scale maps, produced by the Australian Surveying & Land Information Group, are available from many outdoor shops in Australia, or contact AUSLIG, Department of Administrative Services, Scrivener Building, Fern Hill Park, Bruce, ACT 2617 (tel.: 02 6201 4201). The best road maps are produced by the various oil companies—Shell, BP, Mobil, etc.

Guidebooks: *Australia* in the Lonely Planet series gives details of towns in the Outback as well as some interesting sights that can be seen in conjunction with your tour.

Background Reading: There are some moving books on travel in the Australian Outback and stories of Aboriginal life, such as *Tracks* by Robyn Davidson (Picador) and *The Songlines* by Bruce Chatwin (Vintage).

Accommodation & Supplies: In between towns you must be totally self-sufficient for all water, food, and camping gear till the next resupply point. There are gas stations along the way, and a support vehicle should get by on a full tank and a reserve supply— but this does not allow for detours or poor conditions.

Currency & Language: Australian dollars; English, but the Outback Australians have a specific dialect of their own—see the glossary in the Lonely Planet guidebook.

Photography: Black-and-white prints are fantastic for showing up the contours of the landscape, but also carry color film for the rich reds of the desert.

Area Information: Western Australia Tourist Centre, Albert Facey House, Forrest Place, Perth (tel.: 08 9483 1111). If you are traveling alone you can join an organized tour with Remote Outback Cycle Tours (tel.: 08 9244 4614; fax 08 9244 4615).

Websites: www.cycletours.com.au; www.omen.com.au/roc

The first day, on the most western edge of Australia, offers a soft sand start to the trip. You will learn new riding skills along the way on this route.

TIMING & SEASONALITY

 Best Months to Visit: The cooler winter months— July to September—are the most pleasant; June and October are a little hot but bearable.

Climate: Central Australia has very stable weather patterns, which are basically hot! However, occasional flash floods in the desert can gouge huge channels in the earth and wash away anything that lies on the surface.

HEALTH & SAFETY

 **Vaccinations:** A visit to your doctor and dentist for general checkups before undergoing such an isolated trip is wise.

General Health Risks: Prepare yourself for very hot weather and beware of sunstroke and dehydration—wear sunscreen, cover up in the heat of the day, and always wear a helmet (this keeps the sun off your head and provides excellent ventilation); keep well hydrated and allow for an intake of 2.6 U.S. gallons (10 liters) of fluid a day.

Special Considerations: None.

Politics & Religion: No concerns.

Crime Risk: Low.

Food & Drink: Food in the main Outback towns (where you can resupply) is good and cheap. Boil water in the Outback, or treat with iodine for a cooler drink.

HIGHLIGHTS

Taking time to ride through this vast country and meet the wonderful people, who are worlds apart from urban Aussies, is time well spent.

Scenic: The ride crosses the Gibson Desert, one of the biggest deserts on the planet, which has a unique beauty that needs to be seen firsthand to be appreciated. The red dusty center of Australia, with one of the great natural wonders of the world, Uluru (Ayers Rock), is a sight to behold.

Wildlife & Flora: After heavy rain the desert becomes a sea of color from all the flowers. Australia has the most weird and wonderful wildlife: from kookaburras and kangaroos to feral camels and goannas (a type of lizard). Be aware that kangaroos can be aggressive if annoyed.

↓ temperature and precipitation

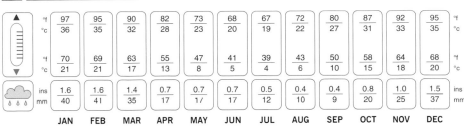

	JAN	FEB	MAR	APR	MAY	JUN	JUL	AUG	SEP	OCT	NOV	DEC	
°f	97	95	90	82	73	68	67	72	80	87	92	95	°f
°c	36	35	32	28	23	20	19	22	27	31	33	35	°c
°f	70	69	63	55	47	41	39	43	50	58	64	68	°f
°c	21	21	17	13	8	5	4	6	10	15	18	20	°c
ins	1.6	1.6	1.4	0.7	0.7	0.7	0.5	0.4	0.4	0.8	1.0	1.5	ins
mm	40	41	35	17	17	17	12	10	9	20	25	37	mm

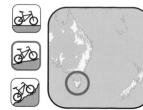

the TASMANIAN TRAIL

TASMANIA, AUSTRALIA

Sue Webber

ACROSS THE CENTER OF AUSTRALIA'S SMALLEST STATE, THE TASMANIAN TRAIL TRAVERSES A SECTION OF THIS UNIQUE ISLAND. TASMANIA IS UNLIKE THE REST OF AUSTRALIA: WITH ITS NORTHERN EUROPEAN CLIMATE, SPECTACULAR WILDERNESS AREAS, AND LOW POPULATION, IT PROVIDES SOME OF THE BEST PLACES FOR CYCLE TOURING ON THE AUSTRALIAN CONTINENT.

You will often have the luxury of empty roads in this sparsely populated area of Tasmania.

Following bush tracks, old railroad lines, and forestry routes, the Tasmanian Trail winds its way through some spectacular countryside, from the lush northern farmlands through to the alpine high plateau and down through the southern half of the State to Hobart.

This route describes the Trail from Devonport to Hobart, over 266 miles (429km). The Tasmanian Trail continues south to Esperance River over another 80 miles (129km) of backcountry. The entire route is mapped and signposted, although maps and guidebooks are still necessary, owing to the complexity of the route and the alternatives available.

The route is shared by cyclists, walkers, and horse riders and crosses private land where a key is necessary to open gates (see Itinerary below). The Tasmanian Trail gives cyclists access to places that they could not normally reach and the inhabitants of towns along the route have agreed to allow cyclists to camp in their towns and use facilities free of charge.

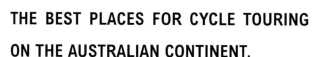

↓ itinerary

•DAY 1   29 miles (47km)

Devonport to Sheffield

Little red and yellow triangles mark the Tasmanian Trail but a map is still essential as the signs can be hard to find. From Devonport, the trail heads south, away from the sea, and follows the estuary of the Mersey river upstream. At Latrobe, pick up the trail key at Sullivan's Milk Bar—you'll need to leave a cash deposit (refunded when the key is returned). This key will open the gates into private property through which the trail passes. The trail soon leaves the

The wide, open road near Bracknell is a typical Tasmanian back road. Western Tiers is visible in the background.

sealed road for a section through a eucalyptus plantation and across sheep paddocks to the road to Railton.

The story of Norm Sykes of Railton is an inspiration for the rest of the ride. Norm lived near Railton without many of the comforts we take for granted; he used his bike for transport and pedaled to power a light so that he could read at night. The trail crosses his land, now the Sykes Sanctuary. A disused railroad line provides an excellent ride into Sheffield, where you can camp by the sports oval.

■ **DAY 2** | **32 miles (51km)**

Sheffield to Deloraine

The climbs begin today, and you'll discover that there are no easy ways to Paradise as you climb the Old Paradise Road past quiet farms. After crossing Minnow Creek the trail divides. The main trail follows logging tracks—some of which are incredibly steep with fallen trees as obstacles— through a State Forest. The alternative is to follow the Union Bridge Road and rejoin the trail after some 2½ miles (4km). The Gog Range Road allows some fast dirt cycling and leads down to the Mersey River crossing. There's a strong current here, so take care pushing your bike through.

A very steep track leads up the far side of the river and into a forest. There's some hard riding and pushing until a long-awaited downhill along a forestry road leads to Mole Creek Road. Follow this road to Red Hills, from where it's only 4 more sealed miles (7km) into Deloraine for shops, restaurants, and a campground with hot showers.

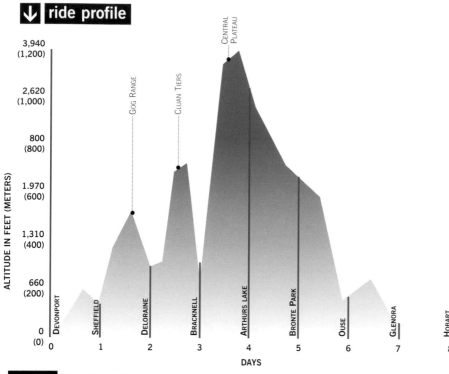

ride profile

↑
Some sections of the Caves
Track are simply unridable with
a heavily loaded bike.

•DAY 3 37 miles (59km)

Deloraine to Bracknell

A very quiet cross-country day along the Cluan Tiers. As you return to Red Hills, a back road leads to Montana Falls. You can visit the falls, which are on private property, by paying at the honesty box at the gate. Cross-country dirt roads lead to Quamby Brook and the climb up along the Cluan Tiers, a logging road with great views down to the plain and the mountains beyond. There's a technical descent down to Myrtle Creek and a sawmill, and then a hard-packed dirt road for the rest of the descent. Easy riding takes you to the little town of Bracknell, where you can camp behind the pub or along by the Liffey River swimming hole. It's worth staying an extra day at Bracknell and riding up to the Liffey Falls. This 36-mile (58-km) day trip involves a long climb into the mountains (650–2,300 feet/200–700m), to the Liffey Falls parking area, a short walk under a forest of giant tree ferns to the falls, and then the most amazing descent back to the plain.

•DAY 4 30 miles (48km)

Bracknell to Arthurs Lake

This is the big climb from the plain up to the high plateau; if you think of a cross-section of Tasmania being shaped like a hat, this is the climb from the brim to the crown.

The trail occasionally crosses paddocks, and riding through long grass is unavoidable.

 key

 route of ride

major road

minor road

ferry route

▲ peak

 campground

 hotel/guesthouse

✕ provisions

✈ airport

 bike shop/repairs

There's some easy back road cycling from Bracknell to the start of the Caves Track. The Caves Track leads up through forests, climbing from 980 to 3,600 feet (300m–1,100m) over 2½ miles (4km). The track surface is often rough and rocky and there are fallen trees to climb over. Be prepared to push, pull, or drag your bike through some sections. On the plus side, the trail is very pretty with lots of wild flowers, including Tasmanian orchids. There is a small place to camp at an old log camp but, if you can, press on to join the main road over the top of Tasmania. The alternative is to ride from Bracknell to Poatina and up the sealed road from there. The weather on top is very different from that of the plains below—while they're enjoying the summer sunshine you may be freezing up here. The trail leads to a fishing camp by Arthurs Lake, one of a series of lakes dammed for a hydroelectric scheme. Despite all the available electricity, the campground's showers are heated by a wood fire.

•DAY 5 34 miles (55km)

Arthurs Lake to Bronte Park

The trail follows an enjoyable gravel track alongside a pipeline to the Great Lake, where mountains rise up in the distance. It then rejoins the main road to Miena, where the Great Lake Hotel is a good chance to stop for a break. The trail takes some deviations from the main road between Miena and Bronte Park; these detours are poorly marked and difficult to find. Bronte Park is an old hydro workers' settlement that has been turned into a holiday resort.

It you have an extra day it's worth riding from Bronte Park to Lake St. Clair along the Lyell Highway. Lake St. Clair, at the southern end of Cradle Mountain National Park, is one of the acclaimed wilderness areas of Tasmania. You can camp by the lake, enjoy some short walks, and experience the beauty of the lake at sunset and sunrise.

If the Mersey River is too high
to cross like this, you may have
to take an alternative route.

The Tasmanian Trail passes
through some lovely Tasmanian
farmlands.

•DAY 6 **34 miles (55km)**

Bronte Park to Ouse

From the high plateau you begin the descent to the south of Tasmania through forests and farmland, along quiet back roads. The best of this day's riding comes south of Victoria Valley when the trail winds along a dirt track through a eucalyptus forest. The trail descends to Ouse at 655 feet (200m) above sea level, where there is a supermarket and free camping in the recreation ground.

•DAY 7 **33 miles (53km)**

Ouse to Glenora

The trail heads out of Ouse, up to the Lake Repulse dam and through a State Forest pine plantation with some steep sections. There are two options in this section. Riders looking for a challenge should take the Mount Bethune track and climb up to 1,640 feet (500m), otherwise take the sealed road to Ellendale, which follows the valley. The two tracks meet on the Rockmount Road and then the trail heads up into a forest and then over grassy paddocks with

views over the countryside. A farm track leads back down to the Tyenna river and then to a road into Glenora, where you can camp in the school grounds. There is a shop at Bushy Park about half a mile (1km) further on.

•DAY 8 **37 miles (60km)**

Glenora to Hobart

Before you leave the hop fields of Bushy Park it's worth taking some time to visit the text kiln built by Ebenezer Shoobridge in 1867, with scripture text plaques set into the walls. As you approach Hobart the road becomes steadily busier. The A10 east of New Norfolk is a narrow, winding road with fast traffic and it's possible to take a detour along back roads to Molesworth and Glenlusk. If you do take the A10, then stop at the Watch House at Granton and cross the highway and follow the road to Austin's Ferry for a route into Hobart that avoids riding along the freeway. Follow Ken White's notes in his guidebook (see Factfile) to reach the cycle path that will take you into the center of Hobart.

factfile

OVERVIEW

The Tasmanian Trail is a collection of routes traversing Tasmania. While there is a marked official route, there are often alternative routes that can be used when weather conditions make the marked route impassable. Using Tasmania's great network of back roads, you can also visit towns and areas of interest along the way and return to the trail to continue your tour. The route described here, from Devonport to Hobart, is 266 miles (429km) over 8 days.

Start: Devonport.
Finish: Hobart.

ABOUT THE TRAIL

The Trail takes in a mixture of sealed back roads, lots of unsealed gravel or dirt roads, and some good single-track through forest and farmland.

Major Climbs & Descents: While there are plenty of hills in Tasmania, the major climb is the Caves Track from 980 to 3,600 feet (300m–1,100m) over 2½ miles (4km). On the south side of the central plateau there is a gradual descent over several days. The altitude ranges from sea level at the start and finish to 3,600 feet (1,100m) on the central plateau.

Difficulty & Special Features: The trail can be extremely hard in places, notably the Caves Track, but there are always easier alternatives. You will find fallen trees across the track in some of the State Forests, and expect to push in some of the steeper sections. The speed and depth of rivers will depend on recent rainfall but expect to push over the Mersey River crossing. It would be possible to ride the trail with vehicle support meeting you at the end of each day but you would still need to be self-sufficient during the day.

ACCESS

 Airports: There are airports at Launceston and Hobart. Ansett and Qantas offer fares from mainland Australia that allow you to fly into Launceston and out of Hobart.

Transport: The *Spirit of Tasmania* runs between Devonport and Melbourne on the Australian mainland. Redline coaches run a service from Launceston to Devonport and from Hobart to Launceston and Devonport. Check when you book whether they will accept your bike.

Passport & Visa Requirements: All visitors to Australia need a full passport and visa, except those holding a New Zealand passport.

Permits & Access Restrictions: The Tasmanian Trail passes through some privately owned land and you will need permission to ride certain parts of the trail. Details and phone numbers are all included in the official Tasmanian Trail guidebook (*see below*), which also provides details on where to get a key to open gates along the trail.

LOCAL INFORMATION

Maps: The Hema map of Tasmania gives a good overview of the State but does not mark the trail itself. More detailed are the Tasmanian 1:100,000 topographic maps published by Tasmaps.

Guidebooks: *Cycle the Tasmanian Trail* by Ken White (Blanche Publications) is a guide written especially for cyclists. *The*

Tasmanian Trail (Tasmanian Trail Association) is the official guide written for horse riders, cyclists, and walkers.

Accommodation & Supplies: Many of the towns along the Trail allow free camping and use of toilets and showers at sports grounds and schools along the route. You will need to phone ahead to make sure the toilets and showers are open; the phone numbers are in the official guide. There are fee-paying campgrounds at Deloraine, Bronte Park, and Arthurs Lake, and plenty of free bush camping at designated sites along the trail. Youth hostels are to be found at Deloraine and Hobart. Hobart has the full range of accommodation from five-star down. There are shops at Devonport, Railton, Sheffield, Deloraine, Bracknell, Miena, Bronte Park, Ouse, Glenora, New Norfolk, and Hobart. There are bicycle shops at Devonport and Hobart.

Currency & Language: Australian dollar; English.

Area Information: Tasmanian Visitor Information Centre, Hobart, 20 Davey Street, Hobart (tel.: 03 6230 8233). Bicycle Tasmania, Environment Centre, 102 Bathurst Street, Hobart, Tasmania 7000. **Website:** www.tourism.tas.gov.au.

TIMING & SEASONALITY

 Best Months to Visit: December to March.

Climate: Be prepared for a wide range of weather. It may reach the high 80sºF (30sºC) on low-lying areas while it can be snowing on the high plateau. Be prepared for rain and use alternative routes if it has been heavy, since rivers may be swollen and dangerous to cross.

HEALTH & SAFETY

Vaccinations: None required.

General Health Risks: Be aware

← *Wallabies can be spotted at Lake St. Clair, which has abundant wildlife; make sure your food is safely packed to avoid it being stolen in the night by foragers.*

of the dangers of hypothermia in cold, wet conditions.

Special Considerations: To enjoy the trail you need a good level of fitness and some experience in off-road riding with a loaded mountain bike.

Politics & Religion: No concerns.
Crime Risk: Low.
Food & Drink: Treat all naturally occurring water to prevent giardiasis.

HIGHLIGHTS

 Scenic: Tasmania has wonderful wilderness areas. Take the time to go up to the Liffey Falls above Bracknell for a great day's riding, or take an extra day to visit Lake St. Clair. The highlands of the Tasmanian plateau provide some of the most amazing views of the trail; take the time to stop and look over the Great Lake to the mountain ranges beyond.

Wildlife & Flora: Much of Tasmania's native wildlife is nocturnal and you'll probably hear more than you'll see. Nighttime campground visitors in search of food may include possums, wallabies, and Tasmanian devils—carnivorous marsupials that live only on this island. Watch out, too, for Tasmanian tigers—some claim to have seen them, although they have been classified extinct.

↓ temperature and precipitation

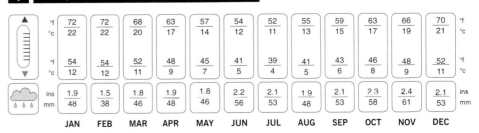

	JAN	FEB	MAR	APR	MAY	JUN	JUL	AUG	SEP	OCT	NOV	DEC	
ºF	72	72	68	63	57	54	52	55	59	63	66	70	ºF
ºC	22	22	20	17	14	12	11	13	15	17	19	21	ºC
ºF	54	54	52	48	45	41	39	41	43	46	48	52	ºF
ºC	12	12	11	9	7	5	4	5	6	8	9	11	ºC
ins	1.9	1.5	1.8	1.9	1.8	2.2	2.1	1.9	2.1	2.3	2.4	2.1	ins
mm	48	38	46	48	46	56	53	48	53	58	61	53	mm

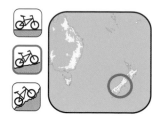

the RAINBOW ROUTE

SOUTH ISLAND, NEW ZEALAND

The Kennett Brothers (Additional photography by Andrew McLellan and Dave Mitchell)

FROM THE STUNNING NELSON LAKES NATIONAL PARK, THE RAINBOW TRAIL FOLLOWS A MOUNTAINOUS PYLON ROAD THAT WAS ORIGINALLY AN OLD DROVERS' ROAD. THE LANDSCAPE INGREDIENTS OF THIS EXPEDITION ARE SIMPLE: THREE HUGE VALLEYS—THE RAINBOW, CLARENCE, AND AWATERE—DIVIDED BY THREE HIGH PASSES THAT PROVIDE AWESOME VISTAS OF MOUNTAINS BEYOND MOUNTAINS.

At the small town of Hanmer Springs, on the edge of the Canterbury Plains, there is the chance to have a rest day, soak in thermal springs, and check out their brilliant, purpose-built mountain bike tracks. The ride then changes tack and heads northeast through Molesworth, New Zealand's largest sheep station, and among the massive Kaikora mountains.

Although it's technically easy, riders will need a fair degree of fitness to tackle the three main passes and several other short but steep climbs. There is a total of 11,500 vertical feet (3,500m) to be climbed in this one-week, 228-mile (366-km) trip. Navigation is straightforward; however, this is big country and a simple map-reading error could cost you the best part of a day. The area is renowned for its unpredictable extremes of weather. Riders must be self-sufficient, with camping equipment and suitable food, for at times you will be at least a day's ride from civilization.

↓ itinerary

•DAY 1 40 miles (64km)

St. Arnaud to Coldwater Creek/Island Gully Hut

From St. Arnaud climb east on Highway 63 for 5½ miles (9km), before turning right at the Rainbow Skifield sign. From there, a narrow road (sealed at first) dives down into the Wairau Valley, crossing many side creeks en route. Some of the larger fords, especially Rough Creek, are impassable after heavy rain, so approach them with caution. (Drowning is known locally as "the New Zealand death!")

A solitary mountain biker crosses a side stream in the Wairau Valley, with the St. Arnaud mountain range looming impressively in the background.

You will fly down from Island Saddle on an exhilarating descent.

Much of the lower valley is cloaked in pristine beech forest that reaches from the riverbanks up to a timberline over 3,300 feet (1,000m) high. Beyond the forest, a legion of mountains, many over 6,550 feet (2,000m), guard the magnificent Nelson Lakes National Park on your right and the rugged Raglan State Forest on your left.

After breaking out of the forest, the pylon road crosses a plateau-like section of the valley before entering Wairau Gorge, where the tumbling river squeezes impossibly through the Turk and Mangerton ridges. Just above the gorge you'll find Coldwater Creek where there is a campground set among the last patch of beech forest. Camp in the forest, or, if you are still feeling fresh, push on to Island Gully Hut (see below).

•DAY 2   40 miles (64km)

Coldwater Creek/Island Gully Hut to Hanmer Springs

Beyond Coldwater Creek, the track climbs gently into an alpine environment that knows no season. Be prepared for all extremes—icy snow to shimmering heat. A rough musterers' and hunters' shelter, known as Island Gully Hut, provides a welcome reprieve from the elements on a stormy day, or an idyllic spot to camp on a calm clear evening. It's an hour's ride (9 miles/15km) south of Coldwater Creek and about a quarter of a mile (400m) off the track on your right.

From the hut, a very low gear climb leads to Island Saddle (4,500 feet/1,372m) nearly 4 miles (6km) away. Every ounce of sweat is paid for by the stunning views of countless mountains flanking two of the largest valleys in New Zealand—the Wairau to the north and the Clarence to the south. It's hard to believe they both flow into the Pacific Ocean a mere 40 miles (64km) from each other.

Check your brakes before diving into the Clarence Valley. The road is steep and many a rider has passed the turn-off to Lake Tennyson in a blur. If the weather is fine it's worth taking the short detour to a scenic picnic spot beside the lake. At the bottom of the descent, the first bridge across the Clarence river provides shelter if necessary, but the predominant wind is from the north and most cyclists fly past, letting it push them toward Hanmer.

A fairly bumpy vehicle track follows the valley floor for 22 miles (35km), before an incongruous road sign marks a fork in the road. Here you must choose between the shorter route to Hanmer Springs (Jacks Pass, 2,820 feet/860m) and the more exciting one (Jollies Pass, 2,780 feet/850m). Both passes involve short climbs followed by long descents that lead right into the welcome resort of Hanmer Springs, Canterbury.

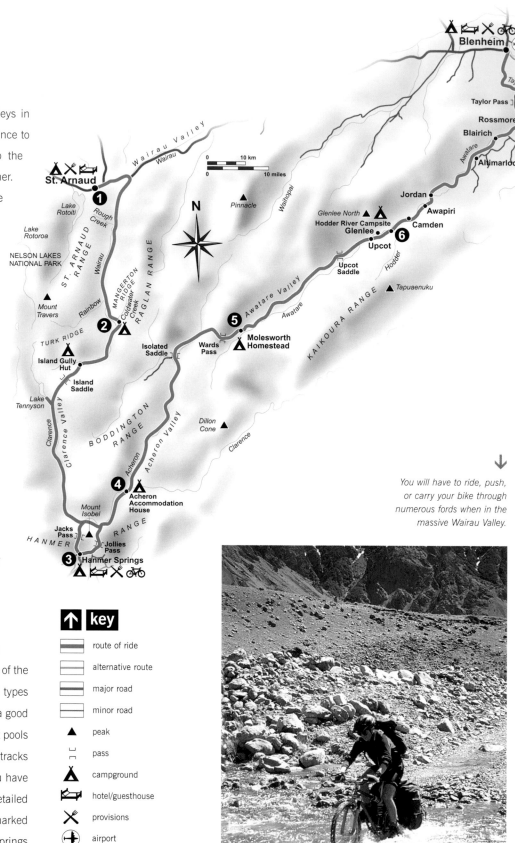

You will have to ride, push, or carry your bike through numerous fords when in the massive Wairau Valley.

•DAY 3 | **31 miles (50km)**

Hanmer Springs to Acheron Accommodation House

Hanmer Springs was a popular health resort for much of the last century. Now it's a magnet for people who love all types of outdoor activities, especially cyclists. Not only is it a good place to stock up on supplies, but it has wonderful hot pools and an extensive network of mountain bike single-tracks throughout the pine forest on the edge of town. If you have time for only a short ride, check out Jolliffe Saddle (detailed in *Classic New Zealand Mountain Bike Rides* and marked on a map that you can buy at the Hanmer Springs Information Centre). You may be tempted to stay in town for an extra day—it's a great place to kick back and relax.

When you finally leave Hanmer Springs, you are once again faced with the choice between the Jacks or the Jollies Pass. Jacks is long and "easy;" Jollies is a steep hill-climber's challenge. They both lead over to the Clarence

key

route of ride

alternative route

major road

minor road

▲ peak

□ pass

▲ campground

🛏 hotel/guesthouse

✕ provisions

✈ airport

🚲 bike shop/repairs

day the views of the Raglan Range to the west and the Kaikoura Range to the east are magnificent. On a lousy day, the wind and rain will make it a challenge to cross the pass without being forced to walk; it's a wild alpine environment where the weather dictates all.

The descent from Wards Pass to Molesworth Homestead on the boundary of the station takes no time at all. At the original homestead, about half a mile (1km) past the new homestead buildings, you will find more historic cob huts and a pleasant Department of Conservation (D.O.C.) camping area. Drop into the D.O.C. caravan for information and to pay for a camping spot.

With a prevailing northwesterly wind on their backs, three cyclists fly down the terraced Clarence Valley.

Valley, where you ride east, down the valley, to the Acheron Accommodation House. This historic house is a grand old cob (a building material of clay and chopped straw) hut, once used by musterers and travelers alike. It's no longer fit to stay in, but there is lovely camping on the grass beside it, or among the willows nearby. Cyclists gather on the porch to discuss the trail and share stories from afar.

•DAY 5 **31 Miles (50km)**

Molesworth Homestead to Hodder River

For the next day or so you will be following a gravel road, like a dragon's back, down the Awatere Valley. It is very hilly, but the downhills are longer and more numerous than the uphills. Take it easy on the steep descent from Upcot Saddle.

At the Hodder River bridge there is a public toilet and some good trees to rest under on hot days. Cyclists and climbers often camp here for the night. Climbers tramp up the Hodder Valley to climb Tapuaenuku (lazily called

•DAY 4 **40 miles (64km)**

Acheron Accommodation House to Molesworth Homestead

Molesworth Station is the largest sheep farm in New Zealand. The countryside is so rugged that mustering the sheep takes weeks, and is still done on horseback. If you left your horse at home, don't worry: a bicycle is almost as good a way to explore this massive landscape.

There is no camping allowed in Molesworth Station, so from Acheron Accommodation House you have a long day ahead. You must make it to the Molesworth Homestead by nightfall. Leaving the Clarence river behind, ride up the Acheron Valley, and over the aptly named Isolated Saddle to avoid a deep gorge. The farm track then drops back down to the Acheron river, and a patch of willow trees beside a bridge provides a good place to stop and contemplate the pass that now towers above you. Ahead, the track climbs steeply up to Ward Pass (3,740 feet/1,140 m). On a fine

↓ ride profile

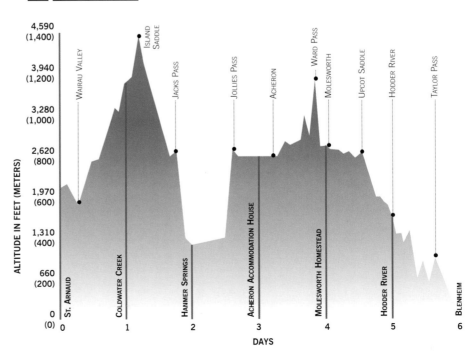

Mount Tappy), which at 9,460 feet (2,885m) is the highest mountain outside the Southern Alps. This was a training ground for Sir Edmund Hillary before he climbed Mount Everest.

In wide open country such as this, mountain bikers should always be prepared for all weather conditions.

•DAY 6   46 miles (74km)

Hodder River to Blenheim

From the Hodder River, the road climbs a few more hills then drops down to Jordan (not much more than a name on a map, but renowned as the hottest place on record in New Zealand: back in 1942 it hit a blistering 108°F/42.2°C) and crosses the Awatere river. Before you know it, you've dealt with the last couple of hills and are flying toward the coast on a smooth, seldom-used, tar-sealed road.

Two or three hours from the Hodder you'll reach a fork in the road signposted "TAYLOR PASS." If you are sick of hills, continue following the Awatere Valley out to Highway 1, then ride north to Blenheim, a couple of hours away. If the idea of lots of traffic seems just too horrible, turn left and climb over Taylor Pass (1,050 feet/320m) to follow a quiet back road right into Blenheim.

 factfile

OVERVIEW

The first 2 days of the Rainbow Route (80 miles/128km) follow a historic route and make up the most popular multi-day mountain bike route in New Zealand. The next 4 days (148 miles/238km) follow the Molesworth Trail along farm tracks and backcountry roads through the country's largest and most rugged sheep station.

Start: St. Arnaud, Nelson Lakes National Park.
Finish: Blenheim, Marlborough.

ABOUT THE TRAIL

The whole trail comprises 5 percent single-track, 10 percent four-wheel-drive track, 75 percent gravel road, and 10 percent sealed road.

Major Climbs & Descents: Despite a lot of climbing and descending being done on an easy gradient in the valleys, there are still many very steep, short- to medium-sized climbs on the route. The climb out of Hanmer Springs is the hardest.

Difficulty & Special Features: The trail is technically easy and the day lengths generally short. However, most of the trail is completely open to wind and rain—elements that can quickly sap a rider's energy. Traveling further than the recommended distances will give you the option of sitting out a stormy day if need be. Isolation is its most special feature! For much of this route you will be mile upon mile from any houses, shops, or public roads. You may not even see another cyclist. Self-sufficiency is essential.

ACCESS

Airports: Christchurch is the nearest international airport, but internal flights can also be made from Auckland and Wellington international airports. From Blenheim, internal flights can be made to most other major towns in New Zealand.

Transport: The public transport network in New Zealand is quite extensive. If you don't have time to cycle to St. Arnaud you can catch a daily bus or shuttle there from main towns in almost any direction—Nelson, Blenheim, or the West Coast. You will be charged an extra $10 (N.Z.) for your bike, unless it's in a bike bag.

Passport & Visa Requirements: All visitors to New Zealand require a valid passport and most visitors will also require a tourist visa; contact your local New Zealand embassy for details.

Permits & Access Restrictions: Permission to cross Rainbow Station must be obtained from Mr. or Mrs. Grahams (tel.: 03 521 1838). The station is closed for mustering in November and March, and in winter because of deep snow. Fire can sometimes close the stations in summer. If the station is closed, ask at the information center in St. Arnaud about riding to the West Coast on the Pioneer Highway. Molesworth Station is open to the public for 6 weeks in January and February, but this is a hot and dusty period for cycling. Outside of this period, permission is required from Don

Reid, Molesworth Station, Private Bag, Blenheim (tel.: 03 575 7043). Always leave farm gates as you find them (imagine how long it would take to collect stray stock!). If you encounter a herd of sheep being mustered, slow down, and pull well off the road.

LOCAL INFORMATION

Maps: Terrainmap 11 Kaikoura.

Guidebooks: *Classic New Zealand Mountain Bike Rides*, written and published by the Kennett Bros, includes 400 rides around the country.

Accommodation & Supplies: St. Arnaud is a small holiday town nestled among the hillocks at the end of picturesque Lake Rotoiti. It has a good campground, a motel, and a few backpackers' hostels. There is a large information center, a gas station, and a general store. Nelson Lakes National Park offers several wonderful trekking opportunities. There is an ecologically significant "mainland island" next to the town, at Kerr Bay, Lake Rotoiti; the 45-minute Honeydew walk passes through some of the best bird life on mainland New Zealand.

Currency & Language: New Zealand dollars. English and Maori are the official languages; everyone speaks English.

Area Information: Hanmer Visitor Information Centre (tel. toll-free in New Zealand: 0800 733 426); Blenheim Visitor Information Centre (tel.: 03 578 9904). For specific track information contact the Department of Conservation in Renwick (tel.: 03 572 9100); Department of Conservation in St. Arnaud (tel.: 03 521 1806); Department of Conservation in Hanmer (tel.: 03 315 7128). For information about canoeing, horse trekking, skiing, bungee

jumping, etc., contact Hanmer Springs Adventure Centre (tel.: 03 315 7233). The Rainbow Rage bike race, which attracts over a thousand riders but is still very laid back, is held the third Saturday in every March; contact Stoke Cycles in Nelson (tel.: 03 547 6361) for information and entry forms.

Website: www.mountainbike.co.nz for local, up-to-date advice, and for purchasing *Classic New Zealand Mountain Bike Rides*; www.hurunui.com/adventure.html.

TIMING & SEASONALITY

Best Months to Visit: November to March.

Climate: During winter (June to September) the passes, and higher parts of the valleys, will be covered in snow. It can snow in summer, but usually not for long. The lower parts of the valleys can become incredibly hot and dry

during summer. The prevailing wind is northwest, but the occasional southerly brings cold, wet, and windy weather.

HEALTH & SAFETY

Vaccinations: None required.

General Health Risks: Hypothermia during winter, heatstroke and dehydration during summer, drowning at the fords after unusually heavy rain. Take plenty of sunscreen, because the ozone layer is thin in this part of the world and sunburn is quite common. There are lots of annoying sandflies at St. Arnaud and in the beech forest: either cover up or apply insect repellent.

Special Considerations: Take a camp stove, since open fires are not allowed on Molesworth Station or at Coldwater Creek campground. Protect plants and animals; keep streams and lakes clean; take care

with fires, camp carefully, and consider others. Please respect the cultural heritage, and *Toitu te whenua*—leave the land undisturbed. It is important that you use toilet facilities provided at campgrounds and towns, or, when in the bush, ensure that toilet sites are well away from streams and rivers, and bury toilet waste.

Politics & Religion: No concerns.
Crime Risk: Minimal.
Food & Drink: Take an extra water bottle or a water filter/iodine.

HIGHLIGHTS

The Rainbow Route is famous for its pristine beech forest and massive open valleys set among a seemingly endless mass of mountains that make up the spine of the upper South Island.

Scenic: Each of the major passes affords panoramic views of the sheep stations, National Parks, and forest parks that surround the route. Lake Tennyson is one of the country's highest lakes and the source of the Clarence river.

Wildlife & Flora: There are countless sheep and cattle; a variety of native birds in the beech forest; paradise ducks, geese, and rabbits in the open valleys; wild pigs in the forest near Hanmer Springs; and rainbow trout and native eels in the rivers.

⬇ temperature and precipitation

		JAN	FEB	MAR	APR	MAY	JUN	JUL	AUG	SEP	OCT	NOV	DEC	
	°f	75	75	70	65	55	50	50	53	56	60	65	69	°f
	°c	23	23	21	17	13	10	10	11	14	16	19	21	°c
	°f	48	47	45	40	33	30	30	30	29	40	42	47	°f
	°c	9	8	7	4	1	−1	−1	−1	−2	4	6	8	°c
	ins	2.3	1.9	2.0	2.1	2.8	2.7	2.6	2.2	2.1	1.9	2.0	2.1	ins
	mm	58	48	52	54	72	68	65	56	53	49	51	54	mm

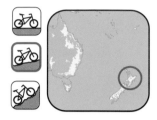

the HEARTLAND TOUR

NORTH ISLAND, NEW ZEALAND

The Kennett Brothers (Additional photography by Charlie Palmer)

THE HEARTLAND TOUR EXPLORES AN INTIMATE LANDSCAPE OF RICH RAIN FOREST, DERELICT GHOST TOWNS, AND DEEP SANDSTONE VALLEYS. FROM TAUMARUNUI, ON THE EDGE OF THE NORTH ISLAND'S VOLCANIC PLATEAU, THE TRAIL FOLLOWS A MIXTURE OF BACKCOUNTRY ROADS, FOUR-WHEEL-DRIVE TRACKS, AND SINGLE-TRACK EN ROUTE TO THE FOOT OF THE MAJESTIC MOUNT TARANAKI.

A flexible itinerary through a region loaded with scenic and historic highlights makes this trip ideal for groups of varying abilities. The route includes two of the best mountain bike rides in New Zealand—the Mythical Moki and the Bridge to Somewhere. Both follow overgrown roads that were cut during the 1930s depression, across land that refused to be tamed. Halfway through the trip, the self-proclaimed Republic of Whangamomona provides a fascinating insight into a small community resilient enough to eke out an existence in the Heartland. Due to astoundingly inaccurate maps, a guidebook is essential.

←

It is possible to reach quite high speeds on the dive down to the start of the Moki Track.

↓ itinerary

•DAY 1 11 miles (18km)

Taumarunui to Ohinepa Landing

Taumarunui is best known as a quiet pioneer railroad town, and indeed the train is still the best way to travel there (after cycling, of course). From either Wellington or Auckland, the major cities of the south and north, the train weaves a wonderfully scenic route through the center of North Island and arrives at a relaxed pace. The running commentary is a slice of classic "kiwiana" that will have you in stitches—or tears. You can learn a lot from a little train trip.

Originally, Taumarunui was an important meeting place

for three Maori tribes, and their influence can still be felt today. To avoid coasting straight past important historical sites, drop into the information center at the railroad station and pick up a "Heritage Trail" booklet.

You don't have to cycle far on the first day, so take time to stock up well before leaving behind the last supermarket and bike shop you will see for six days. Riding west on the River Road, you will soon sneak past Herlihy Bluff, a half-mile-long (1-km), slow-motion landslide that has challenged road engineers for a century. Its alternating layers of sandstone and mudstone were laid down beneath the sea millions of years ago and are almost a mile (1.5km) thick.

Ohinepa Landing, beside the Whanganui River, has been used by canoeists for centuries. It's one of many stopping points along what was once one of New Zealand's busiest trading rivers. The Whanganui River is more like a 140-mile-long (230-km) canal and as such is the country's longest canoeable route. Until a century ago, it provided the best traveling route through Taranaki's rough hill country. These days Ohinepa Landing is used by recreational canoeists, and is a lovely place to camp.

•DAY 2   49 miles (78km)

Ohinepa Landing to Moki Forest

When you hit Highway 43 you should turn left to ride the Heritage Trail. Go past the hamlet of Tatu (blink and you'll miss it) and into the forest on a gravel road. Heading south, the seldom-used Highway 43 soon climbs over Paparata Saddle and descends through native forest beside the serpentine Tangarakau River.

The Heartland is cloaked in lush rain forest and lazy, teak-colored streams; but exploring off the beaten track is not for the faint-hearted.

→

About 9 miles (14km) after the saddle you'll see Mount Damper Road on the right. Follow this for 3 miles (5km) before turning left onto Mangapapa Road. There is a basic, but very scenic D.O.C. (Department of Conservation) camping area a couple of miles (3km) down this road.

•DAY 3 Easy: 13 miles (21km); Hard 28 miles (45km)

Easy: Mount Damper Falls

The impressive Mount Damper Falls are 280 feet (85m) high with a backdrop of native bush. Ride from the campground back to Mangapapa Road and then northeast for 5 miles (8km) before following a half-mile (1-km) walking track across farmland to the falls. Return the same way.

Hard: The Rerekapa and Moki Tracks

The Moki Track is seriously difficult and requires both expert riding skill and outdoor acumen. There are several narrow bridges spanning small rivers that have cut far deeper into the sandstone than you would ever expect. A fall in the wrong place could be fatal.

From the camping area, ride north across a bridge and take the first left onto a four-wheel-drive track called Rerekapa Road. It runs up the valley, past a shack and some cattle yards, on to Rerekapa Track and up to the Boys' Brigade Hut about 4½ miles (7km) from Mangapapa Road. The track is mostly unridable from there to a small saddle; then it improves again as it dives through forest and farmland to Kiwi Road.

At Kiwi Road, turn left and cycle along the well-formed gravel road for about 9 miles (15km) to the start of the Moki Track, next to a bridge on the Waitara River. There is a small parking area beside a "MOKI ROAD, NO EXIT" signpost and a locked gate. Hop over the gate and pedal in the direction of the "MOKI TRACK" sign.

After cycling through a mudstone tunnel you'll reach a swing bridge, where the track proper begins. Cross the swing bridge and walk, then ride, into the forest and onto a long overgrown coach road. This track isn't marked on any maps these days, but, rest assured, it does exist and it follows the windy Waitara River all the way to the eastern half of Moki Road.

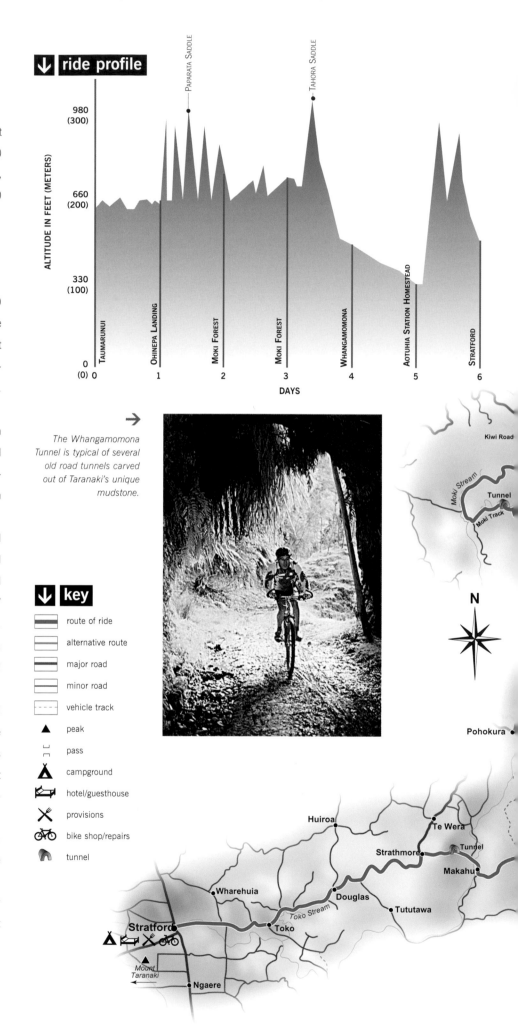

The Whangamomona Tunnel is typical of several old road tunnels carved out of Taranaki's unique mudstone.

←

For mountain bikers who relish technical single-track, the Moki Track is an option not to be missed.

The track narrows as it weaves through dense bush, juxtaposed by unexpected grassy clearings. Steep drop-offs, slippery rocks, and fallen trees are just part of what makes this such a great single-track adventure. A fair section of the track about halfway through is pretty rough, and requires some walking.

When you reach the bush edge, hop over a fence and follow the main farm track past some farm buildings, over a stile, and on to the start of the Moki Road. At the first T-intersection turn left and cruise down to the campground about 1½ miles (2km) away.

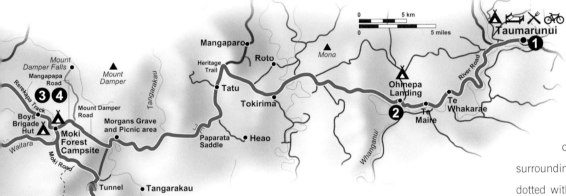

•DAY 4 | 19 miles (31km)

Moki Forest to Whangamomona

Leave the peaceful campground behind and head down to the capital of the Heartland—Whangamomona. Ride out to the highway on Moki Road and south through one of the region's largest mudstone tunnels. The surrounding countryside is now one of scrubby farmland, dotted with patches of bush and rundown farm buildings. You'll find an exception on Tahora Saddle. Here a farmer →

→

If you choose the "Hard" option on Day 3, be sure to travel light in order to cover the difficult ground safely.

has hedged his bets and opened a café and cabins. The food is good and the views are fantastic! For a quiet night, this is the place to stop. Otherwise, freewheel into the Whangamomona (Valley of Plenty) Valley.

Whangamomona is a one-pub town with attitude. It's the heart of the Heartland—a self-declared republic since 1989 and a cultural gem not to be missed. Information boards around the town outline its interesting history. The details can be filled in that night at the pub.

•DAY 5   25 miles (40km)

Whangamomona to Aotuhia Station Homestead

From the pub, leave the highway behind and ride down Whangamomona Road. After about 1½ miles (2km) the gravel road becomes a grassy four-wheel-drive track. The route follows the old road to the Bridge to Somewhere, about 12 miles (20km) away. The track keeps to the true right of the Whangamomona River all the way. There are countless bogs and washed out bridges—the track is best ridden when bone dry.

The history of this route is similar to that of Mangapurua Valley and the Bridge to Nowhere in Whanganui National Park—the road was built in the 1930s to allow returned servicemen to settle the land. After battling for ten years, the government gave up fixing the roads and the settlers walked off the land.

Ride left over the bridge and on into Aotuhia Station Homestead, 1 mile (1.5km) away. Accommodation there is in the shearers' quarters—a great place to learn about daily life on a backcountry farm. The Whanganui River is only a few miles away, just over the bushy hill to the east.

•DAY 6   45 miles (72km)

Aotuhia Station Homestead to Stratford

Coast back to the Bridge to Somewhere and ride south up the Taumata Valley. On your left is the Matemateonga Range, a prominent part of the Whanganui National Park. A famous New Zealand walking route traverses the range and drops down to a landing site on the Whanganui River. Before long you will climb out of the valley and up to the start of the Matemateonga Walkway. If you have the

time to spare, follow the scenic walkway up to Mount Humphries, two hours away. The track follows the ridge through thick forests and occasionally affords stunning views of Taranaki wilderness.

From the Matemateonga Range, the road whisks you down the Mangaehu Valley and on toward Strathmore. A short climb leads to the last tunnel of the tour, once again carved out of sandstone and surrounded by rich green forest. A photo stop is obligatory.

The last 18 miles (30km) to Stratford follows the heritage highway, which leads directly to the foot of the perfect volcanic cone of Taranaki, 8,260 feet (2,518m) high. Myth has it that the mountains Taranaki and Tongariro (near Taumarunui) once fought over the lovely Pihanga. Taranaki, wild with grief and anger, wrenched himself away from the central volcanoes and fled to his present site. The path he followed made a long wound in the earth, which filled with a stream from the side of Tongariro. Green forests, alive with the songs of birds, grew throughout the valley of the new river, which we now know as the Whanganui.

Don't look down! This narrow bridge on the Moki Track crosses a deep, dark ravine.

factfile

 ← *The weather can change from one season to another within a few hours, so always travel with adequate gear and clothing.*

OVERVIEW

 The Heartland Tour combines one of the country's best cycle touring routes with three great mountain bike rides. Riders can meander along the heritage highway, taking a leisurely 6 days to complete 177 miles (284km), with no huge hills or technical riding.

Start: Taumarunui, on the edge of the central volcanic plateau.

Finish: Stratford, at the foot of Mount Taranaki.

ABOUT THE TRAIL

The track is roughly divided as follows: 10 percent single-track, 10 percent four-wheel-drive track, 45 percent gravel road, 35 percent sealed road. A few miles of the single-track is unridable.

Major Climbs & Descents: Several climbs are between 330 and 660 feet (100–200m)—nothing to worry about.

Difficulty & Special Features: This trip is flexible enough to suit riders of all levels. The worst of it involves gnarly single-tracks, tricky route finding, and a couple of long days in the saddle. "Papa mud" is a problem—add rain to Taranaki tracks and mix with a bicycle wheel to create an unridable carborundum-based cement. Avoid single-track and four-wheel-drive tracks after a heavy dose of rain.

ACCESS

Airports: Airports close to Taranaki are at New Plymouth and Taupo. There are international airports at Auckland and Wellington.

Transport: From both Auckland

and Wellington trains follow the main trunk line to Taumarunui every day. If traveling by bike, the 25-mile (40-km), mostly downhill, and very scenic ride from National Park Village, Tongariro to Taumarunui is recommended. A more adventurous entry would be via the famous 42 Traverse; this fantastic mountain bike ride is reasonably technical so ask at the National Park to have your luggage ferried to Owhango. There are several daily buses from Stratford to Auckland and Wellington, and all the major cities in between. To return to Taumarunui by bike, the quiet and scenic Whanganui River Road is recommended; the highway down to Wellington is car infested.

Passport & Visa Requirements: All visitors to New Zealand require a valid passport, and most foreign nationals also require a visa. Contact your local New Zealand embassy for further details.

Permits & Access Restrictions: Always leave farm gates as you find them. If you encounter a herd of sheep or cattle being mustered, slow down and pull off the road.

LOCAL INFORMATION

Maps: 1:50,000 Topomaps: R18 Ohura, R19 Whangamomona, and R20 Matemateonga. The 1:250,000 Terrainmaps 4 Waikato and 6 Taranaki provide a useful overview.

Guidebooks: *Classic New Zealand Mountain Bike Rides*, written and published by The Kennett Bros. includes 400 rides around the country. Pick up a Taumarunui Stratford Heritage Highway booklet from an information center.

Accommodation & Supplies:

Campgrounds do not need to be booked ahead. The Boys' Brigade Hut can be booked through Graham Armstrong (tel.: 06 754 6005). You can camp or rent a cabin at Tahora Saddle (tel.: 06 762 5858). The café there is always open and there are 360-degree views of the surrounding wilderness. There are campgrounds, cabins, and a hotel at Whangamomona (tel.: 06 762 5823). Contact the Aotuhia Station (tel.: 06 762 5868), for permission to stay in the shearers' huts. Stratford Motorcamp has tent sites and cabins (tel.: 06 765 6440).

Currency & Language: N.Z. dollars. English and Maori are the official languages.

Area Information: There are information offices at Taumarunui (tel.: 07 895 7494), and Stratford (tel.: 06 765 6708). Whangamomona celebrates its republic status every year on the Saturday closest to November 1.

Website: www.mountainbike.co.nz for up-to-date, local advice.

TIMING & SEASONALITY

 Best Months to Visit: November through April.

Climate: The weather is generally mild. Snow and sub-zero temperatures are occasionally experienced in winter (June to September). In summer you should be prepared for a little rain and a lot of sun.

HEALTH & SAFETY

Vaccinations: None required.

General Health Risks: Take plenty of sunscreen; the ozone layer is thin in this part of the world and sunburn is common.

Special Considerations: Protect plants and animals; keep streams and lakes clean; take care with fires, camp carefully, and consider others. Please respect the cultural heritage, and *Toitu te whenua*—

leave the land undisturbed. Use toilet facilities provided at campgrounds and towns, or, when in the bush, ensure that toilet sites are well away from streams and rivers, and bury toilet waste.

Politics & Religion: Many people in Taranaki, both Maori and Pakeha, are fiercely independent and should be treated with respect.

Crime Risk: Minimal.

Food & Drink: Filter stream water or treat it with iodine, but avoid it altogether if there is a farm upstream. Take an extra water bottle.

HIGHLIGHTS

The Heartland is renowned for its thick forest and rivers that seem to choose the longest, twistiest route to the sea. The roads and tracks are quiet, and the region is sparsely populated, but rich in both natural and cultural history.

Scenic: The route passes through mudstone tunnels and the forested Tangarekau Gorge, and over passes that afford expansive vistas of seldom-explored wilderness.

Wildlife & Flora: Taranaki is home to many native birds, including the kiwi, tui, and kereru. You may also come across wild cattle and pigs, which should be avoided, and, of course, the possum, New Zealand's most common mammal. There are stands of virgin rain forest at Moki.

temperature and precipitation

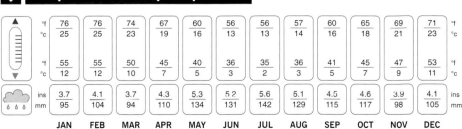

	JAN	FEB	MAR	APR	MAY	JUN	JUL	AUG	SEP	OCT	NOV	DEC
°f	76	76	74	67	60	56	56	57	60	65	69	71
°c	25	25	23	19	16	13	13	14	16	18	21	23
°f	55	55	50	45	40	36	35	36	41	45	47	53
°c	12	12	10	7	5	3	2	3	5	7	9	11
ins	3.7	4.1	3.7	4.3	5.3	5.2	5.6	5.1	4.5	4.6	3.9	4.1
mm	95	104	94	110	134	131	142	129	115	117	98	105

THE AUTHORS

NINA BJORDAL of Norway first experienced the joys of biking as a teenager in Denmark, and has since traveled in Africa and South America. She now works along Norway's premier biking route, Rallarvegen.

GENERAL EDITOR

NICKY CROWTHER has worked in the world of mountain biking, her passion, for the last ten years. During this time, she has been the editor of *Mountain Biking International* magazine, and co-written the Lonely Planet *Cycling Britain* book. She has raced on the British National Mountain Bike Squad and has ridden routes in New Zealand, the Rockies, and the Alps, as well as all over the U.K. She currently works as a freelance editor and reporter specializing in mountain biking and cycling, when she isn't actually in the saddle.

JAMIE CARR is an adventurer who has participated in a dozen biking and mixed endurance events around the globe, ranging from pedaling parched through Australia to mushing with nails in his tires in Alaska. A qualified mountain bike guide in Nepal, he is also handy with ropes, rafts, and kayaks.

STEVE CALLEN thrives on the challenge of outdoor pursuits and has biked all across the Himalayas and in America, and loves to participate in Mountain Biking endurance challenges. He has also trekked and climbed the world's greatest mountain ranges and visits Asia regularly.

CONTRIBUTORS

JUDY ARMSTRONG is an award-winning feature writer, specializing in adventure travel and outdoor pursuits. She travels widely—not only by bike, but also by foot, horse, boat, and bus—through North and South America, Africa, Europe, and Asia.

JOHAN COETZEE started cycling in 1996 and immediately became hooked on mountain biking. Shortly after, he founded the Free State Mounties Mountain Bike Club and the Free State Mountain Bike Association. He became President of the South African Mountain Bike association in 1999, and in 2000 he started up his own company: Mountain Bike South Africa.

EMMA BARRACLOUGH studied in China for two years and has traveled by bike through China, Thailand, Vietnam, and Laos. Emma is currently living in Hong Kong.

CHRIS FORD has spent most of his free time since leaving school on a mountain bike. He's explored much of Europe, crossed the Andes, followed the Ganges into the Himalayas, and delved into remote corners of Africa on his many travels. Chris now runs CycleActive, a company specializing in mountain bike and multi-sport holidays in all corners of the World.

 **BRENT HENRY** is an avid mountain biker, sea kayaker, and skier. He has a passionate love and respect for the outdoors, which he shares with his two young daughters. When not enjoying the great outdoors, Brent works as a school bus driver and writer on a small island in British Columbia.

 **CARLTON REID** is the editor of *BicycleBusiness* and its associated website, www.bikebiz.co.uk. He wrote the *Berlitz Discover Guide to Israel* and Kindlife's *Lebanon: A Travel Guide*, having researched them from the saddle of a mountain bike. He has also written books on mountain biking.

 **TOM HUTTON** is a freelance writer and photographer who is equally at home biking, walking, climbing, or skiing. His passion for the outdoors, in particular remote or dramatic landscapes, is matched only by his love of nature.

 **SEB ROGERS** is a self-confessed single-track junkie with itchy feet and an attraction to anywhere mountainous. Seb is also an experienced photographer and writer. He has left tire tracks in the dust as far afield as Borneo, British Columbia, the Pyrenees, and the Canary Islands, and he is a regular contributor to British mountain bike magazines.

 **THE KENNETT BROTHERS**, Paul, Simon, and Jonathan, have mountain biked extensively throughout the world, as well as thoroughly exploring their home country of New Zealand. They run Wellington's Makara Peak Mountain Bike Park and the www.mountainbike.co.nz website. All three are keen conservationists and strong advocates for cycling, both on and off the road.

 **CHRIS SCOTT** has been biking for ten years, during which time he has built a World Cup downhill course, started a mountain bike club with fellow cyclists, and raced and ridden all over the country. In every wonderful place he has ridden he has always yearned to return to Virginia and his favorite riding in the world where he operates Shenandoah Mountain Touring.

 **MIKE McCOY** is a bicycle-route designer and conceived the Great Divide Mountain Bike Route, which took four years to put together. He has also written numerous articles and eight books. He is managing editor of *Jackson Hole* magazine.

 **SUE WEBBER** is editor of *Australian Cyclist*. She has traveled extensively in Australia by bicycle as well as undertaking tours in Europe and Russia.

 **STEVE MEAD** owned a bike shop in England for four years before moving with his family to the French Pyrenees in 1994 where he runs the mountain biking holiday company, Pyractif.

 **DAVE WILLIS** has photographed the outdoors all his life. First a press photographer, then an expedition photographer in Patagonia, he later returned to his home in the English Lake District where he set up Mountain Sport Photography. He covers all outdoor action from mountain biking and mountaineering to windsurfing and snowboarding.

TRAVELER INFORMATION

AUSTRALIA
Australian Tourism Industry
  Association
P.O. Box E328
Canberra ACT 2600
Tel.: 00 61 2 6273 1000
www.aussie.net.au
www.australia.com

Tourism Queensland
243 Edward Street
Brisbane 4000
Tel.: 00 61 7 3874 2800
www.tq.com.au

Northern Territory Tourist
  Commission
4th Floor — Tourism House
43 Mitchell Street
Darwin NT 0800
Tel.: 00 61 8 8999 3900
www.nttc.com.au

Tourism Tasmania
G.P.O. Box 399
Hobart
Tasmania 7001
Tel.: 00 61 3 6230 8169
Fax: 00 61 3 6230 8353
www.tourism.tas.gov.au

CANADA
Tourism British Columbia
Parliament Buildings
Victoria BC
V8V 1X4
Tel.: 00 1 250 387 1642
www.tourism-vancouver.org

CHILE
National Tourism Board of Chile
SERNATUR
P.O. Box 14082
Santiago
Tel: 00 56 2 696 7141
www.sernatur.cl

CHINA
China National Tourist Office
350 Fifth Avenue, Suite 6413
Empire State Building
New York
NY 10118
U.S.A.
Tel.: 00 1 212 760 8218
www.cnto.org

DOMINICAN REPUBLIC
Ministry of Tourism
Government Offices Block D
Avenida Mexico corner 30 de
  Marzo
Santo Domingo
Tel.: 00 1 809 221 4660
www.dominicana.com.do

ETHIOPIA
Ethiopian Tourism Commission
Ras Mekonin Ave.
P.O. Box 2183
Addis Ababa
Tel.: 00 251 1 44 74 70

FRANCE
Maison de la France
8 Avenue de l'Opera
Paris
Tel.: 00 33 1 42 96 10 23
www.maison-de-la-france.fr

INDIA
Government of India Tourist Office
88 Janpath
New Delhi 110 001
Tel.: 00 91 11 332 0005
www.tourisminindia.com

ISRAEL
Israel Ministry of Tourism
24 King George Sreet
PO Box 1018
Jerusalem 94262
Tel.: 00 97 2 2675 4811
www.infotour.co.il

MALAWI
Malawi Department of Tourism
P.O. Box 401
Blantyre
Tel.: 00 265 620 300
www.malawi–tourism.com

NEPAL
Nepal Tourism Board
Tourist Service Center
P.O. Box 11018
Bhrikiti Mandap
Tel.: 00 997 1 256 909
www.welcomenepal.com

NEW ZEALAND
New Zealand Tourism Board
Fletcher Challenge House
89 The Terrace
P.O. Box 95
Wellington
Tel.: 00 64 4 472 8860
www.nztb.govt.nz

NORWAY
Norwegian Tourist Board
P.O. Box 2893 Solli
Drammensveien 40
N–0230 Oslo
Tel.: 00 47 22 92 52 00
www.ntr.no

RUSSIA
Rostourism
2/1 Kutuzovsky pr–t
9th Floor, 121249
Moscow
Tel.: 00 7 95 933 6969
www.russia–tourism.org

SCOTLAND
Scotland Information Centre
4 Rothesay Terrace
Edinburgh EH3 7RY
Tel.: 00 44 131 473 3600
www.holiday.scotland.net

SOUTH AFRICA
SATOUR
442 Rigel Avenue
South Erasmusrand 0181
Private Bag X164
Pretoria 0001
Tel.: 00 27 124 826 200
www.satour.co.za
www.satour.org

SPAIN
TourSpain
Jose Lazaro Galdiano, no.6
28036 Madrid
Tel.: 00 34 901 300 600
www.spaintour.com
www.tourspain.es

SWITZERLAND
Switzerland Tourism
Toedistrasse 7
P.O. Box 695
Zurich 8027
Tel.: 00 41 1 288 11 11
www.switzerlandtourism.ch
www.switzerlandvacation.ch

U.K.
British Tourist Authority
Thames Tower
Black's Road
London
W6 9EL
Tel.: 00 44 20 8846 9000
www.britishtouristauthority.org

U.S.A.
California Division of Tourism
P.O. BOX 1499
Sacramento
CA 95812
Tel.: 00 1 916 322 2881
www.gocalif.ca.gov

Nevada Commission of Tourism
401 North Carson
Carson City
NV 89701
Tel.: 00 1 775 687 4322
www.travelnevada.com

The Utah Travel Council
Council Hall, Capitol Hill
Salt Lake City
Utah 84114–1396
Tel.: 00 1 801 538–1900
www.utah.com

Virginia Tourism Corporation
901 East Byrd Street
Richmond
VA 23219
Tel.: 00 1 804 786 4484
www.virginia.org

INDEX

Page numbers in *italics* refer to illustrations

INDEX

CREDITS

Key: *b* bottom; *bl* bottom left; *t* top; *tr* top right

We would like to acknowledge the use of photography by the following persons: p1 Jamie Carr; pp2–3 Steve Callen; pp4–5 Jamie Carr; p6*t* Steve Callen, *b* Jamie Carr; p7*t* Trevor Creighton, *b* Chris Ford; p8 Chris Ford; p9 Brent Henry; p10*t* Jamie Carr, *b* Brent Henry; p11*t* Carlton Reid, *b* Jamie Carr; p12*bl* Brent Henry; p13*tr* Chris Ford, *bl* Carlton Reid; p16*t* Mike McCoy, *b* Steve Callen; pp16–17 Brent Henry; p56*t* Seb Rogers, *b* Dave Willis; pp56–57 Steve Mead; p98*t* Emma Barraclough, *b* Jamie Carr; pp98–99 Jamie Carr; 126*t* Carlton Reid, *b* Carlton Reid; pp126–127 Carlton Reid; p156*t* Trevor Creighton, *b* Trevor Creighton; pp156–157 Jamie Carr; p.192 Chris Ford.

All photographs in the rides were reproduced with the kind permission of each ride's author; additional ride photography was supplied by Chuck Haney, p23t; Esben Haakenstad, pp88–91; Trevor Creighton pp92–97, 158–163, and 168–173; Andrew McLellan & Dave Mitchell pp174–179; Charlie Palmer pp180–185.

All other photographs and illustrations are the copyright of Quarto Publishing plc.

Both Quarto and Nicky Crowther, General Editor, would like to thank Neil Simpson for the kind loan of his montain bike for photography.

Disclaimer

Mountain biking is potentially dangerous, and each individual cyclist is responsible for his or her own safety and well-being at all times. While the editor, contributors, and publisher of this book have taken great pains to ensure the accuracy of the information presented, they cannot accept responsibility for loss or injury sustained, however caused, by people using this information. Circumstances change constantly, and the fact that a route, equipment, or techniques are described in this book does not mean that it is necessarily safe or suitable for individual cyclists or groups at any particular time. The publisher does not warrant or endorse the techniques and methods presented in this book, and the authors and publisher will assume no liability for any injury or damage to persons or property which may result from the use or application of any of the contents of this book.